A HISTORY OF READING AND WRITING

D0022031

A HISTORY OF READING AND WRITING

In the Western World

MARTYN LYONS

© Martyn Lyons 2010

All rights reserved. No reproduction, copy or transmission of this publication may be made without written permission.

No portion of this publication may be reproduced, copied or transmitted save with written permission or in accordance with the provisions of the Copyright, Designs and Patents Act 1988, or under the terms of any licence permitting limited copying issued by the Copyright Licensing Agency, Saffron House, 6-10 Kirby Street, London EC1N 8TS.

Any person who does any unauthorized act in relation to this publication may be liable to criminal prosecution and civil claims for damages.

The author has asserted his right to be identified as the author of this work in accordance with the Copyright, Designs and Patents Act 1988.

First published 2010 by
PALGRAVE MACMILLAN

Palgrave Macmillan in the UK is an imprint of Macmillan Publishers Limited, registered in England, company number 785998, of Houndmills, Basingstoke, Hampshire RG21 6XS.

Palgrave Macmillan in the US is a division of St Martin's Press LLC, 175 Fifth Avenue, New York, NY 10010.

Palgrave Macmillan is the global academic imprint of the above companies and has companies and representatives throughout the world.

Palgrave® and Macmillan® are registered trademarks in the United States, the United Kingdom, Europe and other countries.

ISBN 978-0-230-00161-9 hardback

ISBN 978-0-230-00162-6   ISBN 978-1-137-06096-9 (eBook)
DOI 10.1007/978-1-137-06096-9

This book is printed on paper suitable for recycling and made from fully managed and sustained forest sources. Logging, pulping and manufacturing processes are expected to conform to the environmental regulations of the country of origin.

A catalogue record for this book is available from the British Library.

A catalog record for this book is available from the Library of Congress.

10   9   8   7   6   5   4   3   2   1
19 18 17 16 15 14 13 12 11 10

Contents

List of Tables and Illustrations

Tables

Illustrations

Abbreviations

AESC	*Annales – économies, sociétés, civilisations*
AmHistRev	*American Historical Review*
CHBB 3	*Cambridge History of the Book in Britain*, 7 vols., ed. D.F. McKenzie, D.J. McKitterick and I.R. Willison, Cambridge UK (CUP), 1999– *Vol. 3, 1400–1557*, ed. Lotte Hellinga and J.B. Trapp.
CHBB 4	Ibid., *Vol. 4, 1557–1695*, ed. John Barnard and D.F. McKenzie with Maureen Bell
CUP	Cambridge University Press
EHQ	*European History Quarterly*
HEF1	*Histoire de l'Edition française*, 4 vols., ed. Roger Chartier and Henri-Jean Martin in collaboration with Jean-Pierre Vivet, Paris (Promodis/Cercle de la Librairie), 1982–1986, and new ed. Paris (Fayard), 1989–1991. *Tome 1, Le livre conquérant, du Moyen Age au milieu du XVIIe siècle*
HEF2	Ibid., *tome 2,*
HEF3	Ibid., *tome 3,*
HEF4	Ibid., *tome 4, Le livre concurrencié, 1890–1950*
HELE	*Historia de la Edición y de la Lectura en España, 1472–1914*, ed. Víctor Infantes, François Lopez and Jean-François Botrel, Madrid (Fundación Germán Sánchez Ruipérez), 2003.
HOBA2	*A History of the Book in Australia, 1891–1945: A National Culture in a Colonised Market*, ed. Martyn Lyons and John Arnold, St. Lucia (University of Queensland Press), 2001.
HOBAmerica1	*A History of the Book in America*, 5 vols., 2000–, General editor David D. Hall.

	Volume 1: The Colonial Book in the Atlantic World, ed. Hugh Amory and David D. Hall, Cambridge (CUP and American Antiquarian Society), 2000.
HOBAmerica3	Ibid., *Volume 3: The Industrial Book, 1840–1880*, ed. Scott E. Casper, Jeffrey D. Groves, Stephen N. Nissenbaum and Michael Winship, Chapel Hill, NC (University of North Carolina Press and American Antiquarian Society), 2007.
HORW	*A History of Reading in the West*, ed. Guglielmo Cavallo and Roger Chartier, Cambridge, UK (Polity), 1999.
HUP	Harvard University Press
IMEC	Institut Mémoires de l'Edition Contemporaine
JMH	*Journal of Modern History*
MSH	Editions de la Maison des Sciences de l'Homme
OUP	Oxford University Press
P&P	Past and Present
PUF	Presses Universitaires de France
PUP	Princeton University Press
UCP	University of California Press
UP	University Press
YUP	Yale University Press

1
What is the history of reading and writing?

At the beginning of the twenty-first century, we have convinced ourselves that we are going through an information revolution unique in history. In the field of information technology, the rate of change seems astonishingly rapid. One by one, 'revolutionary' technologies are adopted and quickly sink into obsolescence: the electronic typewriter (does anybody even remember them?), the fax machine, the video cassette recorder. We are living, it is said, in an information society, in which the rich and powerful are no longer the 'captains of industry' admired by the nineteenth century, but the CEOs of media and entertainment corporations.[1] It is a good idea to take a historical view of rapid change in textual and visual communication, both to put recent changes into perspective and to be more precise about what is actually new about them. In reality, every society since ancient Egypt has been an 'information society', in the sense that those who control and restrict access to knowledge in any society thereby control a key component of power.

The purpose of this book is precisely to adopt a much-needed historical perspective on books, reading and writing in the West. It charts the changing conditions which have determined access to textual communication and the uses to which it has been put. In order to do so, it does not adopt the viewpoint of authors (who were often unidentifiable) or even of publishers, scribes and printers, although their role in textual production has been crucial and will not be neglected. The principal focus will be on the consumer rather than the producer; in other words, this will be a history of literature and textual communication in general from the standpoint of the reader. It aims to show how the relationship of readers (and writers, too) with their texts has changed over time, and how those changes have been influenced by the technological, economic, political and cultural developments which are central to Western history.

This book devotes more space to reading than writing, but this balance simply reflects the current state of scholarship. Whereas cultural historians have developed quite sophisticated approaches to the study of the act of reading, scholars are only just beginning to realise the importance of writing practices at all levels of past societies. The richness of scribal cultures is now starting to surface. This book is written, however, in the conviction that we should no longer separate the historical study of reading from that of writing, but should explore them together and investigate the connections between them. In so doing, we must also connect the history of reading and writing to wider historical problems. This book accordingly devotes chapters to some of the major turning points in the history of the West, including the Renaissance, the Protestant Reformation and the origins of the French Revolution. The role of print production and the contribution of reading and writing to these events will be discussed.

This introductory chapter will review some of the main ideas and approaches used in the history of reading and writing.

Concepts in the history of reading

The history of reading is concerned with all the factors which have determined the reception of texts. It asks what was read in any given society, by whom and how. In what social situations did people read? Did they read silently and alone, or aloud in groups? Did they read casually, purely for diversion, in a fragmented and disengaged manner, as Richard Hoggart described the approach of English working-class readers in the 1950s?[2] Or did they read obsessively, in a dedicated and concentrated way, seeking self-improvement, enlightenment or emancipation? What exactly was the purpose of reading for the readers under consideration – did they read for distraction and escape, for learning, for reference, for practical advice or out of religious devotion? Did they carefully re-read a few well-worn texts, or did they fast-read and then throw away their reading, as magazine readers do today, in a perpetual search for novelty? For example, the historian Carlo Ginzburg laments the disappearance of 'slow reading', alluding perhaps with tongue in cheek to the Italian 'slow food' movement, arguing the need for close textual examination and criticism and deploring crash courses in fast-reading.[3]

The history of reading includes a study of the norms and practices which determine readers' responses. Certain reading models incorporating recommended reading material, rules and taboos have been promoted by churches, trade unions, educators and other groups intent on directing or mobilising the reader. How have readers responded to such recommendations? We need to ask these questions if we are to evaluate how readers integrate their reading into the cultural or educational capital they have already accumulated. At the heart of this agenda lies an investigation into how meaning is ascribed to texts. Only in the act of reading, in the confrontation between reader and text, does literature come alive. The history of the reader, therefore, is a socio-historical study of the factors which produce meaning.

The (mainly German) exponents of Reception Theory launched their hunt for the reader in the literary text itself. Embedded in every piece of literature, they argue, lies an 'implied' or a 'hidden' reader.[4] Novels give the reader guidelines on which to base judgements, raise his or her expectations and leave clues designed to mobilise the reader's imagination. On occasion, for example, the eighteenth-century novel would address the reader directly. The text, in this theory, may open up several different interpretive possibilities for the reader, and it assumes his or her active participation. The presence of the reader, and the reader's expectations of a work of fiction, may thus be deduced from within the text.

These ideas unfortunately lack a historical perspective. They assume that literary texts are static and immutable, whereas they are constantly re-edited over time, in different versions and formats and at different prices. Each re-incarnation of a text targets a new public, whose participation and expectations are guided not just by authors but by publishing strategies, illustrations and all the other physical aspects of the book.

In any case, as a historian of reading I am less interested in implied or putative readers than in actual readers. Individual readers have recorded their reactions in their own autobiographies, letters and diaries, or perhaps they have been coerced into explaining their responses (for example, by the Inquisition). I am chiefly concerned not with the implications of canonical texts fossilised in time but with real readers in specific historical circumstances, who can provide us with what Janice Radway calls 'an empirically-based ethnography of reading'.[5] Two initiatives, one in Britain and the other in the USA, pursue further the traces of actual historical readers and their practices. The Reading Experience Database, or RED for short, has assembled a multitude of details from varied sources on individual readers' responses in Britain between 1450 and 1945. The rather different American project, entitled 'What Middletown Read', will provide complete evidence of who borrowed what from the Public Library in Muncie, Indiana, between 1891 and 1902. The results of both these innovative projects will be available online, and the RED may already be consulted.[6]

Reading is a creative process. The reader is not an empty or transparent receptacle who automatically receives the 'imprint' of what is read. Readers select, interpret, re-work and re-imagine what they read; their responses are far from uniform. The principle of the reader's autonomy is fundamental to the history of reading. In Michel de Certeau's metaphor, the reader is a poacher.[7] Readers as consumers hide as it were in the text; they are trespassers, creeping about the proprietor's estate for their own nefarious purposes. The estate is not their property; the landscape has been laid out by other hands; but, undetected, they take what they need from it – a hare here, a thrush there, even a deer if they are lucky – and escape without leaving a trace on the page. In this way, the individual reader insinuates his or her own meanings and purposes into another's text. Each individual reader has silent and invisible ways of subverting the dominant order of consumerised culture. Readers are not passive or docile; they make texts their own, improvising personal meanings and making unexpected textual connections. Sometimes our elites and advertising industries assume that the public is moulded by the consumer products which are offered to it. Consumer passivity, however, is a fallacy. As De Certeau bluntly put it, 'It is always a good idea to remember that we shouldn't treat people like idiots.'[8]

At this point, we hit a snag. If, as this book argues, individual readers engage in a dynamic interaction with what is read, and share in the production of meaning, if, in addition, they develop private interpretations which are not in any way predetermined, then how are we to write their personal histories? The danger is that we will be faced with a multiplicity of individual stories, all of them unique. If we dissolve the history of reading into a myriad of free agents, all arriving at unexpected conclusions, we have a state of subjective anarchy in which no generalisations are either possible or legitimate.

There are ways out of this dilemma. Pierre Bourdieu offers a sociological perspective on the problem. According to Bourdieu, the reader comes to a text with an accumulated 'cultural capital', made up of two components – his or her economic and cultural capital – which determine preferences. Bourdieu posed a pertinent question for the historian of reading, namely what are the social conditions determining the consumption and appropriation of culture?[9] Some key socio-cultural components of class, including one's level of schooling, produce a cultural competence which defines what we call 'taste'. In other words, it allows the reader to 'decode' a literary work, identify its style, period, genre or author. For Bourdieu, even the ways we acquire cultural objects like books and use them are themselves signs of class, through which we identify ourselves with certain groups and distance ourselves from others. Some readers buy books from antiquarian dealers while others subscribe to the fine reproductions edited by the Folio Society, as distinct from others who find their books in supermarkets or second-hand paperback exchanges. In the process of selecting and responding to what we read, according to Bourdieu, we are operating a strategy of distinction and affirming our membership of a particular social or cultural group. Social groups or communities share a common *habitus* which determines their cultural practices and shapes the common characteristics of an entire lifestyle.

Bourdieu's sociology of consumer practices reminds us that readers are not entirely alone: they belong to social groups. They may also belong to 'interpretive communities'. Stanley Fish, the American literary critic to whom we owe this idea, offers a useful corrective to the anarchic tendencies of reading history previously mentioned.[10] To adapt a well-worn phrase, readers make their own meanings, but they do not make them entirely as they wish. Readers do so as members of a community which shares certain assumptions about literature and what it constitutes. Members of a reading community may not know each other or even be aware of each other's existence, and this fact alone stretches our conventional ideas of community. Members of a reading community, however, have a common set of criteria for judging what is 'good' or 'bad' literature, for categorising texts as belonging to certain genres and for establishing their own genre hierarchies. Reading communities may be readers of the same newspaper, they may have an institutional basis like a literary society or a university faculty or they might be defined more loosely in terms of gender or social class. Perhaps as women readers, or as militant communist workers, they employ similar interpretive strategies in attributing meaning to their books. Individual readers may of course belong to several reading communities at once.

Fish would probably be enormously surprised by the distance that historians have since run with his original conception. James Smith Allen, to take a prominent example, took the idea of the interpretive community as the starting point for his analysis of readers' letters to nineteenth-century French fiction writers.[11] He found that, at the beginning of the century, readers' letters valued the noble sentiments expressed in fiction. They envisaged the author as a man of fine aristocratic sensibilities (thus Stendhal received letters addressed to 'Monsieur de Stendhal'). Readers judged writers according to traditional shared criteria, which demanded moral lessons and allegiance to neoclassical virtues of simplicity and restraint. They adapted slowly to the realist ethic, and their correspondence suggested to Allen that for some time they associated realism with immorality. Gradually, the impact of Flaubert and Zola redefined the expectations of the public. Instead of praising a novel's refinement and delicate taste, readers were more likely to appreciate its energy and power. These insights, building on valuable direct evidence of readers' responses, gave Allen's work shape and direction.

Fish's notion, to which Allen's work refers, is only a starting point. It does not give us enough help to define the social realities of reading communities in historical time. For this we need a social context. As Robert Darnton reminded us, ascribing meaning to texts is a social activity.[12] The process is not wholly individual and random, but relies on broader social and cultural conditioning factors. The expectations brought to the book by readers are formed through shared social experience. These expectations may also be encouraged by publishers who adopt marketing strategies aimed at particular communities of readers. This already goes beyond Fish's own formulations, but his ideas need a broad interpretation.

A community of readers can exist on various levels. On one level, it shares a common stock of literary references or images drawn from a shared imaginary library. Thus early British migrants to Australia, faced with the novel and threatening experiences of their new life, refracted them through shared literary analogies. On the long sea journey to Australia, for example, Coleridge was a regular companion. Emigrants' diaries and journals rarely failed to describe one particular landmark experience: the first sighting of the albatross, followed by attempts to kill or capture a specimen, in the style of the Ancient Mariner. 'Who could doubt their supernatural attributes? Certainly not a spirit-chilled lands woman, with Coleridge's magic legend perpetually repeating itself to her', wrote 27-year-old Louisa Meredith, arriving in Sydney in 1839. Louisa was to surround herself with mementos of the reading community from which she felt uprooted. She called her spaniel Dick Swiveller (from Dickens' *Old Curiosity Shop*), and she rode horses called Touchstone and Audrey (from Shakespeare's *As You Like It*).[13]

This agenda for the history of reading developed from the *histoire du livre*, as initiated by Lucien Febvre and the Annales school of history, and continued by Robert Darnton among many others. These scholars showed the importance of placing literary production into a social and economic context. They understood books as material and commercial objects, produced for profit and sent in search of readers. The history of the book thus emphasised the role of the printers, publishers and book-sellers who manufactured books and brought them to the reading public. Darnton developed the notion of the communications circuit (Figure 1.1), which genuflected in the direction of the author, but emphasised as well all the producers and distributive networks which give books a material reality and a social meaning.[14] The paper manufacturers, the composi-tors, the bookbinders, the itinerant peddlers, the smugglers of forbidden literature, librarians, booksellers – all these and other characters in the chain of production now became the objects of historical investigation. Darnton's model of textual transmission invites criticism for its anachro-nisms: it reflects the world of eighteenth-century France, when literature was peddled and smuggled to avoid censorship, and when books were often sold unbound for readers to bind as they wished.[15] In addition, the model is vague about how readers influence publishers. In spite of such criticisms, however, Darnton's scheme effectively dethrones the author from his or her role as sole creator.

L'histoire du livre also incorporates the study of the evolving material forms of the book. Authors, we are frequently reminded, write texts; they do not write books. As Stoddard explained,

> Whatever they may do, authors do not write books. Books are not written at all. They are manufactured by scribes and other artisans, by mechanics and other engineers, and by printing presses and other machines.[16]

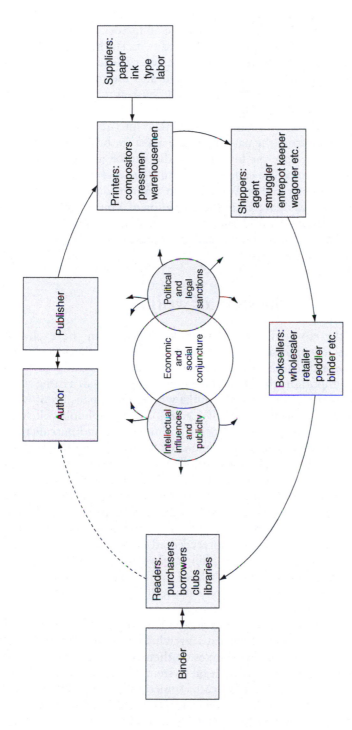

Figure 1.1 The Communications Circuit from 'Kiss of Lamourette' by Robert Darnton. © 1990 Robert Darnton. Used by Permission of W. W. Norton & Co., Inc.

The physical form of the text, on screen or on paper, its format, the disposition of typographical space on the page are all factors which determine the historical relationship between reader and text. The historian of reading attempts to elucidate the relationships between the text in its physical form, the means by which it was circulated and the meaning ascribed to it by its eventual public. Many rules and constraints determine these connections, some of them imposed by governmental or clerical censorship. There are technical limitations to be taken into account, as well as limitations deriving from the nature of the market for books in historical time. We might also trace the invention of the author, as a distinct legal persona, endowed since the eighteenth century at least with some form of intellectual property rights. We may also want to discuss the role of print culture as an essential part of the formation of a public sphere in the late eighteenth century. Considering the historical importance of print in European and Western culture, this agenda concerns all of us whose task it is to read and criticise texts.

The story of writing

We can tell the story of reading as it developed from the exclusive attribute of a few into a necessity of life for all. At the same time, the Western world learned to write, and the democratisation of writing forms an important theme of this book. Reading and writing were not quite simultaneous processes – on the whole, the expansion of writing practices followed the spread of reading – but this book will treat them together as far as possible. Writing had its public and bureaucratic forms: from the monumental inscriptions of ancient Rome to the writing of vast organisations like the Catholic Church, writing was always an essential instrument of power. In Fernand Braudel's famous work *The Mediterranean and the Mediterranean World in the Age of Philip II*, he pictured Philip of Spain at the centre of the greatest Empire the world had ever seen.[17] It was an Empire organised, administered and held together by bureaucratic writing on an unprecedented scale and pursued at an exhausting pace. Braudel imagined Philip at the centre of a global epistolary web, as a graphomaniac overwhelmed by his writing responsibilities. In Braudel's vision, 'writing the Empire' made Philip its victim at the same time as it enabled him to be its master.

The writing of power always engendered fear among the subordinate classes. They saw writing as a means by which governments recorded their land and possessions, levied taxes on them, organised conscription and administered an oppressive legal system. Since writing was an attribute of clerical elites, the uneducated sometimes imagined that it possessed magical powers. In the Caribbean, recounted López de Gómara, the Indians carrying the papers of their European lords hung them at the far end of a pole at a safe distance, because they were convinced that 'they contained some spirit and that they could speak, like some deity speaking through a man, and not by human means'.[18]

Increasingly, however, individuals appropriated writing for their own private purposes. The spread of cursive script, familiarly known as 'joined-up' or 'running' writing, facilitated more private and informal uses of writing technology in medieval Europe. In the modern period, writing was appropriated by every section of society for a wide range of purposes, sometimes pragmatic, sometimes intimate. Even for the humblest peasant, specific crises and moments made written communication absolutely essential. These situations occurred at times of great migrations of peoples, and in times of separation from one's family during war or imprisonment. The nineteenth century, in particular, witnessed a huge expansion of writing activity at every social level. We must therefore consider the West's apprenticeship in writing alongside its acquisition of reading skills.

Aims and objectives

The history of reading and writing goes in search of four main objectives. Firstly, our task is to find the targeted reader, or the audience desired and solicited by both author and publisher. The targeted reader may leave traces in the text itself, but stronger clues are usually found in the commercial or editing strategies chosen by the publisher to reach the desired market. The novels of Walter Scott, for example, which were immensely popular in Europe in the early nineteenth century, were sometimes presented as love stories and sometimes as realistic historical novels. Similarly, some editions of Jules Verne's novels stressed their pedagogic value and treated them almost as geography lessons, while their illustrations sometimes undermined this marketing approach by stressing the adventure and suspense which appealed to young male readers. In the choice of price, format, in the quality of the paper and binding, in the typeface and layout, in the presence or absence of illustration and in the marketing tactics employed to sell the work, the targeted reader can be detected.

Secondly, we are hunting for actual readers and their responses. Various constraints surround them, and we need to consult the normative sources, by which I mean all the pressures, bans and instructions through which elites and other institutions seek to channel and structure an individual's reading and to promote what they think *ought* to be read. To find flesh-and-blood readers, however, we must also plunge into their autobiographies, whether written or oral, spontaneously composed or written under duress from a spiritual confessor. Readers have written about their own reading and reactions to it and in doing so create valuable material for the study of reading practices in the past.

A third and more general aim remains to historicise the encounter between the reader and the text. The material form of the book is an important ingredient in identifying a market and soliciting certain reading responses. The ways in which a text reaches its readers may also affect the way it is received. The reader's own background and culture will further influence how the text is appropriated. The history of reading will then become a study of how meaning is ascribed to texts, and of the norms and practices which determine how in the past we have understood and made use of literature.

The fourth objective is to demonstrate the democratisation of writing practices, in all its ramifications. These include exploring how the growing mastery of the written word served governments and opened up new possibilities for individual communication. The access to writing has contributed to the emancipation of workers and women. This liberating process has always been dependent on the development of writing as an evolving technology. The multiple uses of writing – whether bureaucratic or religious, or domestic and familial – form part of the history of scribal culture in the Western world. They raise questions about the complex relationship between oral and written culture in pre-industrial societies.

Several turning points stand out in such a history, and the revolutions of the book help to frame what follows. One of the first of these was the invention of the codex, whose advantages allowed it to gradually replace the scroll. Another was the medieval invention of silent reading as the normal method of textual appropriation, which gradually took the place of reading as an oral performance and a communal activity. Reading aloud of course did not disappear; it still exists in different and specific contexts and we must be alert to them. These transformations are introduced in Chapter 2. A third landmark was the invention of printing, which, as this book will argue, has been overrated. The invention of printing is discussed in Chapter 3, and the role of print in the European Renaissance, Reformation and early modern popular culture is outlined in Chapters 4, 5 and 6. Chapter 7 analyses the rise of reading and writing literacy over several centuries. In Chapters 8 and 9, the importance of Enlightenment literature and its reception is discussed, as well as the significance of the so-called 'reading revolution' at the end of the eighteenth and beginning of the nineteenth centuries. A fourth revolution in reading and writing occurred in the nineteenth century, which witnessed the industrialisation of the book and the advent of a mass literary culture. These questions form the subject matter of Chapters 10 and 11, while Chapter 12 is entirely devoted to the spread of writing practices in this period.

Lastly, the appearance of computerised text brings us into the present. Some contemporary reactions to hypertext eerily resemble fifteenth-century responses to printing, ranging from hailing a new utopia to dire prophecies of doom. In spite of such parallels, the computer revolution has proved far more profound than Gutenberg's invention, in that it completely changed the material form of the codex which had been dominant for at least 1500 years. It has also invited an unprecedented involvement of the reader in the text, changing the way we write as well as the way we read.

2

Reading and writing in the ancient and medieval world

The origins of writing are lost in the mists of prehistory. From the earliest bark paintings of Australian aboriginal peoples to the palaeolithic cave paintings of Lascaux in south-western France, which date from about 15,000 BC, ancient people created signs and images on a variety of surfaces and for many purposes. Whether they produced their 'texts' to invoke a deity or to perpetuate an ancient collective memory, they were fulfilling some of the essential functions of writing: they wanted to communicate with other beings, either human or divine, and in some sense their signs and images constituted a representation of their world. Ancient societies wrote in pictures or graphic symbols, and they wrote on bark, stone, wood, clay (in Sumer), papyrus (in Egypt), tortoise shells, bamboo or silk (all in China) or animal skins. At some time around 3,500 BC, the people of Sumer in Mesopotamia (modern Iraq) developed cuneiform script, made by stamping reeds into softened clay. Writing has always signified power, and the wealth and power of Sumer helped to spread writing technology throughout the Middle East.

In these ancient societies, however, knowledge of writing was confined to a small minority. Political and clerical elites claimed the exclusive right to produce and interpret the meaning of signs. This chapter will briefly consider the nature of restricted literacy, as well as the importance of writing for traditional societies. Anthropologists have argued that mastery of writing technology marked out the great civilisations from the rest, and enabled new forms of rational thinking to develop. They suggest clear dichotomies between oral and literate cultures, arguing that memory and consciousness work very differently in oral as opposed to literate societies.[1] But what was the relationship between the oral and the literate in traditional societies? Polarised models, in which literacy drives out orality and science overcomes magic, may be of limited value in understanding the cultures of the ancient and medieval West. A more nuanced approach is needed for, as this chapter will suggest, oral cultures coexisted with literacy for centuries, and they enjoyed complex and dynamic relationships with each other.

In medieval Europe, three developments transformed the history of reading and writing in the long term. Firstly, the appearance of the codex in the first centuries of the Christian era gave the book its distinctive and recognisable material form: instead of a scroll (*volumen*) it increasingly consisted of individual pages loosely attached to each other at one side. Secondly, the appearance of consistent word separation changed the format of texts and helped to make individual silent reading the normal mode of appropriation. The so-called Dark Ages were thus responsible for two momentous cultural innovations: the adoption of the codex and the spread of silent reading. This chapter asks how significant was the shift from the scroll to the codex; it also investigates what made the invention of silent reading possible. Finally, the growth of medieval monarchies created new bureaucratic uses for writing in the fields of law, administration and accounting.

Restricted literacy

In the world of 'restricted literacy', as defined by Jack Goody, only a small minority of the gentry or upper class were literate, while the mass of the population lived on the 'margins of literacy'.[2] Reading and writing were the exclusive privilege of landowning and clerical elites. It has been estimated that in ancient Egypt only one per cent of the population could write, and this small group consisted of the Pharaoh, his administrative cadres, the leaders of the army, perhaps their wives and the priests.[3] Monopolistic control by elites was sometimes reinforced by the nature of writing itself. In China, for example, an individual needed to master about 3,000 different characters to acquire basic literacy, and perhaps 50,000 characters to become fully literate.[4] This could take an educated person an entire lifetime, and only the aristocracy had the leisure time for such learned pursuits.

Writing had a magical quality and a religious purpose. It gave privileged access to divine mysteries, in the same way that Latin was to do in the medieval Church. Writing enabled humans to communicate with their Gods. This is how experts explain inscriptions found inside Egyptian tombs: after the tombs were walled up, no human being would ever read their messages. At the same time, Gods could write to mortals, as when Belshazzar King of Babylon saw 'the writing on the wall' and had Daniel decipher its uncomfortable prophecies. Similarly, when Moses brought the tablets of the law down from Mount Sinai, the inscriptions of the commandments were thought to be of divine origin. Such texts became permanent points of reference; they issued from God and carried authority even if worshippers did not always understand their archaic language.

Many sacred texts originate in oral sources, but derive their force as permanent written records of God-given wisdom. Much of the New Testament consists of sayings and sermons recollected and written down by the evangelists, while the Koran similarly contains the divine revelations received from Allah and reported to a scribe by Mohammed, who reputedly was himself illiterate. Writing gave religions resonance and the power to expand. As Goody put it, 'Literate religions [like Christianity, Islam, Judaism]...are generally religions of conversion...You can spread them, like jam.'[5]

Knowledge of writing was an instrument of bureaucratic and priestly power. Priests or shamans claimed they alone were able to interpret divine writing in sacred books or perhaps, as Mesopotamians believed, inscribed in the entrails of animals after ritual sacrifice. Knowledge of writing made such experts privileged intermediaries between earthly existence and the life beyond. In some societies priests acted as the first archivists, storing texts and at the same time protecting their own privileged access to them. The genealogies of the tribes of Israel were enshrined in writing, and the laws of Leviticus defined the religious practices of Judaism for ever.

The logic of the alphabet: oral and written cultures

Anthropologists argue that writing imposes its own 'logic'; in other words, it encourages linear thinking and reasoning, changing human thought processes and enabling more sophisticated social and political organisations to come into being. Writing enabled governments to exert authority at a distance, to enforce impersonalised forms of law and to maintain systematic records of previous decisions. It facilitated tax collection, commercial transactions and the administration of legal systems. Not only did this enormously strengthen the power of any state but, Goody and Ong claim, it also restructured the way we think. It made us more aware of the past, and allowed individuals to think critically about long-standing collective traditions. It helped science overcome myth and reason overcome custom. Writing was integral to Western society and its values.

The introduction of alphabetic script, in this argument, was a decisive advance which potentially made reading and writing skills more accessible. The Chinese used ideograms ('characters'), the Egyptians wrote hieroglyphs and the Cretans of 2,000 BC used Linear A, a combination of signs and ideograms whose codes remain impenetrable even today. The importance of the phonetic alphabet lay in the fact that, unlike these other writing systems, its signs represented sounds of the human voice. This invention gave writing the potential to reach a wider audience for the first time. The Greek alphabet, which was developed in the sixth and fifth centuries BC, has sometimes been considered the key which unlocked the secrets of writing for the Western world. In associating letters and syllables with the pronunciation of specific vowels and consonants, alphabetical script could undermine the elite's monopoly of literacy. Unlike Chinese characters, it did not take a lifetime to learn.

This emphasis on the Greek alphabet as the unique crucible of modern rationality requires modification, and some of its protagonists have themselves recognised that the claim is vulnerable to the charge of Eurocentrism.[6] Phonetic alphabets existed elsewhere, for example amongst Semitic languages like Hebrew and Aramaic, although they used consonants only. The Greeks were neither the first nor the only society to produce a phonetic alphabet. In fact, they learned the idea from the Phoenicians, adding their own vowels. Furthermore, the extent of literacy in ancient Greece should not be overestimated. Sparta, for instance, had little familiarity with written culture. Certainly, an urban minority of Athenians (excluding peasants or slaves) had some elementary reading and writing skills. But this did not mean that books were commonly in circulation: Aristotle accumulated a celebrated library, but this was exceptional and, in any case, paper was very scarce in Greece.[7] According to Rosalind Thomas, to say that Athenians were literate meant rather that they could make out public inscriptions.[8] Ancient Greece was predominantly an oral culture, and many members of Athenian society lived on the margins of literacy.

Although Goody and Ong postulated a link between alphabetical literacy and the progress of abstract scientific thought, this can be questioned. Societies without alphabets and without widespread literacy have nevertheless achieved a sophisticated understanding of their world. Ancient China, for instance, was a non-alphabetic society with relatively advanced scientific knowledge.[9] Intrepid Polynesian navigators, to take another example, sailed thousands of miles across the Pacific: their knowledge of the ocean's geography was perfected long before the existence of maps, and Captain James Cook respected and consulted their expertise.

In oral cultures, people tell stories differently from the way they are told in a literate society. In Ong's analysis, oral storytellers are prone to repetition and redundancy. They rely on memory, which may be prodigious, but needs signposts in the story ('mnemonic clues') to guide the narrator and jog his or her memory about what comes next. Rhyme and rhythm are two techniques which structure the memory in this way. In oral narratives, words have great power, but the structure is 'additive not analytic' – only in writing, Ong argues, can distance and critical reflection be fully accomplished.[10]

A clear polarisation between the oral and the literate is nevertheless hard to swallow. When Ong refers disconcertingly to societies which still have 'an oral residue', the phrase suggests waste matter rather than a dynamic culture.[11] This seems an unsatisfactory way to acknowledge the inevitable blurring which occurs historically between oral and literate modes of cultural transmission.

Does literacy drive out the oral, condemning it to a residual existence? Multiple kinds of contact occur, sometimes based on conflict and at other times on reciprocal exchange. In some cases, as when a literate imperialist power overcomes a non-literate indigenous people, the relationship between the two is very unequal. The British colonisation of Australia, for example, brought severe linguistic erosion in its wake. In 1788, Australians spoke between 200 and 650 indigenous languages. Two centuries later, only 8 survived, if we exclude those spoken only by a few small groups and families.[12]

New Zealand provides another interesting example of the encounter between oral and literate societies. At the beginning of the nineteenth century, British settlers and missionaries tried hard to make the Maori people literate. They devised a Maori alphabet, taught the Maori how to read it and printed the Bible in Maori. And yet the culture of the Maori continued to rest on the spoken rather than the written word, as it had done for centuries. In 1840, 46 Maori chiefs from the north island of New Zealand signed a treaty with the British at Waitangi, which the British understood as a firm written agreement to surrender sovereignty to the crown. But it is far from clear that the Maori leaders placed the same importance on their own written 'consent'. What mattered more to them were the verbal arguments and discussion in which their complaints were presented. As one chief later said, 'The sayings of the Pakeha [white man] float light, like the wood of the *wahu* tree, and always remain to be seen, but the sayings of the Maori sink to the bottom like stone.'[13] In this story of cultural misunderstanding, writing was used to expropriate a predominantly 'oral' people. Oral and literate cultures seemed to coexist almost in parallel universes. In spite of colonial domination, however, oral cultures could still retain their vigour.

Oral culture had its own logic. Plato and Socrates both believed that learning and teaching depended on oral transmission, and could only effectively proceed by means of face-to-face dialogue between teacher and student. The Socratic teaching method rested on a very personal interplay of question and answer between the master and his disciple. As far as we know, Socrates wrote no books – we know of his ideas second-hand, through works like Plato's *Republic* – and he would be sceptical of the current academic infatuation with Web-based learning, which removes the verbal dialogue he thought fundamental. The problem with writing was what it destroyed: it ruined the capacity to memorise, which in some oral societies was very highly developed. In any group, the oral memory of its elders was a vast repository of history and tradition. As one man from Mali said, 'In Africa, every time an old man dies, it's like a library burning down.'[14] Writing furthermore creates a distance between individuals, so that it does not directly respond to criticism and objections, and it cannot defend itself against questions as can a speaker. Later, in Europe's medieval universities, the teaching of rhetoric continued a traditional emphasis on oral communication as a learned art and a powerful means of persuasion.

There is an assumption that the acquisition of literacy is an indicator of modernity and enlightenment. In many pre-modern societies, however, the oral and the literate coexisted; their relationship was sometimes confrontational and rarely equal, but often reciprocal. Unlike anthropologists, historians have not found strong evidence to support the idea of a decisive rupture between literacy and orality. The example of classical Greece can briefly illustrate some aspects of the relationships between the written and the spoken word in ancient societies.

Reading and writing in ancient Greece

Unlike Semitic languages, Greek was written and read from left to right. The script was phonetic, without standardised spelling. Greeks wrote in *scriptio continua*: that is to say, in continuous script, with no space between words and with line breaks which did not respect the end of a word. Such a completely unpunctuated script is very hard to read; but it becomes comprehensible when it is verbalised, and it was the act of speaking the text aloud that gave it meaning. Reading in ancient Greece was generally viewed as oral performance, especially in the case of poetry recitals to private audiences (the 'symposium'). Although silent reading certainly existed, it was a marginal activity in the Greco-Roman world. The writer wrote to create sound, and his task was only complete when his text was transformed into the spoken word. According to Jesper Svenbro, Greeks sometimes thought of writer and reader as a homosexual couple, in which the reader was a necessary but passive instrument of the writer.[15] For the Greeks, then, writing words was like writing music: it meant little until someone gave it voice.

Antisthenes taught that knowledge should be inscribed on the mind and not on paper.[16] The great Greek historians Herodotus and Thucydides produced histories based for the first time on written documents, but they also relied on oral sources, and Herodotus read his history in public performances.[17] Homer's *Iliad*, which appeared by about 700 BC, was based on a long tradition of oral composition by various bards. In fact Homeric scholarship was transformed in the twentieth century by the realisation that this epic poem was essentially an oral composition without a single identifiable author. In spite of the increasing importance of writing in fourth-century Athens, the significance of spoken communication was not thereby diminished.

The fact that Plato launched a polemic against the use of writing in education suggests that it was spreading. Athenians used writing for various practical purposes. They used pieces of pottery for making all sorts of notes – this was their scrap paper.[18] They wrote business contracts and property transactions. In the time of Solon in the seventh and sixth centuries BC, there was a shift from customary to written law. Mortgage stones (*horoi*) registered the existence of a debt on land, and they were removed when the mortgage was fully paid. Written evidence was admitted in court, but it was not necessarily considered more reliable than oral testimony. In about 405 BC, a city archive was established at the Metroön, which stored documents in various media – stone *stelai*, wooden tablets and papyrus scrolls. But you had to know where to look if you wanted to consult the archive. Records of legal cases were simply put in jars and then sealed up – a far cry from modern practices of information retrieval.[19] Female literacy remained unusual. According to Menander, 'Whoever teaches a woman the alphabet . . . is giving poison to a terrible serpent.'[20]

Following Zumthor, we might think of oral cultures in three categories.[21] At one end of the spectrum are societies in which writing is completely absent, which may historically have included parts of the Pacific and sub-Saharan Africa; at the other extreme lie societies like the modern West, in which print culture is dominant and oral communication is pushed to the margins. Somewhere in between the two extremes lies a third group of mixed cultures, in which oral and written cultures coexist and influence each other. Classical Athens and medieval Europe provide examples of such hybrid states.

Word separation and silent reading

Although silent reading certainly existed in antiquity,[22] a decisive shift in the history of reading began to occur in the early medieval period. In St. Augustine's *Confessions*, the author was amazed to observe St. Ambrose, bishop of Milan, reading exclusively in silence, for 'When he read, his eyes followed the pages and his heart pondered the meaning, though his voice and tongue were still.'[23] Perhaps, thought Augustine, Ambrose is just resting his voice, or perhaps he is fed up with being pestered with questions about scholarly problems, and is giving us the message that he does not want to be interrupted for a while. Augustine could not find a good explanation for Ambrose's behaviour, because he thought of reading as an oral activity, involving a whole textual community in a common attempt to understand scripture.

In the seventh century, Isidore of Seville declared that reading aloud hampered comprehension of the text, and he suggested quiet reading, in which readers moved their lips and murmured the text.[24] This indicates a transition from reading aloud to a more individualised appropriation of the text. Reading in a low voice was increasingly considered an aid towards profound meditation and memorisation.

From about the seventh century onwards, according to Paul Saenger, the separation of words significantly assisted the spread of individual reading in silence.[25] In the ancient world, as we have seen, Latin and Greek texts were usually written in continuous script, with uniform capital letters, and they had none of the aids to silent reading which we now take for granted in modern transcription. The process of change first developed on the fringes of the Roman world, where expertise in Latin may have been thin on the ground. Monks and their scribes in Ireland and the British Isles initiated the practice of separating words, introducing a range of writing techniques which clarified the meaning of Latin texts and aided silent, individual readers to decode them. New writing practices made reading faster and began to transform the relationship between author, reader and text. In a ninth-century vernacular poem, an Irish monk at the abbey of Reichenau compared reading to a cat silently stalking a mouse: an astonishingly modern evocation.[26]

After the collapse of Roman teaching institutions, the Church played a leading role in promoting written culture, but evolution was very gradual. Dots (called interpuncts) were sometimes inserted between syllables and words. Spaces were inserted to 'aerate' the text, but not at first in a thorough or systematic way. But by the twelfth century, word separation was universal in Europe, and a range of punctuation marks and signposts in the text assisted its comprehension. Sometimes scribes even returned to older manuscripts written in *scriptio continua*, and added slashes to indicate breaks between words.[27]

Other breakthroughs followed. The cathedral schools of the twelfth century developed the use of silent reading. In the fifteenth century, the rule of silence was adopted for the first time in the libraries of Oxford University and the Sorbonne; until then, readers went to libraries to 'speak', or to dictate their texts, not read them silently. Oral reading, of course, is much slower than silent reading, and monastic libraries would often lend their readers a single volume at Easter, to be returned one year later. Monastic experts on the act of reading began to recognise private and silent reading as a sign of sincere devotion and serious meditation, whereas the chanting in common of psalms and responses could become mechanical, did not spring 'from the heart' and did not necessarily reflect a superior inner spirituality. In the fourteenth and fifteenth centuries, representations of the Annunciation in French and Flemish paintings increasingly portrayed the event as a revelation experienced by Mary as she was absorbed in solitary contemplation of a sacred text.[28]

Silent reading had become associated with deep spiritual devotion. By the fourteenth century, for example, books of hours had become immensely popular. They contained programmes of prayers and psalms for individual use at fixed times of the day. They were easily portable, much employed by the educated laity, and some were luxury items with sumptuous illumination. The book of hours illustrated the way that books had acquired a more private and intimate focus. Its images and devotions opened up a private spiritual world. Reading now demanded greater individual engagement with texts, whether the reader was empathetic or sceptical towards what he or she read.

The codex: a revolution in reading and writing

In the first century AD, the Romans started to adopt parchment, named after Pergamum (in modern Turkey), where it was supposedly invented. Parchment, made from animal skin, was hardier than papyrus, which had the added disadvantage for the Romans that it had to be imported from the Middle East. Unlike papyrus, parchment could be scraped clean and re-used (the original meaning of the palimpsest). Parchment technology, however, was labour-intensive and for this reason expensive. Drafts were made with a stylus on wax tablets before being entrusted to a scribe. Animal skin had to be scraped, smoothed with pumice stone and then polished with goats' teeth. Parchment was made from the skins of cattle, sheep, goat, rabbit and even squirrel. But calf's skin (*vellum*) was superior. The Winchester Bible needed 250 calfs' skins, but these would be selected from over 2,000 hides, rejecting all those with a blemished surface.[29]

The monastic scriptoria of the early Middle Ages brought together multi-talented scribes and manuscript illuminators. Between the seventh and the thirteenth centuries, scribes had to know many scripts among the various uncials and minuscules in use in what Armando Petrucci calls Italy's 'multi-graphic environment'.[30] They had to be competent to copy religious works in Latin, Greek or Hebrew, and they had to master the difficult technology of writing. Before copying, they first lined the page using a plumb line. They were armed with a razor, pumice stone and chalk to erase errors and make corrections, and they needed a supply of both black and red inks. As they worked, they would hold a knife in one hand, to scrape the paper if necessary and to keep the paper firmly in one place. The knife was also used to sharpen their bird's-feather quill pens (the original 'penknife').

The scroll or *volumen* had been the accepted form of writing for centuries: the great library of Alexandria contained about half a million scrolls before it was burned down by Aurelius in 273 AD.[31] The scroll, however, was very unwieldy: some surviving scrolls were ten metres long.

Because they were in *scriptio continua*, without page breaks, chapter breaks, page numbers or an index, orienting oneself within the text of a scroll was not easy.

Between the second and the fourth centuries AD, a major landmark in the history of reading and writing occurred: the codex was increasingly preferred to the scroll, and was to give the book the enduring form it retained for 17 centuries to come. In the codex, the book has individual pages of the same size, attached at the left-hand side and covered with cloth, wooden boards or some richer material. The Romans had already started to attach sheets of parchment to one another, but the codex proper is usually attributed to the Christian world, and papyrus codices of the Bible have survived from as long ago as the second century.

The codex possessed several technological advantages over the scroll. For one thing, both sides of the paper could be used, so the codex could hold much more text. Before long, the entire Christian Bible could be contained within a single codex. Greater capacity, however, did not guarantee greater coherence. Many early codices were miscellanies, or collections of different books, perhaps written in different languages by different authors. Unlike the scroll, the *codex* did not need to be held in both hands, liberating the reader who could read and take notes, scratch, eat or drink at the same time. The word processor has re-introduced a screen version of the scroll, although now we read it from top to bottom, not perpendicularly as early readers did. Above all, finding one's way in a codex was easier because page numbers could be added, as well as meaningful indexes and summaries of the contents. Scholars could find quotations, and refer to specific parts of a text which they could compare to other texts in other codices. The surprising thing is that the codex took so long to become accepted. The *volumen* was still in use throughout the Middle Ages, and it was long favoured by the English monarchy for reasons which are unclear. The scroll was also used in the theatre, which is the origin of the actor's 'role'.

The spread of bureaucratic literacy

In the early Middle Ages, all governments made greater use of writing, to assist and record their administrative and legal decisions. As Marco Brava de la Serna pithily put it several centuries later, 'Monarquía sin letras, Imperio sin luz' – a monarchy without letters is an empire without light.[32] He referred to the Habsburg Empire, but its medieval predecessors were gradually discovering how to derive greater strength from the uses of writing. Michael Clanchy has analysed the passage from memory to written record between the eighth and the fourteenth centuries, and described various forms of literacy in early medieval

Europe.[33] His often-quoted work is fundamental, and it shows that the expansion of government engendered forms of bureaucratic writing which left the mass of the population on the margins of literacy.

Today we think of literacy as combining the skills of reading and writing in a symmetrical relationship. It is considered a mark of education and social integration and to be illiterate carries a powerful stigma. But historically as well as today, literacy took many forms, including reading literacy, writing literacy, listening literacy, literacy in particular languages and the ability to count. In medieval Europe writing was unnecessary for most educated people – they paid a professional scribe to do their writing for them. They dictated what needed to be written, demonstrating the essential difference between the author (who spoke the text) and the scribe (who wrote it down). Perhaps authors would eventually add their personal seal or their signature, but often this consisted of a cross. Once a mark of Christian allegiance, signing with a cross now indicates illiteracy (Figure 2.1).

Religious incentives to literacy were very strong. The main purpose was to read one's prayers and follow the Christian liturgy. Prayers and worship were group activities in which texts were spoken or sung together, so that listening and reading aloud were vital aspects of learning

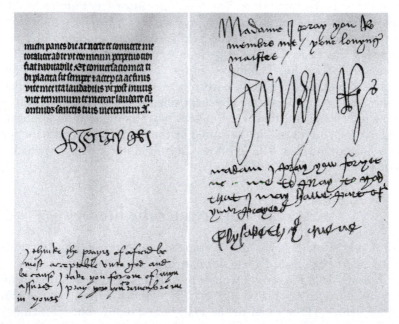

Figure 2.1 Varieties of medieval handwriting.

Note: These English royal signatures appear in a book of hours. On the right are the signatures of Henry VII and Elizabeth of York; and on the left the writing of Henry VIII and his first wife Catherine of Aragon, whose signature has been removed. © Alamy Images.

to be literate. So, too, was learning Latin. In medieval Europe, to be *litteratus* meant to be familiar with Latin; the illiterate were those who knew no Latin. In 1301, letters from Pope Boniface VIII had to be read to the Parliament at Westminster 'in Latin for the literate and in the native tongue for the illiterate'.[34] A *litteratus* was a cultivated man, but he was not necessarily able to read or write, while an *illitteratus* was not necessarily completely illiterate in a modern sense. When John of Salisbury famously wrote 'rex illitteratus est quasi asinus coronatus' – an illiterate king is like a crowned ass – he meant that without Latin a ruler would not have access to the texts from which he might receive God's guidance.[35] Latin remained the language of the Church and thus an international language. It remained the language of the dominant elites, and the subordinate classes identified written Latin culture as one ingredient in their oppression. In 1022, for instance, heretics were burned at the stake in Orléans for attacking the books of the clergy as merely artificial inventions 'written on the skins of animals' and not the true word of God.[36]

As Clanchy demonstrates, oral communication and memory continued to play a powerful role in medieval law and government. The Magna Carta of 1215, for example, was, in retrospect, a significant constitutional milestone in English history, but for it to have any meaning for contemporaries it had to be orally proclaimed throughout the kingdom, in both English and French (the written original was in Latin).[37] Important documents could always be forged or lost in transit; the voice of a messenger seemed more reliable and authentic. The King's word was law, whether someone happened to write it down or not. The law courts regularly relied on oral witness to adjudicate disputes. In England, in order to resolve an issue, they might resort to consulting a jury of 12 local knights. The managers of great estates had their accounts regularly 'audited' – which meant that they were read aloud. What made contracts into binding agreements were verbal promises and the symbols which accompanied such pledges. For instance, a deal might be clinched by the exchange of knives or swords. This practice survives in the ceremonial exchange of wedding rings between bride and groom. Financial transactions were recorded on wooden sticks or 'tallies'. Documentary evidence might accompany all such agreements, but it did not yet carry the force of law. Custom and oral wisdom remained authoritative.

In twelfth- and thirteenth-century England, however, the authorities began to make greater use of documentary records. They drew up lists of tax liability, while monasteries and the great estates inventoried their assets in writing, recorded the annual harvest yield and used written accounting systems. The monasteries copied their title deeds into written registers (cartularies) for greater long-term security. Under Henry II (1133–89), the English monarchy employed more clerks than ever before, and started to issue royal decrees (writs) in standard written formats. This generated a new form of secular literacy, which was independent of the Church and spread in response to the day-to-day needs of the king and his administration. In theory, the development of written law inspired greater transparency and less arbitrary decision-making. In practice, it also paved the way for new generations of legal specialists. Sometimes the advent of greater literacy could be liberating; at other times it entrenched the power of castes.

In the eighth and ninth centuries, the Empire of Charlemagne (768–814) made use of writing as an instrument of power, and closely associated religious intellectuals like Alcuin of York with the apparatus of state. The emperor needed lists of property to be taxed, of soldiers to be mobilised and of the lords who had sworn him allegiance. A new kind of handwriting, the Carolingian minuscule, speeded up the work of government scribes. The Carolingian empire stretched from the Pyrenees to Saxony and from northern Italy to the Netherlands, including much of present-day France, Belgium, Germany and Switzerland. Only written Latin could transcend the linguistic mosaic of such a disparate kingdom. Latin literacy had two important functions: it united the government of the empire and distinguished the dominant elite from mere commoners. Ordinary people were on the margins of Latin literacy, but they could understand documents if the need arose; their literacy in Latin was passive rather than active. For Charlemagne, writing was an instrument of government. Its uses expanded to meet administrative requirements, but the literacy thus produced was of a narrow and bureaucratic kind.

England, meanwhile, stood on the periphery of Christian Europe. In the early Middle Ages it was already a melting pot of Celtic, Latin, Anglo-Saxon and Danish cultures. But Britain as a whole had a tenuous grasp of Latin; the Viking raids had destroyed centres of scholarship, and in the Carolingian period there was a brain drain to the continent.[38] In relation to the Latinised world, England seemed backward and remote. As far as most of Christian Europe was concerned, it might as well have been in outer space. Conquest by Duke William of Normandy in 1066, however, brought England into the orbit of continental Europe and enormously boosted the significance of written culture. In 1086, the Domesday Book attempted a systematic written survey of land ownership and taxable assets across the country. By the reign of Henry I in the early twelfth century, a substantial royal secretariat was producing about 4,500 royal letters annually (an average scribe could write three letters per day).[39]

Britain imported books from France, in French or Latin, and lay readers could enjoy poems, songs and histories as long as they mastered these languages. After the Norman Conquest, therefore, the Anglo-Saxon gentry faced the challenge of becoming trilingual. The Church and the royal bureaucracy functioned in Latin, but the everyday language of the new Norman upper class and its literature was French. Meanwhile, English remained the spoken language of ordinary people. Each language had its own purpose and the language in which one wrote was not necessarily the language one used in everyday conversation with family, friends or vassals. Royal decrees had to be publicly read aloud in English if the king's subjects were to understand them. In the law courts, testimony delivered in any language had to be translated into Latin, until in the thirteenth century French became the language of legal record in England.

The margins of literacy

Reading, writing and listening were quite separate skills, and in most of Europe, they might have involved different languages and alphabets. Christian evangelism spread the use of Gothic and Cyrillic script in Central and Eastern Europe, while in Al-Andalus (Moslem Spain) Latin, Arabic and Hebrew were used side by side.[40] By the fourteenth and fifteenth centuries, public inscriptions on monuments were starting to proliferate, and there were signs that an archive mentality was developing. Royal archives, for example, were established at Valencia in 1419 and Aragon in 1436.[41] As governments increasingly adopted the techniques of writing and keeping written records, ruling elites started to lose their monopoly over literacy. The expansion of royal bureaucracies in itself demanded the recruitment of large numbers of literate scribes and copyists. At the same time, royal subjects inevitably resorted more frequently to written records. They needed documentary contracts of sale and title deeds to their property, while writing a will was a secure way to organise one's succession.

The consequences of expanded bureaucratic literacy at the level of the monarchy were thus felt further down the social scale. Members of the gentry who owned property needed writing skills to manage their affairs effectively, and even peasants occasionally needed writing to buy and sell land. Many 'family books' survive from the fourteenth and fifteenth centuries, mainly from Tuscany, Provence and Catalonia. In their pages, peasants and artisans kept their accounts, wrote the genealogy of their family and recorded notable events. The world of restricted literacy, therefore, contained within it the potential to erode monopolies on literacy even if, in the early Middle Ages, the lower classes remained at best passively literate, or at worst on the margins of written culture.

3

Was there a printing revolution?

The invention of printing is often considered a revolutionary event with far-reaching consequences for the development of Western thought. The title of Elizabeth Eisenstein's influential book *The Printing Press as an agent of change* was in itself a manifesto for the thesis of the printing revolution.[1] The invention of moveable type, in this view, heralded a new typographical culture, in which texts could circulate more widely, enjoy a more permanent existence and facilitate great advances in scholarship – all of which had allegedly been impossible in the world of scribal culture. Printing, it was argued, had major consequences for the diffusion of the Scientific Revolution of the seventeenth century, the Protestant Reformation and the Renaissance. In fact, it is hard to imagine these intellectual developments without the printed word to spread their influence.

The 'printing revolution' thesis enjoyed further support from an unexpected source: the Canadian sociologist and media guru of the 1960s, Marshall McLuhan. In his *Gutenberg Galaxy*, McLuhan claimed that the invention of print changed not just the way we read, but the way we think.[2] McLuhan associated the rise of print with thinking with the eye; that is to say, it developed linear thought patterns quite different from those based on sound or touch. Furthermore, McLuhan saw print as a medium which individualised the reader, and distanced his or her private perceptions from the common values which held together a group or a whole society.

These were enormous claims to make on behalf of the invention of moveable type by Johannes Gutenberg and his colleagues at some time in the middle of the fifteenth century. But what did Gutenberg actually change? This chapter will examine important aspects of the so-called 'printing revolution', and question whether such a revolution actually occurred. Arguments about the revolutionary nature of the invention of printing need to be looked at very closely and their limitations made clear. For one thing, they apply mainly to the transformation of the life of the scholar. Printing did not touch the lives of ordinary people, who remained part of a rich oral culture, largely outside the world of print, for centuries after Gutenberg. Secondly, print did not immediately change either the nature or the subject matter of the book itself. It did not of course change the material – paper – on which books were produced. It took the arrival of the computer to make a radical break with 17 centuries of traditional book production. The form of the book, as a series of pages stitched or bound together, was unaltered. Some exaggerated claims have been advanced for the 'printing revolution' thesis, and they need to be carefully scrutinised. Before this, however, we should establish the history and mythology of Gutenberg's invention.

The Gutenberg myth

Little is known about precisely when and where printing was invented. In fact, the fragmentary nature of the evidence has encouraged the proliferation of myths about the origins of printing in Europe. The current consensus on the exact date when printing appeared, and on where it was invented, has developed over centuries of argument over disputed evidence. The consensus view favours the German city of Mainz as the place of origin, and the invention is of course conventionally attributed to Johannes Genszfleisch, usually known as Gutenberg. In this domain, as in many other provinces of the history of technology, the myth of the individual creative genius is alive and well.

Yet it has not always been so. It took half a century, for instance, before chroniclers invented and consecrated the date (1440) which would thenceforth be celebrated as the origin of printing.[3] Although several late-fifteenth-century texts named Gutenberg as the inventor, the emergence of the revolutionary hero is a comparatively recent phenomenon. When the bicentenary and tercentenary of the invention of printing were celebrated in Leipzig in 1640 and 1740, respectively, Gutenberg's associates Fust and Schöffer were named as the main inventors, together with their 'assistant' Gutenberg.[4] Only in the mid-eighteenth century did Gutenberg emerge as the primary protagonist, with Schöpflin's collection of documents on Gutenberg in 1760.[5] From this moment on, the myth developed that Gutenberg's backers and colleagues Fust and Schöffer played only a minor role in the story. In the romantic era, Gutenberg was portrayed as a misunderstood genius, dedicated to the cause of universal education, but dying in poverty after being cheated by the parasitical capitalists who exploited him. This, for example, was the theme of the work on Gutenberg by the French poet Lamartine, which he wrote for Hachette's railway bookstalls.[6]

One is entitled to question this myth of the inventor-genius, which is based on the fallacy of 'The Eureka Factor'.[7] In this popular version of scientific progress, 'discoveries' are 'made' by individual geniuses who have sudden and unexpected brainwaves, rather than as outcomes of a cumulative process of learning. Thus alongside Archimedes and his bath and Newton and his apple we also class Gutenberg and moveable type. One pamphlet of 1840 called Gutenberg, with enormous exaggeration, 'inventor of the book', ignoring two millennia of book production before print.[8] The reality is more mundane. A range of developments converged to make possible the invention of moveable type in the 1440s. One was the growing demand for secular and humanist learning among social elites, together with the rise of universities, which had already caused a rise in production of the scribal book in the decades before the invention of printing.[9] Growing urbanisation helped to make a real market for books possible. Improvements in paper-making and the development of metallurgy were further technological conditions necessary for the invention of moveable type. Gutenberg spent years experimenting to find the right mixture of metals for the moulds out of which his characters would be formed in even stronger steel. He worked not as an isolated hero, but rather as a member of a team, and he worked in a cultural and technological context which made his success both achievable and worthwhile.

Modern scholarship has re-examined some further myths, suggesting, for example, that Gutenberg was by no means a victim of financiers, but an active entrepreneur in his own right.[10] In addition, it now seems difficult to align Gutenberg with the development of the humanist culture of the Renaissance. As was the case for so many printers of his time, his primary customer was the Catholic Church, which provided his bread and butter. Nineteenth-century myths of Gutenberg sometimes appropriated him for Protestantism, or else represented him as a liberal progressive breaking through the choking fog of clerical bigotry. Gutenberg, however, was a jobbing printer for the ecclesiastical authorities. Not only did he produce the 42-line Bible, but he also printed the Papal Indulgences, which had been one of the main targets of Lutheran polemics.

This brief excursion into the mythology of Gutenberg's invention has aimed to show how the notion of the printing revolution has been manufactured and nurtured over the centuries. The modern ideology of the print revolution is chiefly a construction of the French Revolution and the nineteenth century. For the French revolutionaries, print production separated modern thinking from the barbaric, 'Gothic' and irrational Middle Ages. For them, modernity began with print, which had made possible the diffusion of those eighteenth-century philosophers whom the French Revolution selected as its intellectual ancestors. In September 1792, the Prussian-born revolutionary Cloots asked the French National Assembly to transfer Gutenberg's ashes to the Pantheon, where great republican heroes were honoured. Cloots praised Gutenberg as the first true revolutionary, without whom Voltaire and Rousseau would be unknown.[11] Subsequently, nineteenth-century commentators echoed the utopian discourse of the French Revolution, with its emphasis on the advance of reason and liberty, attributing to Gutenberg the role of standard-bearer for the emancipation of all humanity. Paradoxically, it did so just at the moment when mechanisation was beginning to make Gutenberg's techniques obsolete.

Moveable type had already been in use in East Asia, long before Gutenberg's invention. The first mobile characters made in metal appeared in Korea probably two centuries before 1440. Kai-Wing Chow suggests that the Chinese and Koreans deliberately preferred woodblock technology because it was more suitable for their paper, which did not require a firm press to transfer the ink.[12] Since wood was then abundant, this was a rational choice. It was in Europe, therefore, rather than in Asia, that printing was to have widespread social and cultural consequences, and it was from European bases that printing colonised the world. It is generally agreed that Gutenberg rather than the Koreans made the first printing press, and the idea that Gutenberg borrowed from the Koreans is pure fancy. In the printing mythology of the nineteenth century, Europe used printing to spread its civilising influence to the primitive (i.e., non-European) world, to Christianise the natives and educate the ignorant.

Several attractive interpretations may be offered to explain why printing took off in Europe and not in Asia. A technological interpretation points to the easy and cheap access to woodcut technology in China and to the practical difficulty of mastering the thousands of characters which make up the Chinese 'alphabet'. A more socio-political perspective might contrast the Chinese imperial elite's exclusive grip on written culture with Europe's greater willingness to see the social and political benefits of more widespread literacy. Lastly, and perhaps more decisively, an economic historian might associate the development of print literacy in Europe with the gradual rise of a capitalist market economy, and the very different trajectory taken by the slowly developing economies of Asia.

The early world of print

Gutenberg's associates and fellow workers spread the new printing technology, taking work commissioned by great aristocrats and wealthy burgers, the churches, law courts and universities. The great international fairs of Leipzig and Frankfurt, not forgetting the Spanish fair of Medina del Campo, helped to advertise the potential of print. Every year at such fairs booksellers and printers met to display their wares, settle their accounts with each other and pay their debts. They usually paid in kind rather than cash, exchanging parts of their stock. At the same time, large numbers of almanacs and brochures would be sold to the general public. In the first wave of printing, the technology was adopted in the thriving urban centres of Germany, northern Italy and the Netherlands, many of them prosperous commercial cities like Leipzig, Antwerp and Venice, which dominated Italian book production. By 1480, printing workshops existed in 110 towns of Western Europe.[13]

They included London and Oxford, although Britain generally lagged behind the continent. The first printed book in English was produced in 1474 by William Caxton, working in Bruges before he established his own shop, with royal patronage, in Westminster Abbey. Until the 1530s, most printers working in Britain came from continental Europe, so that from the British point of view, printing was a newfangled foreign invention. The first presses established in Oxford did not last long, but in London a network of booksellers and artisans grew up in and around Paternoster Row near St. Paul's Cathedral. Close by were the schools, convents and law courts which demanded printed material.

The generation after 1480 took printing into Switzerland, Spain and France, where Basle and Geneva, Toledo and Valladolid, Paris and Lyon now developed as centres of print production. In the sixteenth century, print technology spread further afield to Scandinavia, Eastern Europe and beyond. Moscow had the printing press by the 1560s, and Constantinople by 1727. Spanish and Portuguese missionaries were responsible for establishing printing in Mexico in the 1540s, Peru in 1584 and Japan (Nagasaki) in 1590. The first press arrived in New England in 1638.

Printing spread wherever there was a demand from merchants, the Church or political authorities. Trading centres were important printing centres, which is why Antwerp, Venice and Lyon led the way. In France, the centralisation of political and judicial institutions in Paris, together with the presence there of the Sorbonne, produced the capital's peculiar concentrations of print-shops and booksellers, who gathered in the Palais-Royal and the Latin Quarter. By 1530, Paris and Lyon were together responsible for 90 per cent of all publications in France.[14] Parisian printers specialised in liturgical works and books of hours while Lyon, which supplied the Italian and Spanish markets, concentrated on medical and legal reference works. In Spain, the early centres of printing included Toledo, the great ecclesiastical centre, Valladolid, city of the royal court, Alcalá, because of its university, and Seville, the gateway to the Americas.

The speed of dissemination should not be overestimated, for demand was still limited. Paris had 183 printing presses in 1644, and the university town of Leiden in the Netherlands had only 29 presses in 1651.[15] Most firms, however, only possessed one or two presses each. Half a century after the invention of printing, print runs only averaged about

Figure 3.1 The Gutenberg Bible.

Note: Gutenberg experimented for years with inks and metals before he could perfect his 42-line Bible, an early printing masterpiece from 1455. Note the deep black ink, Gothic font and personalised decoration. © The Print Collection/Alamy.

500 copies. Gutenberg's 42-line Bible itself, produced in two columns and in large in-folio format, had a print run of between 160 and 180 copies only (Figure 3.1).[16] In the sixteenth century, between 1,000 and 1,500 copies became the norm, and this remained the situation until the nineteenth century. In England, the Stationers' Company (the powerful guild of booksellers) formally agreed in 1587 that 1500 would be the maximum print run for ordinary books.[17] A few genres always exceeded this relatively limited circulation, like catechisms, works of piety and prayer, and annual almanacs which were produced in runs of tens of thousands to be sold cheaply by itinerant peddlers (*colporteurs*). Customers were

responsible for their own binding; it was cheaper to both transport and sell books unbound.

Paper was still made from rags mashed to pulp, according to a technique originally derived from the Arabs. An army of ragpickers was needed to collect waste cloth (*chiffons*) and a good supply of clean water was essential. Paper was by far the largest cost. In Christopher Plantin's workshop in Antwerp, paper regularly absorbed between 60 and 70 per cent of production costs, and this proportion rose in the case of large print runs.[18] In other words, increasing the print run did not enable cost savings, as is the case today; it simply made it harder to make a profit. In contrast, the wooden press itself did not require a great capital investment. A good stock of characters was vital and expensive, especially for a printer working in several languages like Plantin, printer/publisher of the polyglot Bible, with texts in Latin, Greek, Hebrew, Syriac and Aramaic. While classical scholars and Renaissance humanists favoured 'roman' characters, the Church and the general populace used Gothic

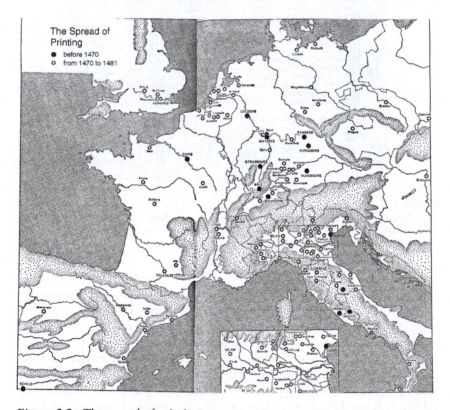

Figure 3.2   The spread of printing.

Note: In half a century, Gutenberg's invention had spread to the main commercial and university centres of Europe. © The Gutenberg Institute.

script, which survived strongly in Germany and Austria. The ink, concocted mainly from oil, soot and gum, was spread by ink-balls, made of leather and stuffed with horsehair, with wooden handles. Each printing press employed four or five workers to prepare the type (compositors), ink it and operate the press. In seventeenth-century Paris, they might produce 2,500 printed sheets in a day's work.[19] They worked as a team, for 12 or 14 hours per day, but they had a nomadic existence, moving cities frequently to find work. Printers and their apprentices were normally literate and had an unusually good knowledge of Latin; they also had a reputation for indiscipline and binge drinking. A map illustrating the spread of printing is shown in Figure 3.2.

The 'printing revolution' defended

Printing ensured a wider diffusion of literature than ever before to the cultivated elite, and for this reason it has been labelled a 'communications revolution'. Print made possible a much faster rate of production than before. Scribes usually copied three to four pages per day, but the printing press could produce at a much faster rate than this and therefore disseminate texts more widely. Whereas in the world of scribal culture, intellectuals had to hunt down rare copies of manuscripts in monastery libraries, and then have them laboriously copied for consultation, now there might be several hundred copies in general circulation.

The 'print revolution' did not simply mark a quantitative jump in the rate of production and the number of copies of a text in circulation. There were qualitative changes involved, too. The protagonists of the printing revolution thesis, like Elizabeth Eisenstein, argued that print made texts more permanent. It contributed to the standardisation of language and the appearance of fixed, uniform editions. There had been revivals of Greek learning in the past, according to this thesis, but the essential texts of ancient authors had often been lost. What we know as the European Renaissance, however, rediscovered ancient learning once and for all. It put it into print, giving it a permanent life and thereby making repeated cycles of loss and rediscovery redundant.

Print produced uniform editions, with standardised spelling, instead of the textual corruption which had characterised the hand-copied editions of tired scribes. Even a good scribe was prone to human error, and could be expected to make at least one mistake per page. Instead of copies which all varied in some way from each other, now in the print world (in theory at least) all copies were identical. Of course, serious mistakes could still be made. One Bible of 1631 printed the seventh commandment omitting the vital word 'not', telling readers 'Thou shalt commit adultery.' This was the so-called 'Wicked Bible', whose printers were subsequently fined.[20] Uniformity in print was nevertheless a vital development for reference works like maps and dictionaries. A map or an anatomical diagram would have little credibility if the reader knew that every copy was unique. At the same time, alphabetical order became generally accepted, even if some purists regarded it as contrary to nature (had God, after all, created the species in alphabetical order?). For the first time, ecclesiastical authorities could envisage the same prayer book in the hands of all the faithful, which guaranteed standardised forms or worship everywhere.

The life of scholars was thus transformed. They could consult texts more freely and, importantly, could more easily compare different texts and build on the work of past scholars. Print made their work accessible as never before, and so knowledge could advance in a cumulative process. Scholars could consider and revise the wisdom of the past: they would not always be compelled to reinvent it. Thus the Polish monk Copernicus reworked the calculations of the Greek astronomer Ptolemy with the position of the Earth and the Sun reversed, to postulate the heliocentric universe.[21]

The standardised vocabulary of the printed book helped to formalise vernacular languages. It could give oral languages a literary existence, and it helped to spread the use of languages like French, English, Italian and German, eroding popular dialects. This alleged connection between national consciousness and the advent of print will be further discussed below.

The idea of the 'printing revolution' thus interprets the arrival of print as a step forward for enlightenment, science, rationality and modernity. In the hands of Marshall McLuhan, however, this liberal-progressive viewpoint disintegrated. Although McLuhan made enormous claims for the influence of print, he was ultimately very pessimistic about the consequences. Print, he argued, had changed the balance of human sense perceptions. *Homo typographicus*, for McLuhan, experienced a decline in aural and tactile perceptions and relied increasingly on sight. As a result, he became alienated from his own natural perceptive self, as learning through the senses became more and more compartmentalised.

McLuhan was far more sensitive than were the 'printing revolution' historians to the cultural loss which printing caused. Admittedly, the wider circulation of printed texts further eroded the clerical monopoly of knowledge. At the same time, a new world of widespread individual reading tended to undermine communal values, make individuals more critical of accepted norms, and loosen the ties of social consensus. So for McLuhan, print signalled a double alienation: not only was the reader alienated from his or her own senses of touch and hearing, but he or she was also increasingly estranged from the social group. Literacy, then, meant cultural loss. But all was regained in the world of the electronic media, which once again restored the importance of touch and hearing, and re-united us with the widest of all communities, McLuhan's 'global village'. In McLuhan's modern 'acoustic paradise', the linear thinking of print culture no longer dominates, sensory perceptions are in better equilibrium and we have re-joined the tribe. For McLuhan, print destroyed 'the Africa within', but the electronic media have reconnected us with it.

McLuhan's wild and sometimes brilliant insights will not bear too much exposure. McLuhan never considered the politics of print. The questions of who was empowered by print, and whom it deprived of power, escaped him. He never differentiated between different levels of society, education or literacy in historical time. Furthermore, much of what he wrote of the impact of reading on sense perceptions could have been said about the scribal book as well as about the print version. In the next section, some more claims for the 'printing revolution' will be critically considered.

The 'printing revolution' examined

In acknowledging the power of Gutenberg's invention, we should consider its short-term and medium-term social impact. For a long time, the 'printing revolution' only affected a narrow scholarly elite. It barely touched the mass of the people of Europe who remained for the most part illiterate. According to the evidence of *post mortem* inventories in which the possessions of deceased citizens were catalogued, very few people owned books in the two centuries following Gutenberg. In the Spanish city of Valencia in the 'golden age' from 1474 to 1550, the proportion of individuals who owned any books at all were as follows:[22]

9 out of 10 ecclesiastics
3 out of 4 members of the liberal professions (e.g., lawyers and doctors)
1 out of 2 aristocrats
1 out of 3 merchants
1 out of 7 textile artisans
1 out of 10 manual workers

The world of the book was very familiar to men of the Church, and to the cream of the educated laity, but amongst the lower classes it was virtually unknown. If we compare this example with similar evidence from Canterbury (England) in 1620–40, we again encounter wide social variations in the degree of contact with book culture. Here 9 out of 10 members of the liberal professions owned books, as did three quarters of the nobles, but fewer than half (45 per cent) of textile workers and only one-third (36 per cent) of building workers recorded books among their possessions.[23]

Print was not necessarily revolutionary for the European peasantry, except in the sense that the printed word offered new means of domination to the governments, aristocrats, clerics, lawyers and tax-collectors who oppressed them. The impact of printing therefore needs to be judged carefully in relation to different levels of literacy and socio-professional status, as well as in relation to gender differences. For, as will be discussed in Chapter 7, literacy rates of men were much higher than those of women in early modern Europe.

There were naturally sections of the elites who challenged and resisted the spread of print culture. The clerical elite no longer enjoyed a monopoly of knowledge, as book production shifted further away from monasteries to princely courts, universities and commercial centres. Print, as both Eisenstein and McLuhan emphasised, offered individual readers new ways of reflecting on the world and its orthodoxies. Traditionalists were bound to react against criticism and against any process which undermined authority. For such conservative thinkers, print was a pernicious influence because it spread ignorance and prejudice and could poison the minds of the unwary. Umberto Eco's novel *The Name of the Rose* offered a dramatic fictionalised example of a medieval attempt to preserve hidden knowledge, and to prevent curious readers gaining access to works considered dangerous. In this medieval mystery, contact with forbidden books literally did poison the reader, who died from touching the poisoned pages. Print, too, could be viewed as corrupt and immoral. *Est virgo haec penna,* ran the Latin motto, *meretrix est stampificata*: the pen is a virgin, print is a whore.[24] Print was promiscuous, putting untruths into every undiscriminating reader's hands.

Manuscript culture survived best among the social and cultural elites. Evidence from England and Spain suggests that the advent of printing did not interrupt a vibrant circulation of manuscript books, especially works of poetry and chivalric romances. Poets like Donne, Marvell and Rochester wrote specifically for scribal transmission. As Harold Love has shown, this could sometimes be more profitable than print publication, was free from censorship and ensured circulation among well-defined reading communities.[25] Resorting to print was considered demeaning for a gentleman and carried a stigma. Manuscript newsletters continued to circulate from London to the provinces, sometimes issued in several hundred copies. In France, the number of manuscript books in circulation did not start to fall until the 1490s.[26] Monastic libraries remained, with a few exceptions, bastions of conservatism. An English survey of 4,900 extant books which have been traced to monastic houses between 1400 and 1557 suggested that only 6.5 per cent of their holdings were printed books.[27] One should not necessarily look to the educated upper classes to embrace the modernity of print; in practice, they often clung to traditional forms of communication.[28]

In many ways, the printed book was not markedly different from the scribal book. Continuities persisted in technological terms and in terms of content. Paper was still made from rags and ink from plant dyes, while the shape of the codex did not change. The fundamental technology of the book remained the same. For some time yet, scribes would continue to copy printed books by hand. Content also changed little, and slowly. The same kinds of books that had circulated in scribal form were put into print. Of all books printed before 1501 (the *incunabula*), 77 per cent were in Latin, and 45 per cent of titles were religious texts.[29] Geoffrey Chaucer's *Canterbury Tales* is a good example of scribal book which made an uninterrupted transition to print. Over 80 manuscripts of the *Canterbury Tales* still survive, and it was one of the first titles printed by Caxton after he settled in Westminster.[30] Another consequence of printing was the proliferation of works of personal devotion. Here, too, little had immediately changed. Paris was the arsenal of counter-reformation publishing, churning out books of hours, prayer books and missals. The result of the diffusion of print, therefore, was as much to strengthen existing prejudices as it was to publicise new ideas.

The printed book inherited many of the conventions of the scribal book, but gradually imposed and developed its own methods of organising typographical space. New printed forms of punctuation, for example, had to be developed. Early printed books often invited readers to supply their own reading aids, asking them to number the pages, accent capital letters in red and add their own punctuation. Electronic texts restore some of these lost opportunities for reader involvement. At first, printed texts resembled scribal texts, but printers assumed more and more editorial control. In 1502, when the great Venetian printer Aldus Manutius published his new edition of Ovid, he invited the reader to paginate it and put the page numbers in the table of contents. After 1502, however, he almost always did this himself.[31]

Printing thus reduced the participation of the reader in editorial functions. He or she lost the freedom to manipulate and 'signpost' the text. Soon readers had no more to do except make separate notes for personal use. There was a significant change in the relationship between text and notes. Marginal glosses were very common in manuscript books; but Aldus Manutius adopted the technique of printing notes at the end of the text. This was in stark contrast to some medieval books, in which the text might be surrounded on three sides by marginal notes, and was dwarfed by the extensive commentaries which effectively became the main item on the page. Renaissance printers like Aldus removed the notes and gave the text back its primacy. This procedure also suited the writers of the Protestant Reformation, who wanted to demote scholastic commentary and return to the fundamentals of the Scriptures.

Question marks (?) had already appeared in scribal culture, but brackets ([]) and exclamation marks (!) were of fifteenth-century origin. The title page was an innovation of the printed book. So were right-margin justification and running titles (headers) at the top of the page. Paragraph breaks had hardly been used before the sixteenth century, so that early printed books presented the reader with a dense mass of unbroken text, divided only perhaps into two columns, a daunting prospect for the modern reader. One of the first works to adopt paragraph breaks fully throughout was Descartes' *Discourse on Method*, because the philosopher wanted to reach a wider audience of readers with different reading competencies, rather than limiting his appeal to a narrow circle of intellectuals. In his other works, however, Descartes was reluctant to use paragraph breaks, partly because he was happy to write for an academic readership, and partly because he simply wanted to economise on paper, which normally absorbed about one half of book production costs at this time.[32] The modern division of the Bible into chapters and verses also dates from the printed book. Although the Bible had been divided into chapters in the thirteenth century, there was no accepted, standard way of doing this until the version of the French printer Robert Estienne, produced in 1649.

Fixity and uniformity, as we have seen, were two consequences of printing claimed by exponents of the 'printing revolution' thesis. For Eisenstein, the emergence of standard, permanent and authoritative texts distinguished the world of print from scribal culture. Librarians would certainly dispute the argument that print brought permanence. In their view, the permanent preservation of any text owes something to the professional expertise and resources of librarians. Other aspects of Eisenstein's claims also look a little shaky. Today, when we open a book like this one, we make several unspoken assumptions. We assume, firstly, that the author who is named on the title page has written it. We also assume it has been published with the author's permission. We further assume that all copies of this edition of the text will be identical. In seventeenth-century England, however, none of these assumptions could be guaranteed. As Adrian Johns argues, reliability and authority were not inherent in the printed form.[33] They were acquired by hardworking authors, publishers and learned societies who defended criteria of integrity against plagiarists and illegal (pirated) editions.

The early world of print was a cut-throat world of unscrupulous profit-seekers. Works were frequently pirated in unauthorised editions, illegal imitations or abbreviated versions. Books were not necessarily written by the named author, not necessarily 'authorised' by him or her and copies were not necessarily identical. Scientific findings did not easily acquire universal value and credit. Galileo's images of the lunar surface, first published in Venice in 1610, were reprinted without permission in Frankfurt and London editions, from woodcuts which were recycled and did not reproduce identical images each time they were used.[34] Shakespeare's first folio is another notorious example; it had 600 different typefaces, non-uniform spelling and punctuation, erratic arrangements of layout, mispagination and poor proofreading. No two surviving copies are exactly the same.[35]

In seventeenth-century Britain, authors had little control over the production of their work unless they specifically made an effort to be involved. Compositors were expected to correct the text they were composing. Proofreaders did exist, but often the first sheets would be checked as the text was already being printed. In these circumstances, texts inevitably had many variants. The King James Bible, for instance, had 24,000 textual variants up to 1830.[36] Authors would sometimes come to London to live in the printing house in order to oversee their proofs. Figure 3.3 reproduces an image of a printing house. Piracy, Johns has demonstrated, was a normal hazard of the London publishing world. The Stationers' Company alone litigated against alleged pirates

Figure 3.3   The printing press.

Note: This example is from Coster's print shop in Haarlem, Netherlands. The man on the left holds the ink-balls, while the compositor sits on the right. © The Bodelian Library, University of Oxford.

over 40 times, between 1600 and 1720, while hundreds of other allegations were dealt with in the Stationers' private court.[37] English titles might be reprinted with impunity on the continent and then imported into England with false imprints. Uncertainty, then, rather than stability, was a characteristic of British print culture, especially in the period between the lapsing of government controls in 1695 and the first copyright legislation in 1710. Fixity, Johns argues, was not a technological given, but was culturally produced, out of multiple interactions between printers and booksellers, proofreaders and engravers, learned societies and coffee-house debaters.

Plagiarists and impostors abounded. One bookseller, John Dunton, invented the proceedings of a fictitious learned society, the Athenian Society, which even had Jonathan Swift fooled.[38] Authenticity was the result of authors' and publishers' struggles to secure the credit of royal patrons, trustworthy academic societies and ultimately readers themselves. There are obvious parallels here with the World Wide Web. Contemporary web surfers are similarly faced with problems of authenticity, copyright and unauthorised appropriation of material which mirror those encountered in an earlier era by users of the new print culture.

Lastly, the claim that print boosted national languages and national consciousness can also be challenged, although some analysts of modern nationalism have readily seized on this hypothetical connection. Benedict Anderson's much-quoted emphasis on print nationalism, for instance, has been taken too much for granted.[39] Print culture did not produce modern nationalism: a causal relationship seems impossible to sustain given the 400-year time lag between the invention of printing and the appearance of nineteenth-century nationalist movements! Furthermore, there is a missing link in the postulated chain between print and nationalism, namely the reader. Any speculation about the impact of printed literature must proceed via a study of literacy, reception and the readers' responses. So far it has rarely done so. In addition, nationalism often spread through oral rather than printed channels, in spoken verse and song. Scandinavian examples are instructive. Swedish romantic nationalism was disseminated in songs, which were published in print form but intended to be performed aloud. In Norway, scholars collected folk songs. In Denmark, the priest and poet Nikolaj Grundtvig translated the early medieval sagas and epic poems which he considered to be lost treasures of 'Danishness'. But his work was disseminated largely through oral media: sermons, psalms and the 1,500 songs he composed to be sung by his Lutheran followers.[40]

Many claims have been made about the revolutionary nature of the invention of printing, and some of them are exaggerated. The printed book reached a limited audience in the sixteenth, seventeenth and eighteenth centuries. Not until at least four centuries after Gutenberg did a mass culture of print emerge in Western Europe. What is more, there were many continuities, in both technology and content, between the scribal and the printed book. It was difficult to establish stable and authoritative versions of, for example, Shakespeare's *Henry VI* or Newton's *Principia*. Acceptance and legitimacy, according to Adrian Johns, came from intellectual circles rather than from printing technology alone. Johns' critique of the 'printing revolution' thesis is geographically limited to the London publishing world. In spite of this limitation, however, it reflects an important shift in historians' concerns away from the technology of book production, and towards the process of reading and the study of readers' responses.[41] Historians always need to be wary of the technological fallacy: that is to say, the notion that technological innovation is in itself a determining factor of historical change. The context, and in this case the readers, also mattered.

Damage control

Reactions to printing were as varied and extreme as first responses to the Internet. On one hand, the invention seemed to open up a new world in which truth and knowledge would be accessible to wider and wider audiences. On the other hand, the invention was decried because it disseminated lies, prejudice and unsubstantiated assertions. For some it heralded a communications utopia in which the democratisation of knowledge could be realised on a limitless scale. For others there was a clear danger that the medium, if free from all effective control, could cause serious damage.

In the aftermath of the advent of printing, attempts were made to assert control over printed matter. Censorship was a special concern of the Catholic Church, since it had always assumed the role of defining orthodox doctrine and defending it against heretical interpretations. Pope Leo X condemned printing in 1513 as an invention leading to errors of faith and morals, and bound to generate 'manifold troubles'.[42] The index of prohibited books identified the Church's blacklisted publications, and the list grew longer in the counter-reformation period. In France, censorship powers were exercised by the Theology Faculty of the Sorbonne (the University of Paris), as well as by the law courts (the *parlements*). After 1563, the monarchy also took control, and henceforth nothing could be legally published in the kingdom without royal permission, in the form of a *privilège* granted to a printer to produce a text. A royal privilege was not just a repressive measure; it also gave publishers protection from illicit competition. Publishers with a royal *privilège* knew that they had a legal monopoly to produce their texts. None of this successfully stifled religious dissent; neither did it prevent an outpouring of pamphlets in a time of political crisis, such as the Frondes in the mid-seventeenth century. If the powerful French monarchy found it difficult to enforce regulation, how much more difficult was it for other regimes in less regulated parts of Europe, like the Netherlands, parts of Switzerland and some German and Italian city states. When the subversive work of Galileo was smuggled out of his prison, it was destined for the more open climate of the Netherlands, where it was published in Leiden by the Dutch publisher Elzevier.

The creation and protection of authors' and publishers' rights was another consequence of the competitive chaos of the world of print. In Britain, the Stationers' Company, founded in 1557, regulated the trade in the interests of printers and booksellers, prosecuted publishing pirates and guaranteed a form of copyright on behalf of the book trade as a whole. But then, as in France, all regulatory frameworks collapsed in the English Civil War (1642–51). In 1662, a Licensing Bill instituted government censorship in place of print anarchy: publishers needed prior government approval and, if it was given, a license to publish was granted. This regime, which installed a kind of dual control of the book trade by both the state and the Stationers' Company, endured until the Act was repealed in 1695. In 1710, the English Copyright Act abolished the censorship of literature prior to publication. It conferred copyright for 21 years for works published before 1709, and for 14 years for works published thereafter. This period could be extended if the author was alive. This legislation marked a significant turning point in the development of intellectual property.

The fact that so much effort was now directed into the surveillance and regulation of the book trade already demonstrated the power of print. Print was an important change, but its revolutionary nature should not be overestimated. It is best regarded as one of many landmarks in the history of reading, along with the invention of the codex, the rise of silent reading, and the industrialisation of the book in the nineteenth century. A history of print technology must be combined with the history of the processes and social circumstances in which readers gave meaning to their texts. In the chapters which follow, readers in two specific contexts will be considered: the Protestant Reformation and the Renaissance.

4

Print and the Protestant Reformation

Protestantism was a religion of the book. Its adherents advocated a return to the fundamental truths of Holy Scripture, instead of relying on the erudite commentaries and interpretations of scholars and theologians. The message of the Bible, Protestant leaders believed, should be accessible to all Christians. These simple ideas inspired Protestantism's use of print propaganda in the Reformation era. The Reformation contributed to the spread of vernacular languages, which all the Christian faithful could potentially understand, at the expense of Latin, whose usage perpetuated the domination of an allegedly corrupt Catholic clergy. Protestants hoped to make the Bible more accessible to believers, and in so doing, leaders like Martin Luther challenged Papal authority. As a result, Protestant posterity has sometimes claimed him as a revolutionary hero who exposed the materialism, hypocrisy and superstitious magic of traditional Catholicism.

The main focus of this chapter is to explore the relationship between Protestantism and print, and the role of the printed word generally in the religious conflicts of sixteenth-century Europe. For both Protestants and Catholics, printed books were designed to persuade the curious and keep the faithful on the true path to salvation. For all the protagonists in the religious conflicts of the sixteenth century, religious texts and liturgical books defined allegiance and unified a community of belief. John Foxe's *Actes and Monuments*, for example, which was a strikingly illustrated and oft-published encyclopaedia of Protestant martyrdom, was a book in which English Protestants read their own identity.[1] The following discussion will examine how Reformation Protestantism disseminated its ideas, and how the Catholic Church reacted to the flood of printed material which flowed from Protestant presses. The image of Luther, as it was communicated to contemporary readers, will be considered. Just as the previous chapter scrutinised some conventional wisdom about the invention of printing, so too some accepted ideas about Protestant Bible-reading must be questioned. An eminent historian already blitzed one tired cliché when he called the widespread popular reading of the German Bible 'a myth and a fable'.[2]

Protestant literacy

Protestantism used national languages, but their audience was limited by the widespread illiteracy of the rural masses and most of the urban labouring classes in Reformation Europe. Rolf Engelsing estimated that only between 3 and 4 per cent of the population of the German states could read at the time of the Reformation, and David Cressy suggested that in England perhaps 10 per cent of men and just 1 per cent of women were able to read.[3] Until the seventeenth century, when parish records in England and France started to yield more solid information, only guesswork about literacy rates is possible. The meaning of 'literacy' and the ways historians calculate the rate of literacy must be considered more fully in Chapter 7. Literacy depended heavily on both social status and gender; in other words, men were generally more literate than women, and both men and women of the nobility or the professions were generally more literate than their social inferiors. The reception of Reformation ideas therefore varied very much according to its social context. Calvinism appealed to skilled urban artisans like the print-workers of Lyon analysed by Natalie Davis.[4] The psalm-singing journeymen printers of the 1550s were educated and well paid, and two-thirds of them could read and write. In Germany, on the other hand, Lutheranism had a rural following amongst poor peasants with a much lower rate of literacy.

The spread of Protestantism sometimes built on old medieval heresies which had enjoyed a literate following. Vernacular scriptures, for example, had been used by the Waldensians in the fifteenth century, by the English Lollard movement and the Hussites of Bohemia. Like their Protestant successors, these heretical sects believed that true Christians did not need the mediation of the clergy or the Pope, since they could find their own salvation through an individual quest for biblical truth. In certain social and regional contexts, therefore, the message of Protestantism fell on fertile ground and was heard by literate communities with a long legacy of religious dissent. Previous heresies, however, had been local in their scope and limited in their duration. Print presented Lutheranism and Calvinism with an unprecedented opportunity to secure a much broader appeal and a long-term future.

The vernacular Bible and vernacular reading

Luther's New Testament in German appeared in 1522. It took him only 11 weeks to translate it and the printers spent less than 6 months printing it. They used the Gothic font, rather than the humanist script with which we are more familiar, to target a broad popular consumption. The Old Testament followed, but at a more sedate rhythm. In fact it took Luther another 12 years to produce it. He needed help with Hebrew and the books of the prophets presented a high degree of difficulty.[5] There had been 18 German-language Bibles before Luther's, but his was by far the most effective and successful.[6]

It was not alone, for in the 1520s and 1530s intellectuals all over Europe were producing Bibles in their own languages. A Dutch Bible appeared in 1526, and an Italian Bible in 1532. In 1526, William Tyndale's English New Testament was imported from Germany, and was promptly burned, but it nevertheless went into 40 editions before 1566.[7] Miles Coverdale's first complete version of the English Bible, probably printed in Cologne, appeared in England in 1535. In 1541, a royal edict ordered that an English Bible be set up in every parish church. The King James Authorised Version swamped all other editions after its appearance in 1611, but in the 1630s a cheap, bound copy would have cost an unskilled labourer an entire week's wages, if he had been able to read it.[8] After 1588, a complete Welsh Bible was also available.

In Portugal and Spain, however, where Protestant influences were more effectively quarantined, vernacular Bibles did not appear until much later in the 1790s. Lefèvre d'Etaples translated the New Testament into French in 1523, and his entire Bible followed between 1530 and 1534, although most French Bibles were imported from Antwerp, Strasbourg or Switzerland. It is one of the many paradoxes of the Protestant Reformation that Luther's German Bible was first translated into Latin so that French readers could understand it (it was later, of course, rendered into French). Jean Calvin wrote his works in both Latin and a personal style of French which became admired by friend and foe alike for its limpid precision.

Translating scripture was not always easy and scholars felt much was lost in translating the Bible into languages considered less noble than those of its ancient authors. Olivétan complained that 'to make the French language speak with the eloquence of Hebrew and Greek' was like 'teaching the sweet nightingale to sing the raucous song of the crow'.[9] They were nevertheless dedicated to the heroic task of making the Bible available for general consumption. It was dangerous work. Tyndale was burned at the stake in 1535, and the French printer Etienne Dolet suffered the same fate in 1546.

How popular was the Lutheran Bible? Before Luther's death in 1546, his German Bible went through over 400 total or partial reprints,

amounting to about 200,000 copies.[10] This represented a huge circulation for the period, but nevertheless the German Bible was out of
reach of most Lutherans. For one thing, many of them were illiterate,
and for another, it was too expensive. An unbound copy of the complete German Bible of 1534 cost the equivalent of a month's wages
for the average labourer.[11] Not until the eighteenth century did its real
cost fall within the purchasing range of an ordinary German working
man. Instead, Luther's Bible was destined for purchase by churches, pastors and Lutheran schools. Sometimes it was bought by governments
who made its usage compulsory. In 1533, for instance, every parish in
Meissen was required to own a German Bible, paid for out of Church
funds, and in Brandenburg every pastor was supposed to have a copy.
In practice, Lutheranism relied on its pastors to interpret the Bible for
believers.

In the Netherlands, the situation was rather different. Here literacy
was more widespread than in Germany, and a greater proportion of
Bibles was bought by families. It is significant that Calvinist printers produced many small-format octavo editions of the Bible for personal use
and greater portability, while the larger in-folio size was more favoured
by Lutheran Bible printers. The larger format was more suitable for use
in Church, the smaller format more suitable for reading at home.[12] In
seventeenth-century New England, too, Bible ownership was probably
much more common than in early modern Germany.

In order to appreciate the true impact of Protestantism in Germany
and elsewhere, we must look beyond production of the Bible, phenomenal though that was, and consider its relationship to other printed texts.
There is no doubt that the Reformation brought about a great increase in
vernacular publishing. It has been estimated that between 1517 and 1523
the number of books printed in German increased tenfold.[13] The proportion of works produced in Latin gradually receded, although 70 per cent
of publications in Germany were still in Latin in the 1570s. In France,
the royal edict of Villers-Cotterêts of 1539 made the use of French compulsory in all official documents. In the Lutheran city of Strasbourg,
Chrisman identified two distinct cultures in the middle of the sixteenth
century: one learned, erudite and Latin-based, the other secular and
based on the German language. The German, secular culture dominated
book production in the city after about 1550.[14] In Strasbourg, however,
Bible ownership remained patchy. Very few townspeople owned a complete Bible, although they perhaps possessed a New Testament or a part
of it, prayer books and anti-Papal pamphlets.[15]

In England, there had been a relatively high proportion of vernacular book production even in the incunabular period. In the 1530s, the
Henrician Reformation and the dissolution of the monasteries dealt an
irreparable blow to Catholic Latin culture. No significant work in Latin
was produced in England throughout the fifteenth and early sixteenth

centuries. This long Latin drought was broken only by Thomas More's *Utopia*, but Erasmus took it to Louvain to be printed there and no English edition appeared before 1551.[16] In Britain, the central struggle was waged not over the vernacular Bible but the English prayer book. The stakes were high since printing now opened up the possibility for the state to prescribe a standardised form of worship throughout the entire kingdom. In the war to control the prayer book, fortunes swung first one way then another. In the reign of Edward VI (1547–53), when Protestantism triumphed, Cranmer's Book of Common Prayer of 1549 was promoted. It was to be produced in over 500 editions in English over the next 180 years.[17] After 1553, however, a period of reaction set in under the Catholic Mary I, and Cranmer's prayer book was condemned and burned. English Protestant printing moved to the continent, where John Knox and other Marian exiles produced the Geneva Bible. It took the accession of Elizabeth I to ensure the passing of the Act of Uniformity and to establish with it the Protestant prayer book.

The spread of Lutheranism relied less on the Bible itself than on a range of pamphlets, brochures and ephemeral flysheets. Broadsheets of a single page, including simple woodcut illustrations, were produced cheaply in their thousands and these *flugschriften* reached a wide audience. Luther's Bible had included very few illustrations, although in the Book of Revelation the Whore of Babylon was represented complete with Papal tiara. In any case because of their cost not every edition reproduced them. Illustrated broadsheets were much more likely to appeal to semi-literate readers. They were a hybrid mixture of image and text which, because of their visual nature, could be 'read' by literate and illiterate alike. Stock images of the False Church, Luther and the Pope, the good shepherd and the debauched monk were accompanied by complementary texts which might be read aloud to anchor the visual message.[18]

Short polemical pamphlets had a mass circulation. Luther's *Appeal to the Christian Nobility of the German Nation* (1520) sold 4000 copies in a few days, and went into 13 editions in two years.[19] There were as many as three million copies of pamphlets circulating in Germany between 1518 and 1525. They made the fortune of printers in Luther's small hometown of Wittenberg. Since they were pirated so often and so unscrupulously, he lost control of his own output. The quality of pirated editions from Augsburg, Basle or Leipzig was extremely poor. Publishers rushed them to the presses so as not to be outsmarted by the competition, and so there was no time for the luxury of accurate proofreading. Luther was seriously aggrieved by some unauthorised editions. 'I do not even recognise my own books', he said.

> They leave things out, they put things in the wrong order, or they falsify the text or fail to correct it. They have even learned the trick of putting Wittenberg at the beginning of some books which have never

been in Wittenberg...greed and envy drive them to deceive people by appropriating our name.[20]

Such was the price of fame. The intentions of the author could be distorted or travestied, and his or her texts were open to unforeseen interpretations. Luther invented special 'seals of quality' – little logos depicting the lamb and flag, or a rose with a cross at its centre – which he hoped would distinguish the approved editions from the unauthorised versions.

Both Luther and his friend and associate, the German theology professor Philip Melanchthon (1497–1560), championed vernacular printing. They also relied on catechisms, which were a much more practical way of teaching the young than using the Bible. Catechisms summarised a few clear and simple dogmas in question-and-answer format and they could be memorised. As the Catholic Church had known for centuries, they were a good pedagogical tool in an essentially oral culture. Thus the Lutheran catechism paradoxically borrowed the tried and tested learning technique of the Catholic enemy. The problem for both of these protagonists was that children who learned a formula by heart might not fully understand the text they were reciting. Calvinism, in its turn, relied on Psalters and promoted the community singing of psalms, which became one of its hallmarks. In a society of limited literacy both Lutheranism and Calvinism relied on oral and visual means of communication as much as on the printed text. The Bible and other texts would be read aloud in markets, inns and private reading groups. In Kitzbühel a group of Tyrolean miners would gather in private houses or, if weather permitted, in the open air to listen to readings of sermons or the gospel.[21] In the Spanish Netherlands, groups read and circulated evangelical books, because, as we know, the conventicle in Louvain was discovered in 1543 and all its members were executed.[22]

Variant readings of the protestant message

Martin Luther's message reached its audience by word of mouth and through cheap woodcut illustrations as much as through the medium of printed texts. Protestants, however, were opposed to an excess of imagery. They were offended by clerical ostentation and their iconoclastic tendencies made them more attuned to print culture than to a culture of images. Surprisingly, however, ordinary people learned about Luther primarily through pictorial representation.

Luther was represented to ordinary readers as quite literally a charismatic figure; in other words, he was shown to be endowed with magical power. This was not at all in conformity with Luther's own notions of spirituality. In some images, he figured as a respected theological authority who was qualified to give expert advice on the scriptures. This representation as a great doctor of the Church also contradicted Protestant ideas on scholasticism and the 'priesthood of all believers'. Nevertheless, these images were essential to his popular appeal, and ordinary people saw Luther in very traditional terms.[23] Like the Catholic saints of legend, Luther was credited with healing powers. In popular imagery, he even worked miracles, for it was believed that people who attacked his portrait sometimes received bad injuries. Broadsheets often gave him a nimbus, the attribute of a Catholic saint, or else he was compared to a biblical prophet and even to John the Baptist. In some woodcuts, he is accompanied by a dove, the symbol of divine inspiration or the presence of the Holy Ghost. In a complete reversal of Lutheran doctrine, even pieces of Luther's coat came to be revered as holy relics. In Eisleben, Luther's birthplace, fragments of cloth from his cloak and schoolboy cap were cult objects. The Inquisition often burned heretical books, and according to the Jesuits, good literature floated upwards and survived the flames intact.[24] The myth developed that Luther's works were equally flameproof. He was the 'Incombustible Luther', in the ironic phrase of Bob Scribner, who did most to uncover the long history of Luther mythology.

This iconography represents some very traditional features of a popular culture steeped in Catholic mythologies. Rather than rebelling against Catholic imagery, constructions of Luther sometimes reproduced it. At one level there was clearly a popular Reformation, propagated through woodcut imagery, which did not always mesh with the kind of Protestantism debated by theologians and scholars. At the popular level, the Protestant discourse was imbued with the vocabulary of saints, miracles and relics. Printing technology had not eradicated differences between social groups with different cultural and educational backgrounds. Perhaps print production had only skimmed the surface of the great ocean of popular mentalities.

Reformation Protestantism had several centres and many leaders. They included not only Martin Luther and Jean Calvin but also Melanchthon in Germany, Zwingli in Switzerland and a host of other more radical figures. The Protestant Reformation was far from monolithic, and a historian of reading is obliged to consider relations between Protestants themselves.

Even Lutheranism lacked consistency, for Luther's own position evolved. At first, he fully encouraged popular reading of the Bible and he regarded print as a great blessing. In 1520, he wrote that all children should receive daily lessons in the New Testament. He recommended that every Christian should read St. John's Gospel and Paul's *Epistle to the Romans* on a daily basis.[25] Zwingli and Melanchthon promoted similar ideas about the priesthood of all believers. But menacing events forced a change of thinking. In 1525, violent rural disturbances erupted in the so-called 'Peasants' War'. Protesters brandished Lutheran slogans while demanding the abolition of tithes and other fiscal burdens. Some, like Thomas Müntzer, accused Luther of condoning the oppression of the poor by the ruling princes of Germany. In 1535, a group of Anabaptists tried to implement some extreme Protestant principles when they briefly seized power in the city of Munster. The Anabaptists believed in adult baptism for all, and in Munster they attempted to purge society of wickedness in anticipation of the Second Coming. They were preparing for an apocalyptic day of judgement in which righteousness would triumph and the mighty would be brought low. In Munster, the Anabaptists seemed to reject the entire intellectual heritage of Christianity. They introduced polygamy, proclaimed the common ownership of goods and, most significantly for our purposes, banned every book except the Bible. These episodes were potentially extremely dangerous for the credibility of Protestantism. Luther needed the support and protection of rulers like Frederick of Saxony, but such support might be withdrawn if Lutheranism turned out to be a recipe for social revolution, bloodshed and disorder. After 1525 or thereabouts, Protestantism needed a closer alignment with the forces of law and order.

The Peasants' War of 1525 therefore revealed the conservatism of Protestant leaders. They became more reticent. They spoke more of the dangers of reading the Bible incorrectly. Calvin did not advocate unlimited usage of the Bible. Instead he compared Holy Scripture to a loaf of bread with a thick crust. To feed his flock, said Calvin, God wants 'that the bread be sliced for us, that the pieces be put in our mouths, and that they be chewed for us'.[26] In Luther's revised view, 'Nowadays every Tom, Dick and Harry imagines he understands the Bible and knows it inside out', and this now posed problems.[27] The directives of both Protestant and Catholic leaders seemed to converge: both warned that readers needed guidance if subversive ideas were to be avoided, although of course they continued to disagree on who should provide the guidance. Radical readers were anathema to Catholicism, and a political embarrassment for Protestantism.

Catholic reactions

The Catholic Church was not slow to perceive the dangers of the wide dissemination of scripture and religious works in local languages. If all the faithful had easy access to the Bible, priestly wisdom would become superfluous. Individuals would interpret scripture independently and the authority of the Church would be undermined. The Church would lose the monopoly it claimed over the interpretation of Christian doctrine. For one traditionalist, Geiler von Keyserberg, giving ordinary people a Bible in German was as dangerous as giving a child a knife to cut its own bread. In 1485, the Archbishop of Mainz banned the translation of theological works into German because this would falsify the truth. The Church hierarchy had a profoundly paternalistic view of its followers; the faithful needed guidance and protection from erroneous ideas. Ordinary believers, therefore, only needed to know what the clergy decided was good for them, and that meant the Our Father, the Ave Maria, the Ten Commandments and the Creed.

In 1546, the Council of Trent emphasised learning through oral appropriation and re-asserted that the right to interpret doctrine belonged to the Church alone. Giving the faithful access to scripture would be unnecessary, and it would erode the fundamental distinction between clergy and laity (which many Protestants sought to weaken or dissolve altogether). The Catholic Church's attitude was to allow vernacular Bible-reading with prior permission and under clerical supervision. In 1593, however, Pope Clement VIII forbade vernacular Bible-reading outright.

At the same time, the Catholic Church multiplied its own propaganda. It produced Latin breviaries, missals and catechisms to encourage conformity among priests who were the main target of this literature. Producing and selling new editions to Spain and the Netherlands made the fortune of the Antwerp printing house of Christopher Plantin between 1590 and 1640.[28] In the seventeenth century, Paris became another powerhouse of Catholic publishing, churning out books of hours, devotional works, lives of the saints and *Imitations de Jésus-Christ*. Print was the instrument of the Counter-reformation as well as of the Reformation.

The Protestant Reformation provoked a wave of measures to censor and regulate the book trade. The Papacy took the lead in imposing repressive controls. In 1487, Pope Innocent VIII banned printers from printing anything impious, scandalous or contrary to the Roman Catholic faith without clerical permission, on pain of excommunication. The Papal Inquisition, originally established in the twelfth century, was extended to Spain, Italy and France in the Counter-reformation. It was a travelling court, reporting directly to Rome, entrusted with suppressing all heterodox views. In Spain, its main job had been at first to target Jews and Moslems, but it became an important means of identifying and punishing all sorts of heretics.

Both political and Papal authorities established censorship apparatus to control and channel print production. In France, the works of Luther and Melanchthon were condemned by the Sorbonne Theology Faculty, which claimed censorship powers but could not enforce them unless the supreme law courts (*Parlements*) endorsed its decisions. In practice, French censorship only took effect in rare moments when the Sorbonne, the Parlement of Paris and the king himself acted in unison. Often they acted independently. In 1523, for instance, the Sorbonne condemned Lefèvre's French New Testament, but since King François

I himself had sponsored the translation, the ban remained nugatory. In 1525, on the other hand, both the Sorbonne Theology Faculty and the Parlement joined forces to ban the production of vernacular Bibles.

Official policy changed after the Affaire des Placards, when anonymous polemical posters attacking the Catholic Mass appeared overnight in Paris. The king now took vigorous repressive action. In so doing, he attacked deviant printers as fiercely as subversive authors. Since authors did not always identify themselves, repressive regimes usually found printers an easier target. There were nine executions in the wake of the Affaire des Placards, and more followed after further provocative bill-posting activity occurred in the following year.

No one, however, could stem the flow of imported Protestant literature into France from Geneva. In 1542, Calvin's *Institutio* was banned in France in any language. The regime of censorship gradually escalated. In 1545, the Sorbonne and the Parlement jointly endorsed a list of prohibited books on which Genevan publishers figured prominently. In 1551 the royal Edict of Châteaubriant banned all imports of literature from Calvinist Geneva, and required printers of all translations of the Bible to seek prior approval from the Sorbonne Theology Faculty. The publication of any anonymous work was banned. Booksellers too were targeted, and a system of inspection was established to hunt down prohibited books and pamphlets. Itinerant peddlers, on the other hand, often escaped police surveillance.

Dissident views could not be completely stamped out. Secret networks linked Geneva with other sympathetic centres like Antwerp, Leiden and Edinburgh. Lyon continued to supply French Calvinists with Bibles, Psalters and Calvin's *Institutio*. Travelling pastors and peddlers continued to spread Calvinist literature throughout provincial France. In 1562, an entire barge full of Calvinist literature was seized on the river Seine and it took eight experts several days to draw up an inventory of its subversive contents.[29] The fact that it had got that far suggested the difficulties involved in trying to quarantine an entire country. Scheming printers sometimes slipped a Protestant text or sermon into an anthology which appeared on the outside to be perfectly respectable and Catholic in inspiration – a technique called 'camouflage printing'. Wherever they could, printers circumvented the regulation of their trade by disguising the true author of a work and its place of origin. Some Protestant pamphlets cheekily claimed to have been printed in Rome itself. Meanwhile, in Elizabethan England, the situation was reversed: here it was the Catholic polemicists and readers who had to resort to smuggling and publishing ruses.

In 1562, the opening of the religious wars in France disrupted book production and shattered Huguenot (French Calvinist) networks. At the same time, and partly as a consequence, there was a drastic collapse in the Geneva publishing industry from which it never fully recovered.

Many printers were victims of the anti-Protestant pogrom of the Saint-Barthélémy massacres in 1572 (although there were printers among the perpetrators as well).[30] After the devastation of the religious wars, the centre of gravity of French Protestantism would shift from Lyon and Geneva to La Rochelle.

In Spain, following the excommunication of Luther himself in 1521, the monarchy joined with the Inquisition to exclude all his works from the Iberian peninsula. In 1558, their efforts were reinforced by Philip II and the Inquisitor-General Fernando de Valdès. Printers needed official permission before producing specific works, and no books could be imported into the country without royal licence. The punishment for violations was death and the confiscation of the offender's property. As a consequence of such measures, the spread of Reformation ideas was stifled, and so at the same time was the Spanish book trade. Another by-product of banning the Bible in national languages was the exclusion of women from direct access to scripture, because few literate women knew Latin. They would turn instead to the *Lives of the Saints* for spiritual edification.[31] Under such a regime, the dominant religious ideology permeated culture and scholarship. No doubt authors and publishers practised a degree of self-censorship which we can only guess at. A climate of suspicion and denunciation prevailed.

Book-burnings were regular occurrences in many parts of Europe. They had a symbolic and pedagogical value, and constituted a warning to readers and printers alike. In the 1520s, public burnings were organised in Louvain and Antwerp. Others were to follow in Lyon. Sometimes, as in Paris in 1562, the bonfire raged for days as carts continued to arrive with more supplies of literary fuel for the flames.[32] The biblical justification for book-burning was found in *Acts*, chapter 19, verse 19:

> Many of them also which used curious arts brought their books together, and burned them before all men.

This text often adorned the title page of the Index of prohibited literature. Books had to undergo an ordeal by fire: the few that contained the truth would remain intact, while pernicious literature would be consumed by the flames.

The urge to burn books is eternal, suggests Francisco Gimeno Blay, and gives a strange fanatical pleasure to those who indulge in it.[33] It is a phenomenon by no means confined to the religious struggles of early modern Europe, as we are reminded by the obliteration of the National Library of Sarajevo in 1992, and the burning of Salman Rushdie's *Satanic Verses* in Bradford (England) in 1989. Book-burning may attack an individual author, and can be a premonition of his or her own destruction. Above all, book-burning was an operation of social hygiene, designed to exterminate intellectual infections. Thus, when Don Quixote's housekeeper participated in the destruction of the books which generated the Don's dangerous fantasies, she also brought holy water and hyssop to purify and protect his room.[34] As long as writing remains a weapon in the struggle to re-shape society, the periodical destruction of literature is probably inevitable.

In 1546, the Council of Trent affirmed that the Latin vulgate Bible was the only authentic Holy Scripture. In 1558, the first Index of prohibited books was published in Rome. The Index was frequently updated, and it became more sophisticated in its classification of authors according to the degree of their supposed toxicity and in signalling specific passages to be expurgated from suspect literature. Sara Nalle examined 836 Inquisition trials between 1570 and 1610 in a single Spanish diocese (Cuenca) – over 20 per year – in which the Inquisitors tried to ban the reading of religious books in the vernacular, and even opposed the reading of romances as well. The ideologues of the Counter-reformation, she found, were hostile to popular reading in itself.[35] The Inquisition demonised the book to such an extent that just owning one was regarded as suspicious. In Venice, the Holy Office accused one artisan of heresy in 1572 simply because he had been caught reading books in a neighbour's house.[36]

In England, the advent of printing had given the English monarchy an unprecedented opportunity to enforce Henrician orthodoxy. But the sequel was very turbulent. On the death of Henry VIII, his successor Edward VI was only a boy, and Edward Seymour, Duke of Somerset, became Lord Protector (1547–49). In these years, there were no restrictions on Bible-reading and there was a brief explosion of Protestant publishing. A system of prior censorship was restored in 1549 and continued under Mary I. The Duke of Somerset himself was indicted and executed in 1552. Whereas 54 editions of the English Bible had been printed in the reign of Edward VI (1547–53), none appeared under Mary I.[37] In Antwerp, the situation was more relaxed, since the Emperor Charles V saw some value in providing good translations. Repressive measures focussed on the printed book. Meanwhile, manuscript copies were subject to no control. They continued to circulate, especially within closed circles including religious communities.

Reformation readers

It is hard to judge how effective the apparatus of repression was. Clearly, it could not prevent the spread of Protestantism and its implantation in Scandinavia, England and Scotland, and important parts of Germany, the Dutch provinces, Hungary and Bohemia. Even the strictest censorship regime found it difficult to enforce its own legislation. In Paris in the first decade of the seventeenth century, Papal nuncios complained to Rome about the spirit of liberty which seemed to reign in the French capital, and the ease with which heretical and subversive literature was secretly sold to the public.[38] The accused who came before the Inquisition in Venice repeatedly told the court that prohibited books were openly on sale in the city's bookshops. It was even reported that an Inquisitor in Piacenza confiscated books from heretics in order to sell them to Venetian booksellers.[39] If there was a profit in it, then loopholes in the system could always be found. On the other hand, the extent to which authors and printers censored themselves to avoid trouble is unfathomable. No wonder in this climate that some publishers like Christopher Plantin decided it would be prudent to seek the patronage of the Spanish monarchy rather than fall under suspicion.

More importantly for the history of reading, neither Protestant writers nor the Catholic hierarchy could predict readers' responses. Lutherans, Calvinists and Inquisitors alike confronted the independence of individual readers who could not easily be influenced or guided in the desired direction. Luther faced and rejected radical readers who had, in spite of the author's professed intentions, drawn a revolutionary message from his works. As we have seen, many readers received his message through the filter of familiar images which derived from traditional Catholic teaching. Readers brought their own 'baggage' to the act of reading.

The Bible was a central Reformation text, but it was open to many interpretations. Kevin Sharpe indicates various possible reading perspectives on the Book of Revelation.[40] For some, its apocalyptic vision was already a reality in the fire and carnage of the 30 Years' War (1618–48). For many English Protestants, it signified the collapse of Rome, while the defeat of the Spanish Armada in 1588 had been foretold in the Book of Revelation's prophecy of the defeat of the Antichrist. On the other hand, Presbyterians might see things differently: for them the handmaid of Satan might be the Church of England itself. The interpretation of scripture could not be controlled, and different religious and national reading communities found in it very different sources of inspiration and affirmation.

The Inquisition encountered equally autonomous readers. For example, many readers of Erasmus, who was on the Papal Index, defended themselves strongly, regardless of the threat of imprisonment or worse. Odo Quarto, a 60-year-old soldier from Apulia in south-eastern Italy, maintained that the Index could not be trusted to decide what was dangerous. In any case, he pointed out, the Papacy could not even make up its own mind – one Pope might put a book on the Index, but his successor removed it. He was right about the inconsistency: in 1518 Leo X had indeed approved Erasmus' New Testament, while Paul IV later condemned it. Odo represented the independent reader's perspective:

It isn't, he told his accusers, because people read that they necessarily believe what they're reading...Most of the time you read out of curiosity and the desire to know something, not to believe in false ideas.[41]

Odo was articulating a form of reader resistance which must be taken into account whenever historians measure the success or failure of intellectual movements. It was echoed in many Italian inquisition trials in which the validity of the Papal Index itself was brought into question, and the refusal of many readers to co-operate with book-burnings was fully demonstrated.

Historians count the number of vernacular Bibles in circulation, but the significance of this statistical knowledge is only revealed by considering how the biblical text was actually assimilated. The division of the Bible into books, chapters and individual verses perhaps facilitated easy digestion. It was nevertheless deplored by John Locke, among others, who pleaded for the text to be published in continuous unbroken form, as he argued it had originally been written. Otherwise there was a danger that the Bible would be plundered for aphorisms taken out of context.[42] Puritans in Britain and New England probably had similar motives when they recommended reading the Bible from beginning to end, preferable on an annual basis, rather than, as Richard Rogers put it, taking 'a leafe of one and a chapter of another, as idle readers used to doe for novelties sake'.[43] This mode of Bible-reading assumed a very intensive relationship with the text, expressing the reader's reverence for the word of God. Superficial dabbling was to be avoided; instead the text should be the subject of deep meditation. Readers frequently memorised large sections of the Bible, especially the Psalms and the New Testament. Sunday above all became a day of religious reading, when passages from the Bible might be read aloud in Protestant households.

The Bible was held in such awe that some readers attributed magical powers to it. It was thought that it could cure those with inexplicable illnesses, or when opened at random it could, like an oracle, reveal the future. Rembrandt's mother was often depicted, by Rembrandt himself as well as by other painters, as poring over a Latin or a Hebrew Bible like a sorceress searching for a spell. The practice of swearing on the Bible, a ritual still retained for witnesses in courtrooms today, is a reflection of this belief in the exceptional magic and authority of the Bible. The Bible, in other words, could be read in multiple ways which often defied the projects of Protestant divines and Papal censors alike.

The Protestant Reformation happened to coincide with the appearance of new communications technology, and it used print as a powerful propaganda tool. Philip Melanchthon thought printing was a divine gift.

The English anti-Papist John Foxe saw a close connection between print and the triumph of Protestantism when he wrote that

> God works for His Church not with sword and target [i.e. shield] ... but with printing, writing and reading ... How many presses there be in the world, so many black houses there be against the high castle of St. Angelo, so that either the Pope must abolish knowledge and printing, or printing must at length root him out.[44]

Such generalisations about the connections between print and Protestantism are as exaggerated as they are common. The spread of Protestantism was always limited by lower-class illiteracy and, as we have seen, access to the Lutheran Bible was not as widespread as has sometimes been supposed. Lutherans themselves did not always think it desirable. In the face of popular revolt, Protestant leaders became increasingly reluctant to recommend untutored access to Holy Scripture. Protestant propaganda, moreover, attributed characteristics to Luther which were far removed from the progressive revolutionary image found in many popular biographies and films about his life. Readers assimilated Luther into their stock of familiar images of saintly theologians with magical powers.

At the same time, Protestantism certainly encouraged and accelerated the spread of vernacular literature. The spread of unorthodox ideas did not rely on Bible-reading alone. A mass of pamphlet literature, popular broadsides and woodcut images reached a wider audience than expensive Bibles ever could. Lutheran catechisms and Calvinist Psalters had a much wider circulation than the vernacular Bible, especially when produced cheaply in small octavo format.

In the religious struggles of the early modern period, reading and publishing were forms of combat. Through print, antagonistic reading communities struggled to affirm their identity. The Counter-reformation responded to Protestantism not only by attempts at repression but also by multiplying its own printed propaganda, and here the Catholic Church had formidable resources to deploy. This undermines the assumptions of John Foxe quoted above: the Pope did not seek to abolish printing but harnessed it for the interests of the Church. Protestants were not the only ones to exploit the new medium and, what is more, vernacular languages did not suddenly oust the use of Latin. The survival of Latin culture, and the purposes it served for Renaissance readers, is the subject of the following chapter.

5

Renaissance books and humanist readers

Renaissance readers had a special relationship with the classical literature of ancient Greece and Rome. Petrarch ritually kissed his edition of
Virgil before opening it, and Erasmus did the same with his Cicero.[1]
Niccolò Machiavelli told a friend that when he entered his study to
continue his 'conversations' with ancient literature he would take off
his everyday clothes and wear something more dignified.[2] The emphasis in Chapter 4 on the spread of the vernacular must be balanced by
an acknowledgement of the continuing importance of the classics, particularly in Latin, for sixteenth-century intellectuals. The re-discovery and
re-application of ancient learning inspired their reading and the formation of their personal libraries. Today we live in a society which places
extraordinary value on what is new, in which innovation is often confused with significance. In this chapter, in contrast, we encounter readers
who valued tradition and who looked to the learning of the past to guide
their conduct in the future. Latin, as a result, was alive and well.

   This chapter considers humanist readers and publishers in the era historians conveniently call 'the Renaissance' – the title literally means a
'rebirth' of ancient knowledge. There had been previous revivals of classical learning, in the argument of Elizabeth Eisenstein, but print enabled
it to survive and make a permanent contribution to Western culture.
Besides asking questions about the importance of the classics to Renaissance readers, we will also consider why Latin continued to play a very
significant role in European cultural life. Whereas in previous chapters
the discussion of the invention of printing and its links with Protestantism
focussed mainly on German-speaking Europe, in this chapter the com-
pass will swing towards the Italian peninsula, where Venice was the most
important centre of book production. It will consider the importance of
Latin for the intellectual elites, the transition towards a more specialised
typography and the growth of a new reading public. This public, made up

of educated laymen and women, aristocrats, government officials, merchants and a few artisans drove the growth of book production and of reading in the Renaissance.

Renaissance book production

Renaissance publishers and printers (in this period the two roles were combined) were certainly innovators. They found new ways to present editions of Virgil, Cicero, Seneca and Ovid to the educated reading public. New fonts labelled 'roman' and 'italic' referred to ancient Rome but offered new and convenient ways of engaging with its surviving literature. The typeface of this book is descended from the elegant scripts invented in the Renaissance. At first, as we saw in Chapter 3, the printed book imitated the manuscript book. In the sixteenth and seventeenth centuries, however, different conventions were introduced. Typographical space was distributed in new ways which gradually turned the printed book into a very different object from its scribal predecessor.

Venice led the way in Renaissance print production. If we consider the publication of all editions of Cicero, of which there were 126 between 1465 and 1479, the dominance of Italian publishing is very apparent. Venice was responsible for 26 per cent of Cicero editions, while another 33 per cent appeared in Rome or Milan. Paris produced only 10 per cent of all Cicero editions in this period.[3] A hundred years later, Italy had lost its pre-eminence, partly because its flourishing output was slowed down by the influence of the Counter-reformation. The Church banned all Machiavelli's works, for example, and promoted expurgated versions of Boccaccio's *Decameron*. Venetian book production went into a relative decline, in comparison even with other Italian cities. Paris was emerging as an important production centre, and Leiden, where the Elzeviers established themselves, became a significant focus for publishing in the Low Countries in the seventeenth century.

Publishers catered for a growing number of readers who demanded both accurate Latin texts and understandable vernacular editions. But identifying the national language was not a straightforward process. Vernacular languages had to be first generally accepted before they could be standardised in print. For example, there was no standard version of the Italian language. Because, however, of the literary prestige of Boccaccio, Dante and Petrarch, the Tuscan language of the fourteenth century which these writers had used became more and more influential, even among Venetian publishers. Even so, vernacular Italian was in a state of evolution. Correct spelling was in dispute, and publishers would sometimes invite readers to make their own manual corrections on the page if they were not happy with the spelling adopted. As the Tuscan language gradually became the literary norm, Latinisms were eliminated from it.

So Italian dropped the 'h', and *homo* (in Latin, a man) would become the modern *uomo*. Similarly, *nocte* (night) was transformed into *notte,* *perfecto* (perfect) into *perfetto* and so on.[4] The reading public needed to be educated in the new vernacular languages. Publishers had to provide grammars and dictionaries as essential reading aids for new secular readers.

As suggested in Chapter 4, vernacular literature became predominant in mid-sixteenth-century publishing. This was clearly the case in Chrisman's study of Strasbourg, where German rather than Latin was used for a wide range of secular literature, including histories, plays, broadsheets and scientific texts.[5] In France a secular reading culture was developing independently of Latin traditions. If we take the catalogue of the British Library as a guide to sixteenth-century French books, we find that the proportion published in French overtook the proportion published in Latin in the mid-1560s.[6] The main casualty of this trend was medieval literature, which gave way in the 1530s and 1540s to Greek and Latin classics, while contemporary French authors became increasingly popular thereafter.

Latin as a European language

The use of Latin in Europe as a whole had expanded with the Roman Empire and its adoption by many of the Empire's enemies, the so-called but misnamed 'barbarians'. Then Christianity spread the use of Latin further. Latin became the language of law, government and religion. It was a *lingua franca*, a common language in which educated people from all ends of Europe could communicate. As with English today, that did not mean that everybody handled it with equal competence, or that they spoke it everywhere with the same accent. Continental Europeans often complained about English, Scottish and Irish attempts to pronounce Latin, and the lack of comprehension was often mutual.[7] The fluent and correct use of Latin carried considerable intellectual capital, and was a badge identifying the speaker as a member of an educated and cultivated elite. Over the centuries, differences developed between formal written Latin and everyday spoken Latin, which evolved into quite different Latin-based languages in Spain, France, Italy and elsewhere.

In the first years of print, the dominance of Latin was overwhelming. Consider the *incunabula*, that is to say, printed books known to have been published before 1501 (*incunabulum* literally means a cradle). There are over 24,000 surviving *incunabula* titles, and 77.4 per cent of them were printed in Latin. Less than 1 per cent was in English.[8] A study of the language of these early printed books can also suggest which parts of Europe were most reliant on Latin as a language of publication. Italy was clearly most familiar with Latin, because only 17.5 per cent of *incunabula* produced in Italy were in Italian. Table 5.1 shows the approximate statistics for Europe as a whole:

Table 5.1 Preferred language of *incunabula* according to country of origin[9]

17.5% of *incunabula* printed in Italy were in Italian
20% of *incunabula* printed in Germany were in German
24% of *incunabula* printed in the Low Countries were in Dutch or Flemish
29% of *incunabula* printed in France were in French
55% of *incunabula* printed in Britain were in English
52% of *incunabula* printed in Spain were in Castilian or Catalan

---

Spain and Britain, therefore, stood out as parts of Europe where indigenous and regional languages relegated Latin book production to minority status.

The status of Latin was certainly in relative decline. In France, the monarchy took deliberate steps to promote the use of French. The Edict of Villers-Cotterêts in 1539 ordered the substitution of French for Latin in all official documents. In Germany and Spain, publication in Latin was gradually overtaken by vernacular publishing. When publishers offered their wares at the Frankfurt book fair of 1568, the catalogue showed that 331 titles were for sale in Latin, more than double the number of new titles (156) offered in German. Two centuries later, in 1778, the number of titles in Latin remained about the same, but the number of titles in German on offer had soared to 1,821. In Valencia, Latin books still accounted for over 50 per cent of production between 1545 and 1572, but in Barcelona the proportion fell from 60 per cent at the beginning of the sixteenth century to 25–35 per cent at the end of it.[10]

This decline, however, was a long-term phenomenon and must be seen in the context of the continuing usage of Latin and the healthy survival of a Latin reading culture. Latin had an important role as an international language, and it was probably at its peak in this European role in the 200 years between 1450 and 1650. Humanist writers like Erasmus of Rotterdam and Thomas More of England were bilingual, and they needed to be if they were to have a significant readership. Erasmus wanted to reach educated people everywhere and he saw himself as a pan-European humanist scholar, but could not achieve this in Dutch – he needed Latin's international audience. Many well-known authors were translated from the vernacular into Latin in order to reach a wider readership, including John Milton and Teresa of Avila. Translations into Latin were probably

at their peak in the first half of the seventeenth century. Latin was also
the European language of science. Newton wrote in Latin, and Galileo
taught in it. There was a medical Latin, a pharmaceutical Latin and (there
still is) a botanical Latin. Navigational treatises in this age of exploration
were translated into Latin. Navarro Brotóns counted 1,080 titles of scientific and technical works published in Spain or by Spanish authors in
the sixteenth century: 41 per cent of them were in Latin, 40 per cent were
in Castilian and most of the rest appeared in French and Italian.[11] This
was the production of a golden age before Catholic repression effectively
removed Spain from the European network of scientific exchange.

Latin was the language of education, in widespread use as a teaching medium. The schools of Old Regime France were havens of Latin
culture. Seventeenth-century children were taught basic literacy in Latin,
their textbooks were in Latin and their teachers taught in Latin. As late
as the 1880s, a French student in his final year of secondary school spent
10 out of 24 classroom hours per week studying Latin.[12] It was hardly
any different in Protestant Europe. In Germany, the Protestant reformer
Melanchthon produced a Latin grammar which went into 248 editions
between 1526 and the eighteenth century. In England, Colet founded St.
Paul's School in 1509, where students received a solid grounding in spoken and written Latin.[13] Latin students everywhere were inducted into a
life of rote learning, parrot-like recitation and harsh punishment in case
of lapses.

Universities were thoroughly steeped in Latin culture. In Oxford, a
study of sixteenth-century probate inventories suggests books in English
made up only 10 per cent of the contents of individual libraries.[14] In the
old university town of Pavia, about two-thirds of book production were
in Latin for teaching university disciplines, with particular concentrations in law, medicine and theology.[15] Latin competency varied, so that
not every student understood it perfectly. In seventeenth-century Pisa,
university professors would deliver their lecture in Latin, and then go out
into the courtyard to explain what they had been saying more informally
in Tuscan.[16] University Latin, however, enjoyed great longevity: it was
still being used as a teaching medium in Dutch universities in the early
nineteenth century, and in 1863 the great historian Leopold von Ranke
gave his inaugural professorial lecture in Latin.

Latin was the language of international diplomacy until it was superseded by French by the eighteenth century. In polyglot Eastern Europe,
Latin retained its value as a common language. Sessions of the Hungarian
Diet, or parliament, were still being held in Latin up to 1848. Latin, furthermore, remained the language of the Catholic liturgy, as the Council of
Trent had insisted, until the Second Vatican Council of 1962. Latin was
preferred for its qualities of majesty and permanence, because it commanded reverence and was allegedly inspired by God. It cemented the
unity of the universal Church and its defenders argued that to abandon it

might lead to fragmentation and schismatic tendencies. For the faithful, it was a language they did not necessarily fully understand, but which they heard as a familiar part of their environment. They perhaps knew the Our Father and the Creed in Latin, and the strange language conveyed the mystery and the magic of the Mass. Clerical Latin has served some extraordinary purposes. Soon after Primo Levi had been liberated from Auschwitz, he found himself starving and disorientated in the Polish city of Cracow. He had to resort to Latin to ask a priest the way to the soup kitchen: 'Pater optime, ubi est mensa pauperorum?' (Venerable father, where is the table of the poor?).[17] For a language often considered useless, Latin has proved a great resource. But in medieval and early modern Europe, it was a language embedded in the power structures of a hierarchical society. It excluded women, unless they were nuns, and defined the dominant social groups who held political, legal and cultural authority.

The humanist reader

A humanist here means a reader with broad intellectual interests, not limited to a specialised field of knowledge such as law or theology. He or she was interested in, and perhaps taught, the 'humanities', made up of grammar and rhetoric, history, philosophy and poetry. The humanist found inspiration in the writers of antiquity and would write in a script believed to be modelled on Roman handwriting. What kind of books made up the private library of a humanist reader in the late sixteenth and early seventeenth centuries? Some of the answers are to be found in the notarial archives, where the contents of the estates of deceased persons were inventoried. Sometimes this was done in preparation for an auction, sometimes simply to put a value on the estate. For statistically minded researchers this is a goldmine, so that it has sometimes seemed that for historians of reading the only good reader is a dead one. There are of course problems with relying on *post-mortem* inventories as evidence of reading. Analysing private libraries this way is only possible for the wealthier strata of society, because they alone had possessions worth valuing or selling. Even in the libraries of the rich, pamphlets and brochures considered of little monetary value might be discarded and so they disappear from the historian's sight. In addition, the sources have an inherent gender bias: with the exception of some rich widows, it is often very difficult to separate a man's library from the books his wife or daughters used. A more fundamental problem is that records of ownership do not tell us whether or not a book was actually read, and if so, what the reader thought about it. Books, after all, find their way into a personal library by various means: some may be inherited, others received as gifts (wanted or unwanted), others eagerly sought out and purchased. These are important limitations on our knowledge of readers in this period, although *post-mortem* inventories give us very valuable clues about upper-class reading culture.

In Paris, book-owners in the first half of the seventeenth century were most likely to be lawyers, administrators, noblemen and intellectuals. Their private collections usually ran to more than 100 volumes, but only a very few possessed over 1,000 when they died.[18] Only half of them had a Bible, while about 30 per cent owned works of personal devotion, such as missals, breviaries, books of hours or lives of the saints. More than 40 per cent of Parisian libraries had some Plutarch, or some editions of classic Roman authors like Livy, Tacitus, Seneca, Virgil and Horace. Lawyers would typically own Cicero and legal commentaries, while doctors' libraries would contain texts of Galen and Hippocrates. The private library of these men was both a working library, with the standard reference works for each profession, and at the same time a symbol of social success.

The humanist reader's library can be roughly divided into four parts. Firstly, there were religious books. As in the Parisian examples just cited, these did not necessarily include the Bible, but they did include devotional works. In addition, there might be some works on ecclesiastical history, such as Josephus' *History of the Jews*, and probably St. Augustine's *City of God*. In Paris, at least, there would be nothing by Luther or Calvin, but quite possibly some Catholic attacks on them. If we entered a little further into the personal books of a hypothetical Renaissance reader, we would encounter a second category of works of classical learning. These would almost certainly include Cicero, the model for rhetoric and eloquence, Plutarch, Seneca and perhaps the historians Livy and Tacitus. We might find some Aristotle and Plato and certainly some of the best-read Latin poets, Virgil, Horace and Ovid. The more scientifically inclined reader might be interested in Pliny's *Natural History*. The third category was that of professional books, especially medical and anatomical treatises for doctors, and legal commentaries for lawyers. The personal library always functioned as an instrument of work. In our fourth group of books we would find a wide range of other literature, of more recent vintage and much of it in vernacular languages. Specifically humanist authors represented here might include Erasmus, Machiavelli, Petrarch, Boccaccio, Thomas More for his *Utopia* and Castiglione for *The Courtier*, which outlined the ideal attributes and behaviour of the educated Renaissance man. This section might include some history: in France, Froissart's *Chronicles* might appear, while in England sixteenth-century gentlemen had works of heraldry and topography, recent history and etiquette books.[19] In Spain, we would find copies of Cervantes' *Don Quixote*, and everywhere a few chivalrous romances, which were part of a shared culture and not yet specifically designed for a lower-class readership. If we try amongst all this to identify specifically women's reading, we might find it in practical manuals, dealing, for example, with house-keeping, childbirth, cookery, sewing, as well as practical medicine and the use of herbs. We may guess that a woman's books also included a pro-portion of romances, poetry and devotional works, but without clearer evidence it is impossible to know if there were any substantial differences in the ways men and women read.[20]

Increasingly, a gentleman's house had a study set aside for the dis-play of his fine books. The Duke of Urbino, grown wealthy on the proceeds of renting out his private army, personalised his books with fine bindings. In a later period and a little further down the social scale, Samuel Pepys amassed a collection of 3,000 volumes. Some astound-ing personal book collections were formed in this period. One brilliant English example is that of Matthew Parker, Archbishop of Canterbury under Elizabeth I, who died in 1575. Parker's collection of books and manuscripts at Corpus Christi College, Cambridge, was established in the wake of Henry VIII's dissolution of the monasteries, from which many rare items derived. Parker's collection was not merely a collection of treasures: his specific aim was to justify the doctrines of Anglicanism. In doing so, he thought nothing of taking old books apart, re-binding and re-constituting them.

Humanist readers tried to reach ancient authors unadorned. They wanted to scrape aside the thick sediment of medieval commentaries on the classics which had accumulated over the years and which they felt obscured rather than illuminated their meaning. They sought sim-ple and straightforward access to their texts. They went, we might say, in search of the naked Virgil. They approached Latin texts with delib-erate purpose. In works of history, politics and philosophy, they sought lessons which they could apply to present-day situations and problems. They looked for moral and practical guidance in the conduct of pub-lic life. In Elizabethan England, members of the political elite employed scholar-secretaries to read to them for this purpose. One such reader was Gabriel Harvey, employed in the 1580s by the Earl of Leicester, whose reading has been studied by Lisa Jardine and Anthony Grafton.[21] Over 20 years, Harvey was employed to read and take notes on a series of texts in which Livy's histories played a key role. This was purposeful reading with political aims. The classical works were studied partly to develop good political rhetoric, in which field Cicero in particular was considered a master of eloquent argument; and they were read for prece-dents, examples and ideas which might have a bearing on the problems which the leader actually faced. Readers knew they could become bet-ter diplomats or military strategists by studying the campaigns of Caesar or Hannibal, for example, and by avoiding their errors and indecisions. This was active reading with contemporary relevance.

Renaissance readers had many reading strategies. The reading wheel enabled them to view several books at once, to facilitate cross-referencing

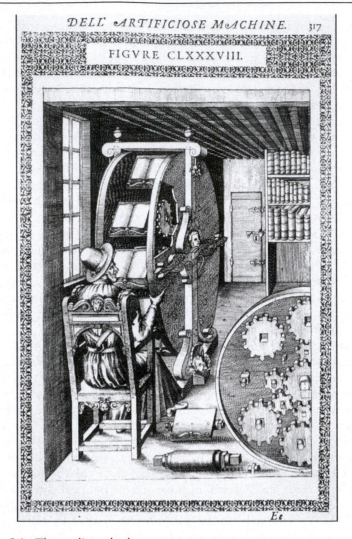

Figure 5.1 The reading wheel.
Note: The reading wheel enabled Renaissance scholars to consult several books at once. © The Gutenberg Institute.

and comparison between texts (Figure 5.1). Memory was highly valued as a means of literary appropriation. Anthony Grafton tells the story of Justus Lipsius, who boasted he would recite the entire works of Tacitus with a dagger held to his throat, inviting his challenger to cut him open if he made a mistake.[22] Selecting and pondering key passages, however, was a superior method of ensuring comprehension. The commonplace book was used by readers to write down arguments, turns of phrase or snippets of information which a reader wanted to think about later or remember.

Shakespeare had such a book, so did Montaigne and the philosopher Bodin.[23] The Buckinghamshire landowner William Drake kept dozens of them in the decades from the 1620s to the 1660s.[24] He recorded notes on his reading of Tacitus and Macchiavelli, as well as the ancient philosophers, historians and poets. He wrote instructions to himself to summarise his reading daily and to read preferably on an empty stomach to improve the concentration. He transcribed legal judgements and parliamentary speeches in the dramatic period leading up to the English Civil War, reflecting on the unfathomable depths of human treachery and cunning. He mined gems of wisdom which he could apply to advance his own career. The commonplace book became a collection of small items of knowledge torn out of their original context and formed into something new by an individual reader who thus created his or her own personal book.

The *florilegium*, meaning literally a bunch of flowers, was in the same tradition. It was a published collection of choice quotations to be plundered for a pithy and entertaining sermon. Renaissance readers turned note-taking into a highly developed art. They copied passages in full, paraphrased or cut-and-pasted choice sections. Like today's undergraduates, they risked plagiarism and reproducing quotations inaccurately. Their strategy was a combination of slavish citation and critical reflection. Thus Leon Battista Alberti, author of a landmark treatise on architecture, raided Cicero for quotations 'with a magpie's zest for brightly coloured objects', as Grafton puts it.[25] Nevertheless, Alberti was more than a clever ventriloquist; he engaged a dialogue with his ancient authorities, building on their learning in order to construct something original and modern. Classical learning was the essential foundation, but the aim was to surpass it.

Their respect for books in general and the ancients in particular was not unmitigated. Although they went in search of the naked Virgil, they often wrote their own commentaries in the margins, and these were not always complimentary. Joseph Scaliger crossed out the text of one book and wrote 'cacas' (shit) all over it.[26] The ideal reader was critical and active, not slavishly devoted to his or her text. Erasmus ridiculed an obsessive respect for Cicero in his *Ciceronianus* of 1528. He imagined a Cicero-addict named Nosoponus who made a dictionary of all the words ever used by Cicero, and even refused to get married or have a family so that he could spend all his time shut away studying Cicero. Nosoponus lived only on currants and coriander seeds while he was studying, trying to memorise Ciceronian phrases which he hoped to trot out at the right moments to make a good impression. As this satire suggests, Erasmus had his own critical version of Cicero. Like many others, he admired Cicero's style and rhetoric, but regarded him as an intellectual locked into the limited world of pagan knowledge. The Erasmian Cicero had to be recruited into Christian culture. Furthermore, Erasmus admired

Cicero as a great example of an intellectual fully involved in public life in the service of the commonwealth. This 'civic humanism' was the ideal of the Renaissance reader. The great error of Erasmus's exemplary nerd Nosoponus was to shut himself away and refuse to accept his social and civic responsibilities.

Uses of the book in the Renaissance

The size and physical form of a book determines its target audience and the uses to which it is put. The most common formats were established in the age of the scribal book and the advent of printing did not change them. Armando Petrucci has usefully classified three main forms and uses of the book in the Renaissance.[27] The first is the *libro da banco*, the book for a reading bench or table. This describes a large format, scholarly book, perhaps for university use. Either scribal or printed, the 'bench-book' would have wide margins for personal comments, and typically a two-column text in Gothic characters. Secondly, the humanist book appeared either in large in-folio format or in the smaller in-quarto. Unlike the first category, the humanist book was not designed for churches, universities or scholarly use, but rather for wealthy laymen and their wives. It would have full-page text without columns, small margins and a distinctively 'roman' font rather than Gothic script. The third and most popular element of Petrucci's classification is the *libro da bisaccia* – the book for a satchel, in small format and easily portable, as its name suggests, in the backpack of a merchant, a preaching friar, a pilgrim or a craftsman. This kind of book would have text in two columns, large print in a Gothic font for popular consumption, and it was very likely illustrated with woodcut prints. All these traditional forms were imitations of scribal books. Petrucci is suggesting that scribal and printed books were both examples of a similar production system. His classification is not one dictated by whether a book was scribal or printed; instead, it is a classification based on how books were actually used.

We may add a further category to this typology – the *libretto da mano*; in other words, the small-format, easily portable version of the humanist book, produced in-octavo for a cultivated lay readership. This innovation was especially promoted by the Venetian printer-publisher Aldus Manutius at the end of the fifteenth century. Renaissance publishers had designed new fonts to replace the popular Gothic script with something clearer, lighter and more elegant. In France, Garamond designed a Roman font, the 'gros romain' in 1543 and many computers have a font available which still bears his name. Similarly, in 1546, Robert Estienne invented a 'Cicero' font to publish his edition of Eusebius. Aldus Manutius similarly claimed to be imitating Latin inscriptions when he designed his 'italic' font. In fact these new fonts had no exact equivalent in Roman times. They looked and were called classical, but this was an invented classicism, designed for the purposes of sixteenth-century readers. Garamond and Aldus Manutius were adapting their interpretation of classical precedents for a contemporary audience, just as paintings of the period might depict Virgil strolling though a sixteenth-century Tuscan landscape. For Grafton, this is best described not so much as a revival of classicism but rather as an imaginative re-construction of a lost society.[28]

The humanist or classical script was an aesthetic revolution in book history. Aldus tried to patent his italic font but nothing could prevent competitors outside his native Venice from adopting it. Gothic was still used for legal and theological works, and it survived for popular readers in the Netherlands and German-speaking Europe. Luther used Gothic when he needed to reach a lower-class audience, and humanist script when he was addressing a more educated readership.

Aldus Manutius revolutionised publishing when, in 1501–02, he produced a series of both Latin and vernacular works in pocket-sized in-octavo editions (the *libretti da mano* already mentioned). These were the first productions in the new italic type. Its small format should not deceive us into thinking that the series was a distant ancestor of the paperback revolution. On the contrary, the Aldine series was expensive and catered most definitely for a cultivated readership. But the series startlingly juxtaposed both vernacular and ancient authors, so that Petrarch and Dante were implicitly given equal status with Virgil and Horace.[29] The Aldine editions were models of simplicity, producing the basic text uncluttered by notes, decoration or commentaries. Humanist readers had found the naked Virgil which they so much appreciated.

In the early decades of print, the printed book imitated the scribal book. The kind of books which were put into print belonged to the same genres for which the manuscript book had catered. For example, about 45 per cent of the *incunabula* were works on theology, following the established patterns of scribal book production.[30] In the sixteenth century, however, a range of new reading aids and publishing practices emerged which were peculiar to the printed book and marked it out as a distinct species. Some of these practices have already been mentioned, like the invention of new 'roman' and italic fonts. Publishers could now use different fonts for different purposes, combine them in the same book or even on the same page. There was no equivalent of this versatility in a manuscript book.

The printed book clearly parted company with its scribal predecessors in its treatment of the relationship between text and illustration. This was to some extent determined by a technological change, in which copper engravings provided far more sophisticated images than the cruder woodcuts. Unlike woodcuts, however, copper engravings demanded a separate press, which immediately caused a divorce between the text and the image.

Early printed books developed a considerable paratextual apparatus, by which is meant the preliminary pages, footnotes and anything in a book which refers to the central text, adorns it or comments on it without actually being a part of it. The title might be accompanied by a Latin tag, the printer's name and the place of publication. There was often a long dedication to the author's patron. The title page was sometimes an elaborately engraved frontispiece, with the title printed within an archway or an entry, inviting the reader to enter a building.

The frontispiece could represent a rich array of symbolic figures, and it spoke a complicated discourse. The scythe, for example, was shorthand for death, the set square was the symbolic attribute of the architect, the sword and scales signified justice and the sextant the science of astronomy. Similar coded illustrations were the main subject of books of emblems, depicting allegorical figures, heraldic devices and mythical and monstrous animals, wyverns, gryphons and so on. The muses, gods and goddesses were favourite subjects, too, each signifying a different talent or quality, together with personifications of the seven deadly sins or the cardinal virtues, and symbolic images for the seasons of the year. New opportunities for the reproduction of artistic illustration created books which employed a wide range of allegorical and symbolic images, which all required deciphering. It is hard to say whether sixteenth-century readers were familiar with all the visual codes used by emblem books and frontispieces. It seems unlikely they could grasp every nuance of this visual language unless the same images were regularly repeated in different books and unless the reader had a long enough memory to remember them. Like all books, visual illustrations were open to multiple readings and different layers of comprehension.[31]

Libraries – a new classification of knowledge

With a greater supply of books in circulation, and the appearance of new titles in the sixteenth and seventeenth centuries, there was a need to impose order on chaos, to organise, list and classify book production. The establishment and growth of libraries, both private and institutional, posed special design and planning problems. The function of the library varied. Some libraries were merely collections of rarities and curiosities. Some were designed to parade wealth and luxury. Leonello d'Este's library in fifteenth-century Ferrara was designed on a Roman model, with painted ceilings, a tiled floor and decorated with images of ancient Rome.[32] Libraries of religious orders like the Jesuits were Christian in their conception and purged of defiling elements. The humanist library, on the other hand, aimed to be both universal and of practical use, providing reference and illumination for scholars and administrators.

All collections needed to be catalogued. The proliferation of catalogues and bibliographies in this period was a sign of what Roger Chartier has called the new order of books.[33] Some of them described actual libraries, while other bibliophiles imagined their ideal library of libraries. But how was any library, actual or imaginary, to be arranged and catalogued? There were many possibilities. Titles might be classified according to their language, in order to highlight the status of the vernacular. Increasingly they were listed alphabetically according to the author's name, although in early libraries the authors' first names rather than their last names dictated the order of the catalogue. Sometimes books were ordered by their size and also by subject, and sometimes by a combination of all these criteria, as was the case in the first printed catalogue of the Bodleian Library in Oxford in 1605, based first on subject matter, then size and then authors' names.[34]

The issue of listing books by subject went to the heart of the Renaissance's classification of knowledge. A library catalogue raised fundamental epistemological questions: what were the recognised disciplines and where did each one sit in relation to God and in the hierarchy of human knowledge? The Renaissance developed a universal scheme of definitions which survived until the nineteenth century. Bibliographies gradually adopted a division into five principal categories, arranged in the following order: Theology, Jurisprudence, History, Arts and Sciences and finally Belles-Lettres. This was a very conservative theory of knowledge. It placed Theology first, and into this category were fitted polemics, spiritual and devotional works, ecclesiastical history, philosophy and grammar. The subsequent emphasis on Law and History (which included biography and geography) seemed to reflect the priorities of the absolute monarchies. The humanities and liberal arts, which were so important to the Renaissance, were pushed down the intellectual hierarchy. Arts and Sciences embraced the natural sciences, physics, chemistry and medicine, as well as practical arts like hygiene, horticulture and animal husbandry. Last came Belles-Lettres, including poetry, literary criticism, essays and theatre.

It is interesting to note what later became of this traditional categorisation of knowledge, as well as what seems to be missing from it in the eyes of a modern reader. Three developments eventually made it out of date. The first was the collapse of the publishing market in the broad category of Theology, which occurred in the eighteenth century and can be associated with the secularising influence of the Enlightenment. It could no longer be assumed that religion formed the overarching framework for all branches of science and learning. Instead, religious publishing became an increasingly marginal category. The second development was the rise of fiction publishing, which we can date from the boom in recreational literature in the second half of the eighteenth century. Novels of course went on to reach a mass readership in the nineteenth century. They filled up the old category of Belles-Lettres and their sheer volume overbalanced the entire scheme of classification, making it effectively obsolete. Thirdly, the traditional classification did not cater at all for the category of Education. The huge expansion in educational publishing in the nineteenth and twentieth centuries would fill a category all on its own.

Humanist readers had different reading practices and a range of strategies for appropriating the learning of antiquity. Sometimes they placed ancient writers firmly within their historical context, and yet they tried to extract models of behaviour and gems of eloquence applicable to their own circumstances. They knew they were studying pagans and struggled to fit them into a Christian mould. Sometimes they plagiarised the classical texts mercilessly and sometimes they used them as the basis for new interpretations.

The Renaissance and the Counter-reformation had both left their mark. Knowledge had been re-organised and, in the hands of a few book-trade entrepreneurs, the printed book had acquired some of the modern characteristics which distinguished it from the manuscript book. Wealthy individual book collectors were amassing important collections. An educated and discerning reading public now existed outside the ranks of the Church. In different ways and with different priorities, the humanists and the Catholic Church had carried respect for Latin culture to its all-time peak in European history. These significant developments, however, mainly concerned a social and institutional elite. In the following chapters, we must put the spotlight on lower levels of society to assess what print and literacy meant for the ordinary people of Europe.

6

Print and popular culture

For the ordinary people of early modern Europe, books were rare and ownership of anything but the very cheapest productions unaffordable. The culture of the poor was nevertheless rich although it is not easily accessible. Unfortunately, very few peasants or urban workers have left personal testimony about their reading. This chapter will discuss the precious artisan autobiographies that survive, as well as the evidence about reading squeezed out of suspects by the Inquisition; but these sources are extremely scarce and historians are usually compelled to approach the study of popular culture indirectly. We are forced to turn for information about popular readers to publishers, governments, judges and the Churches. Paradoxically, we learn most about the culture of the poor from those who wanted to reform it, purify it or suppress it.

The Abbé Grégoire provided a good example of this indirect approach to popular culture in the questionnaire about rural reading habits which he devised in 1790–92, the early years of the French Revolution. Grégoire wanted to know what French peasants read, if anything, and whether local priests had a stock of books to lend to their parishioners. In order to find out more, he turned not to the rural readers themselves, but to his educated colleagues in the Church, the administration and the professions. But for these well-heeled intermediaries, peasants belonged almost to another race: at best they inspired a certain ethnographic curiosity, at worst they were steeped in crass ignorance, prejudice and superstition. In fact, peasants did use almanacs, books of hours and occasionally the *Lives of the Saints*, but as far as Grégoire's informants were concerned, they might have come from another planet.[1] The Abbé had his own agenda, which was not just to 'improve' the peasants but also to eradicate local *patois* and facilitate the spread of the French language. In studying popular culture through such hostile or paternalistic eyes, we must read 'against the grain', separating the cultural assumptions of the intermediary from the real object of our investigation – the lives of the poorest classes.

This chapter investigates the role of reading and writing in early modern popular culture. Popular culture is an elusive quarry, and we need to ask whether there was in fact anything distinctively 'popular' (i.e. lower class) about it. At the same time, the connections between popular and elite cultures must be examined. I use 'culture' to include not just the cultural artefacts which have survived, like the ephemeral chapbooks which were staples of popular reading, but also the cultural practices and beliefs which determined the way texts were assimilated. Popular reading was distinctive not so much for the texts which were consumed, but for the methods of appropriating them. This was an 'amphibious' culture, in which both oral and written communication played significant roles. Peasant literacy had a religious context, and the works most frequently read aloud in a family setting of an evening would be a passage from the Bible or, in Catholic countries, the life of a saint. The workplace provided further reading opportunities: tailors working round a common table would delegate one of their number to read aloud as they sewed. Agricultural workers might use their siesta for collective reading. As one innkeeper told Sancho Panza in *Don Quixote*,

> At harvest-time, a lot of the reapers come in here in the mid-day heat. There's always one of them who can read, and he takes up one of those books. Then as many as thirty of us sit around him, and we enjoy listening so much that it saves us countless grey hairs.[2]

The reading in question concerned those novels of chivalry which had obsessed the Don to the point of lunacy.

The elusive pursuit of popular culture

In this world of traditional literacy, the book was an object of awe and reverence, and writing had miraculous and symbolic uses for those unable to master the hidden secrets of scribal culture. The Bible had special magical powers. It could ward off evil spirits and cure the sick. Many would turn to it as though it was an oracle about to guide the reader on important life decisions. The custom still survives of opening the Bible at random and taking the first verse one reads as a riddle loaded with significance for the future. At the end of the nineteenth century, one Hampshire woman who suffered from fits ate an entire New Testament, putting every page in the middle of her sandwiches. In American Bible folklore, the Bible also cures warts and nosebleeds.[3] Popular culture had many distinctive uses for the book.

'Popular' is used here not in the contemporary sense to mean something that is well liked, but in the sense of something that is 'of the people', that is the lower classes of peasants and the urban poor. When we talk today of 'popular culture', we generally have in mind television soap operas or pulp fiction. This is more helpfully labelled 'mass culture', since it is available to everyone in contemporary society and there is nothing distinctively lower class about it. In discussing popular culture in the pre-industrial period, therefore, we must distinguish practices which emerge 'from the people' from cultural goods which are produced by others for consumption 'by the people'.

In practice, it is difficult to isolate popular cultural forms. They are rarely completely homogeneous or autonomous. Popular culture always contains and absorbs 'foreign' elements. The Italian Marxist Antonio Gramsci characterised the culture of the poor as inarticulate and unsystematic, a mosaic of fragmentary elements long since discarded by the elite.[4] At the same time, popular culture is neither immobile nor a closed heritage; even though we often label it 'traditional', it evolves organically. There was no rigid dichotomy between 'high' and 'low' culture. Such a model of two cultures in opposition to each other, with one dominating the other, is ultimately sterile and static. Instead, this discussion explores ways in which elite and popular culture influenced and infiltrated each other. From this starting point, we discover a wide range of possible relationships and interchanges between the culture of the elite and the culture of the poor. Sometimes they are indeed in conflict with each other; at other times they borrow from and 'contaminate' each other.

In Peter Burke's view, the educated elite once shared a cultural life with their social inferiors. There was a natural intermingling between the cultivated and the disinherited. In the sixteenth century, the upper classes joined the general populace in carnival festivities, bullfights or watching public executions. Even Tsar Ivan the Terrible loved a good ballad as well as the next Russian, not to mention shows by acrobats, clowns and performing dwarves. Burke, however, traces a process in which the upper classes drew away from popular practices.[5] In the seventeenth and eighteenth centuries, he argues, the elites distanced themselves from festivities and certain genres of literature which they had once enjoyed. They asserted their own social distinction by condemning the culture of the poor as coarse, superstitious and obscene. They attacked witchcraft beliefs and other aspects of popular religion. Abbé Grégoire's enquiry in the 1790s showed signs of this attitude of 'enlightened' contempt towards the lower classes. It is difficult in fact to find *any* period when elites did not try to impose moral discipline on popular culture: after the absolutist state and the Counter-reformation came the rationalist impulses of the eighteenth-century Enlightenment, which proved no friendlier to the culture or reading of the poor. In spite of such attempts to stifle it, popular culture had a habit of refusing to obey and of rising defiantly like a phoenix from the ashes.

The possible connections between learned and popular culture can be explored through various genres of reading matter which had wide currency amongst lower-class readers all over Europe, namely chap-books, almanacs and folk tales. In addition, the reading and writing skills of some remarkable individuals from the lower classes will be discussed.

Chapbooks and the *bibliothèque bleue*

The brochures of the *bibliothèque bleue* were cheap and anonymous. They were produced on rough paper, sometimes bound with blue paper commonly used as sugar-wrapping, and sold in their millions. They had their equivalent in every European country; they were known as chap-books in England, and as *pliegos de cordel* in Spain. The *pliego suelto* was a sheet folded once or twice to form a simple four- or eight-page brochure in-quarto. A printer could produce 1,500 copies of them in a day. Although originally destined for an urban audience, by the eigh-teenth century they had acquired a very large rural one. They were peddled in the countryside by itinerant salesmen offering a range of goods besides literature, including items of cutlery and haberdashery. In Shake-speare's *The Winter's Tale*, the peddler Autolycus sells not only books and brochures but mirrors, gloves, ribbons, bracelets, cloth, pins and thread. In Spain, the *pliegos sueltos* were hawked by blind itinerants who held a monopoly of this trade until 1836, organised around the Brotherhood of Our Lady of the Visitation in Madrid. They memorised texts for sale so that they could sing and recite extracts from their wares. Young guides or female companions helped them to identify their texts. The blind Spanish peddler was an early mass medium, transmitting texts orally to the illiterate.[6] Until the second half of the nineteenth century, the itiner-ant *colporteur* was a familiar and regular visitor to most parts of rural France. The chapbooks of the *bibliothèque bleue* which he sold catered for a world outside the domain of the book itself. By 1848, France had 3,500 authorised *colporteurs*, who between them sold about 40 million chapbooks per year.[7] They made the fortune of a few publishers, based in Troyes, who specialised in this cheap and plentiful material. In England, similarly, the trade was concentrated in the hands of a few specialists in the Stationers' Company, which vigorously defended its monopoly.

The repertoire was very enduring. It included almanacs and stories reprinted repeatedly over centuries. The sample of 450 titles analysed by Robert Mandrou gives an inkling of the wide range of this corpus, and it is summarised in Table 6.1.

Mandrou's interpretation requires some revision. For example, he was mistaken in thinking that reading stories aloud was a normal feature of peasant gatherings on winter evenings (the *veillée*).[9] But the gen-res he identified had their equivalents all over Europe.[10] In England, there were folk tales like *Jack and the Giant* or *Dick Whittington and his Cat*. There were chivalrous adventures like the Spanish *El Cid* or

> *Table 6.1* Mandrou's classification of the contents of the *bibliothèque bleue*[8]
>
> ---
>
> Over 25 per cent of titles were pious works, e.g. catechisms, prayers, lives of the Saints, homilies on the art of dying and versions of the *danse macabre*.
>
> About 18 per cent of titles were fiction, farces, burlesques, drinking songs.
>
> About 18 per cent of titles concerned daily life, e.g. calendars, horoscopes, recipes, medical and magical advice.
>
> About 15 per cent of titles were stories of myths and fairy tales.
>
> About 10 per cent were instructions on card and dice games, etiquette books, alphabets for children, instructions on apprenticeships.
>
> Under 10 per cent of titles concerned the history of France, e.g. Charlemagne and the Song of Roland.

the French *Four Sons of Aymon*, all mounted simultaneously on their valiant steed Bayard. There were the exploits of tricksters like Till Eulenspiegel in Germany. Everywhere stories of villains and bandits were popular, including the legendary Robin Hood, the French outlaw Cartouche and a number of roguish Irish highwaymen. Such popular heroes fitted the pattern of the 'social bandit', in that they were sympathetic to the poor, treated women impeccably and, although they were the enemies of exploiters, remained fundamentally loyal to monarchy. Slapstick farce was plentiful, along with 'jest-books' and obscene stories involving cuckolded husbands, shrewish wives, lecherous widows and extraordinary phalluses. Much of this humour was plainly misogynistic.

Mandrou argued that the *bibliothèque bleue* incorporated an overwhelming element of escapism. The emphasis on myth and fable, farce and comedy, magic and romance suggested a body of literature that in no way challenged the social hierarchy but instead strengthened it. Chivalric romances were dominated by generous and brave aristocrats, while the popular *danse macabre* reinforced the theme that all are equal in death, depicted as a skeleton with his scythe, who comes to dance with the rich and powerful as well as the poorest peasant. In this interpretation, the literature preaches patience and submission to the subordinate classes. It acts as a social tranquilliser for the poor. In addition, many texts carried a strong undercurrent of religiosity, and warned of demons and the terrors of Hell. Instructions on the art of a good death were a traditional genre, urging the reader to resist temptation, meditate on Christ and make some charitable donations in his will. Devotional works like catechisms and books of hours, suggesting prayers for the day, always formed a substantial proportion of the catalogue of any chapbook publisher.

The chapbooks, however, had another more practical side. They included manuals with advice for the tasks of everyday life. There were items on gardening and housekeeping. They instructed the reader on how to make soap and sauces, rear chickens or treat common ailments. The more pragmatic titles of the chapbook corpus taught how to write letters of all kinds, whether on matters of love, bereavement or business, and how to address a correspondent who was a social superior or inferior. There was a literature of manners and etiquette, based on Erasmus' model for educating children, advising on how to dress and behave in public, in Church or at the family meal table. These instructional works illustrate what Bollème calls the 'savoir-faire' of chapbook literature.[11]

Mandrou's argument that the chapbooks acted as a social tranquilliser can be critically scrutinised by considering evidence about their audience. The use of crude woodcut illustration suggests that the *bibliothèque bleue* was appealing to semi-literate readers who received the message as much from visual images as from the accompanying text. In France, however, illustration was not always a major part of the text: according to Chartier, only 38 per cent of titles had more than one illustration each, and a half of them had only one.[12] Considering the high degree of illiteracy in France and elsewhere in seventeenth-century Europe (see Chapter 7), it is worth asking where the readers of millions of chapbooks actually came from. Not all customers of the *bibliothèque bleue* were semi-literate peasants, for they included educated readers from the middle class as well as artisans. This would explain some of the 'savoir-faire' literature and the letter-writing and etiquette manuals which seem destined for aspiring artisans rather than a readership that could not write at all. The burlesque literature that glorified individual trades like the tailors or the bakers touched a traditional comic register, in which apprentices played elaborate pranks on their masters and their wives. They drew on the secretive aspects of the guilds, their esoteric ceremonies and jargon. This comic genre essentially glorified the traditional crafts, and was perhaps destined for a readership of artisans. When we encounter almanacs which detail the calendar of the royal court and the sittings of the law courts, it seems again that the publishers did not have the humblest readers in mind. The *bibliothèque bleue* was therefore a meeting point where both learned and popular culture intersected and mingled.

The works which made up the *bibliothèque bleue* were not composed by lower-class authors and we should not therefore consider them as direct expressions of popular culture. There were anonymous, put together by publishers trying to maximise their sales. This was literature written *for* the people rather than *by* the people. The origins of many myths and stories in the corpus derived from erudite literature. Publishers plundered sources like Boccaccio to re-frame their works for popular consumption. *L'Aventurier Buscon*, for example, was a rambling, bawdy burlesque tale taken from the Spanish novelist Quevedo, and transformed for the *bibliothèque bleue* in the seventeenth century. The French publishers made a series of strategic decisions which re-shaped the original text. It was abbreviated and divided into short paragraphs for easy reading. A happy, moral ending was added to the story. Blasphemies and obscenities were eliminated to make it acceptable to the Church. Thus words like *merde* (shit), *pisser* (to piss) and *putain* (whore) were purged.[13] The spirit of Counter-reformation censorship was antagonistic to repeated references to urination and defecation – the comedy of excrement – and the fixation on lower body functions, which Bakhtin identified as a characteristic feature of the medieval sense of humour.[14] There was nothing very original about chapbook literature; in fact it thrived on plagiarism. Works once composed for aristocratic or courtly readers went through many alterations before they found their way into the basket of the *colporteur*. Because of their erudite sources, such stories were not a mirror of popular culture. They were instead a bridge between 'high culture' and a peasant readership.

Chapbook literature was in its heyday in the seventeenth and eighteenth centuries, when it conquered a rural audience. It was under attack from eighteenth-century rationalists and in Britain from reforming Evangelicals. By the middle of the nineteenth century, *colportage* was a declining trade. As the influence of books spread socially and geographically, through serialised novels and illustrated magazines, the world of *colportage* literature correspondingly shrank. In the second half of the nineteenth century, it could not compete with the newspaper press and it disappeared altogether. The railway, the retail bookshop and government censorship all combined to make it obsolete.

Almanacs

Almanacs enjoyed a massive circulation. French almanacs only cost a few *sous* and some had print runs of 200,000 copies.[15] In London in the 1660s, between 3 and 400,000 copies of almanacs were being produced annually for the Stationers' Company.[16] Although peasants very rarely owned a book, they were familiar with the almanac. It hung from the ceiling from a nail in their houses like other household objects.[17]

The almanac had multiple functions. In its traditional model, it was an annual calendar, listing main holidays, saints' days, the movements of the planets and phases of the moon, just as diaries do today. It included horoscopes and prophecies for the coming year. Some Italian almanacs included the horoscopes of eminent people, for example the Pope.[18] So it was not merely a work of reference, but it also had a magical content. Its astrological prognostications gave both agricultural and medical advice. In the eighteenth century, it might also include fables, brief stories and anecdotes about extraordinary events like earthquakes or plagues. The almanac developed into much more than a calendar: it was part-fiction, part-journalism, part-sermon. The general message of such homilies was to accept one's lot in life and prepare for a good death. In the late eighteenth century, *Le Messager Boiteux* (The Lame Courier) recommended sincerity, compassion and submission to the great and powerful.[19] In England, almanacs often had a more political slant. Their prophecies and predictions of the apocalypse reflected a millenarian thread running through the radical tradition. Whereas Tory almanacs predicted the happy birth of a royal heir, radical almanacs prophesied the deaths of kings. 'All monarchs begin to look scurvily', announced the *Levellers' Almanack* of 1652.[20] English almanacs were profoundly nationalistic, with a full range of jokes and prejudices against the Irish, the Scots, the Welsh, the French and all Papists.

At one level almanacs were aimed at semi-literate rural readers. They were the obvious consumers of the almanac's advice on the harvest, changes in the weather or the best time to sow, and one of the most popular of all was specifically addressed to shepherds – *Le Grand calendrier et compost des bergers*, which was well known in England as well as France. The successful English almanac *Poor Robin* (1662–1828) was in its own words 'adapted to the meanest capacity'; in other words, it targeted readers of humble status, which is why in 1828 the *Athenaeum* disparagingly called it 'the oracle of the village alehouse'.[21] In practice, the clientele of the almanac was probably much wider than this. As with chapbooks, it included urban craftsmen and readers even higher up the social scale. Lord Burghley, Queen Elizabeth's leading minister, owned a series of them. The philosopher John Locke owned several issues of *Merlinus Anglicus*, the highly successful 'English Merlin' by William Lilly. Lilly had begun his career in the 1640s with almanacs defending the parliamentary cause, but soon adapted himself to the restoration of Charles II, which he had totally failed to predict. His sales accordingly fell.[22] Almanacs were clearly bought by every social group.

The almanac was a genre in continuous evolution. In the eighteenth century, it absorbed some of the rational spirit of the Enlightenment in striving for greater objectivity and accuracy. It included more historical and scientific information. Astrological prophecies, for example, were eventually excised from Old Moore's popular *Vox Stellarum*. The almanac instead carried descriptions of foreign countries, their customs, flora and fauna, and main geographical features. The genre multiplied – it engendered special almanacs for literary readers, almanacs for pilgrims, almanacs for fashionable women, almanacs for young people and almanacs for lottery-players. Perhaps the lottery-players still needed astrology to find the most auspicious moment to buy their ticket, but the rest of the genres just mentioned were not in the traditional mould and they were not aimed at rural illiterates. The biggest-selling almanac in eighteenth-century Turin was the *Palmaverde*, which offered not only the traditional astrological prognostications, but also a city guide for courtiers and businessmen. It listed the members of the Church hierarchy, and gave the birthdays of the crowned heads of Europe and the prevailing exchange rates for various currencies. It even left several pages blank as modern diaries do, inviting readers to make their own notes.[23] Almanacs, therefore, were a diverse and changing form of literature. Like the chapbooks of the *bibliothèque bleue*, they were not a clear reflection of popular culture, nor were they purely instruments for the control and mystification of the lower classes. They occupied an intermediate area between the culture of the poor and the culture of the educated.

Menocchio and the Inquisition: the micro-history of reading

When Domenico Scandella, known as Menocchio, was first investigated by the Inquisition as a suspected heretic he gave his interrogators details about his reading. The Inquisitors were curious about this because they wanted to discover the origins of his strange and unorthodox ideas. Menocchio was a miller in Friuli in north-eastern Italy and, because we rarely have direct information about the reading practices of a man of his humble status, he has become one of the most famous readers of his time.

What surprised the Inquisition most was Menocchio's version of the creation of the world. According to Menocchio, the world was not made by God or any other divinity. He believed that the earth had existed in a state of chaos, but had solidified by curdling like a cheese, in which huge worms then grew and developed into angels. In 1584, this unique heresy of 'the cheese and the worms' earned Menocchio a sentence of life imprisonment. He was freed after two years but defiantly persisted in his opinions. When he was investigated a second time, the Inquisition was less merciful. Menocchio was executed as a heretic in 1600.[24]

What in the reading of this unfortunate Italian miller had led him to develop such a bizarre and ultimately fatal interpretation of the origins of the world? Menocchio's reading was based on erudite texts, which came his way haphazardly in the small community where he lived, and which he had borrowed. In other words, he had not specifically chosen the works he read, which included a vernacular Bible, Mandeville's fantastic *Travels*, lives of the saints, an unexpurgated edition of Boccaccio's *Decameron*, *Il Fioretto della Bibbia* and a Koran. Nothing in this eclectic and learned selection authorised his amazing version of the creation.

In Carlo Ginzburg's brilliant interpretation, Menocchio's reading nevertheless provided him with the conceptual tools he needed to express his individual world-view. He was an active and selective reader; he took particular words or phrases, gave them new and perhaps distorted meanings and made analogies and creative juxtapositions. But this imaginative contact with learned texts was not sufficient on its own to formulate Menocchio's heresy. The heresy grew out of a confrontation and an interchange between the printed word on one hand and an archaic peasant culture on the other.

Menocchio's views ranged widely and sometimes reflected ancient heresies and a pre-Christian heritage. He professed tolerance and believed in the equality of all religions. He denied the divine status of Christ. He condemned the sacrament of baptism. He regarded all the clergy as noxious parasites, and the Church as a greedy exploiter. None of this, Ginzburg argues, came from Lutheranism or radical Protestantism, of which Menocchio knew nothing. It came from the bedrock of his own ancient peasant culture which was naturally egalitarian and impatient with institutional doctrine. Menocchio brought to his reading 'an obscure, almost unfathomable, layer of remote peasant traditions'.[25]

Ginzburg's suggestive study of the reading of a single individual is an example of Italian micro-history. *Microstoria* sought a way out of the deadening effect of quantitative studies and found it in the minute examination of esoteric and marginal individuals. Through cases like Menocchio, micro-history personalises the historical narrative. Menocchio was a 'normal exception' – an exception almost by definition, because only deviant thinkers and non-conformists attracted the attention of the Inquisition and only their stories survive in the archives; normal, because in spite of his uniqueness, Menocchio also represents something common to the medieval peasantry more generally, its archaisms, its hatred of the rich and its social radicalism which had pre-Christian origins.

Menocchio, it is true, was not quite a 'peasant'. He was a miller, an artisan at the very hub of village life, where all and sundry came to have their grain ground into flour. This intermediate social position, however, gave Menocchio the hybrid status he enjoyed between the oral and the literate, between 'high' and 'popular' culture. Menocchio shows us the wide and totally unpredictable range of responses which could emerge from a fruitful intermingling of the popular and the erudite. He embodies a deeply personal reading response, interpreting what he read imaginatively, energetically and in the light of his own instinctive cultural baggage.

Folk tales: the wolf, the grandmother and the courtier

Folk tales, which the nineteenth century started to call 'fairy tales', also represent an oral folk tradition with roots deep in the past. The stories are mostly familiar to us, although none of them have definitive textual versions. Fairy tales are so mutable that they are texts without texts, and texts without authors, too. We all know the story of Little

Red Riding Hood, the wolf and the grandmother, but every version of it is subtly different. In the medieval and early modern periods, folk tales were told by and for adults. It is only in the modern era that the stories have become exclusively children's literature. Children, then, are the peasants of our time. Folk tales did acquire textual versions, however, and in examining what happened to the stories when they shifted from oral to printed mode and back again, we can focus on the relationships between literary and popular culture. The transformations in the stories worked by Charles Perrault in the seventeenth century (the courtier in the sub-heading), and by the Grimm brothers in the nineteenth, give further examples of the reciprocal connection between print culture and popular culture.

Robert Darnton argued that fairy tales reflected the harsh material realities of peasant life.[26] The tales were obsessed with hunger because peasants were underfed; their characters fantasised about great feasts, giant sausages and enormous catches of fish. They dealt with themes of peasant misery and overpopulation. The unwanted children of The Old Woman Who Lived in a Shoe were thus the victims of over-rapid demographic expansion. Darnton was arguing that the tales were loved because they were real. In complete contrast to psychologists who see fantasy and imagination as the key elements of such children's stories, Darnton was searching for social realism in the folk tales. He was also looking for national themes, suggesting that tales about cunning peasants turning the tables on a cruel and arbitrary world were typical of French culture. Stories like Puss-in-Boots fit this model of the revenge of the downtrodden, using their wits against the rich and the mighty. Darnton, however, should not unduly distract us. As soon as we start to attribute underlying meanings to the stories, we lose sight of how mobile and contingent they are, in different versions and different modes of transmission.

Charles Perrault bequeathed to us many of the stories with which we are familiar. Perrault was an educated administrator in the reign of Louis XIV. He was a cultivated bourgeois and a member of the French Academy, and he worked in the office of Colbert, the Controller-General of Finances. He moved in the highest court circles, and perhaps the ugly sisters in *Cendrillon* (Cinderella) were satires based on personal experience of bitchiness at the court of Versailles. In 1678, he was left a widower with four children under the age of five in his care. He wrote his stories partly to educate his own children, which is one reason why they had a moral and pedagogic purpose. Each story ended with a brief afterthought or 'moralité'; in *Le Petit Chaperon Rouge* (Little Red Riding Hood), the moral was 'don't listen to plausible rogues and seducers'. This was the only story in Perrault's collection which did not have a happy ending – in other words, the wolf triumphed. A marginal note about the ending in the 1695 edition ran: 'Read these words in a loud voice to frighten the child, as if the wolf was going to eat her.' This fierce lesson was a far cry from sugary Disneyland conclusions.

Perrault took tales from oral tradition and recast them, making them conform to the classical aesthetic of rationality and moral decency. He eliminated much irrationality, absurdity and crudity as the stories were transformed for an educated audience. Some of them had precedents in learned literature like the *Decameron* or *Pentameron*; but others like *Le Petit Chaperon Rouge* had no available written version before 1697. In Perrault's hands, the oral literature or ethno-text was given the exalted status of literature and made fit for courtly consumption. In *La Belle au Bois Dormant* (Sleeping Beauty), for instance, some fourteenth-century vulgarities were purged. Prince Charming no longer made love to Sleeping Beauty while she slept, nor did she give birth, still asleep, as a result of immaculate or at least unconscious conception (her childbearing capabilities perhaps make her an ancient fertility symbol).[27] Nor, in Perrault's version, did she awake to find that her future mother-in-law was a wicked ogress. Perrault produced a more sanitised written version.

Perrault added touches of dramatic genius, inventing Cinderella's glass slipper, but deciding that three balls were far too many for the poor girl. He was also responsible for the boots on Puss-in-Boots (a symbol of mastery?) and he added the red riding hood to the story of the girl, the wolf and the grandmother. In previous versions of *Le Petit Chaperon Rouge,* the girl asked a coarse question about the wolf/grandmother's hairy body, which had undesirable sexual overtones. The original story had also included involuntary cannibalism when the wolf offered the unsuspecting girl a piece of her grandmother's flesh as refreshment. Perrault eliminated these grotesque extravagances. In his literary versions of these oral tales, there was less nudity, less sex and less black humour. Perrault also robbed the little peasant girl of her independence and ingenuity. In some versions, she had escaped the wolf by pretending that she urgently needed to urinate in the garden, but Perrault deprived her of this escape route.

Perrault's adaptations crossed the blurred frontier between popular and elite culture. He put oral tradition into writing, and then gave the written versions back to oral tradition to be retold. Ever since Perrault, print and oral versions have coexisted and undergone further transformations. His stories have survived, but not always in the form he intended. His versions were subjected to further editorial changes. Some publishers found the conclusion of *Le Petit Chaperon Rouge* intolerable, and amended it so that the wolf would get the punishment he deserved. Nevertheless, in the oral versions collected in the French countryside by nineteenth- and twentieth-century folklorists, only 7 out of 35 French versions had a happy ending.[28] Many others still retained aspects from the pre-Perrault era, showing that oral versions independent of Perrault still survived.

The folk tales were fluid and unstable. Their transition from oral narrative into literary form at Perrault's hands was a landmark, but one which involved textual modifications. In the nineteenth century, Jacob and Wilhelm Grimm also claimed to be tapping oral tradition when they introduced further modifications into the written corpus of European folk tales. The Grimms did not merely adapt that old tradition, but they continued to adapt their own adaptations. Between the first edition of their compilation in 1812 and the fifth edition in 1843, many textual alterations intervened.

The 1812 collection was a product of the early romantic era. The authors wanted to find for Germany a unique folk culture on which a national literature could be based. They set out to transcribe oral tales gathered from peasant storytellers. That, at least, was the theory and the intention. In practice, their sources were probably found among their own close circle of friends and relatives in Hesse, none of whom were peasants. Some were descended from French Huguenot settlers, through whom were possibly filtered the stories of Charles Perrault.[29]

We owe many fairy tale clichés to the Grimms. Friendly hunters and woodcutters proliferate, as do princes and princesses who live happily ever after. With the Grimm brothers, the incidence of evil stepmothers rises sharply. This has the effect of softening parent–child conflicts, as when a weak but sympathetic biological father is introduced into *Hansel and Gretel*. In the fourth edition of 1840, their mother became a step-mother, so that no natural parents appeared as malevolent.[30] The Grimms also endowed *Snow White* with a stepmother for the first time, and had the heroine rescued not by a prince, but by her father. This new concern for good parenting pushed child characters into deeper dependence on adult benevolence and divine intervention. Whereas Hansel and Gretel had trusted their own considerable ingenuity to solve their predicament, they now, in the Grimms' fifth edition, called on God for help. To empha-sise this entirely new religious dimension, the wicked witch is described as 'godless'.[31] The Grimms stepped up the violence in their treatment of villains, like Rumpelstiltskin, who met a violent end instead of flying away on a spoon, and they were reluctant to endorse successful criminal acts, so that Puss-in-Boots found no place in their anthology.

The Grimms' achievement was hailed as a national literary monu-ment. They had meanwhile demonstrated that popular literary culture had many points of contact with the world of elite literature. Popular culture was neither static nor residual nor passive, but creative, dynamic and always open to assimilation and contamination.

Ordinary writers

One of the most surprising manifestations of popular literary culture is the appearance of accomplished writers from the ranks of the poor. The full flowering of working-class autobiography occurred in the nineteenth-century, when many self-made men traced their personal ascent in writing, but already in the early modern period we find examples of this kind of 'ego-document' by skilled workers. Many peasants and artisans were familiar with writing in other genres; they kept account books or *livres de famille*, or in Italy they used *zibaldoni*, notebooks in which might be collected prayers, recipes, accounts of the vintage, wills or contracts. Sometimes they wrote under coercion. Confessors or Inquisitors might demand an autobiographical document to encourage the scrutiny of the conscience and character of the subject. Sometimes they dictated the text to a scribe, as in the case of Beatriz Ana Ruiz, the illiterate washerwoman from Alicante born in 1666, who dictated her mystical visions to a friend who in turn wrote them down for her confessor.

The texts produced by humble authors did not always conform to what we might now understand by literary autobiography. They often had an oral basis or were illustrated with drawings or composed with the help of other family members. In his study of artisan autobiographers in early modern Europe, James Amelang compared his lower-class writers to the mythical Icarus, who flew too close to the sun, burned his wings and fell to earth.[32] Workers who wrote were usurping a cultural territory which was not naturally their own. They had literary aspirations which were regarded as inappropriate for their inherited position in life. They were interlopers who, without the benefit of extended schooling, improvised their own literary culture.

Miquel Parets was born in 1610 into a family of Barcelona tanners. He was active in the local leather trade and wrote a chronicle in the Catalan language. We should not expect much self-introspection from such chronicles, for they related public affairs rather than personal intimacies. Parets wrote as an eyewitness of local events in his description of the plague of 1651. He copied out public documents like the Treaty of the Pyrenees between France and Spain in 1659 to add historical authenticity to his account.[33] Artisan writers did not necessarily write in great detail about their own work, although much can be gleaned about working conditions in the eighteenth century from the autobiography of Jacques-Louis Ménétra, the Parisian glazier.[34] They described their travels, too, but gave the barest facts about their wives and families, for their writings were essentially about their public role rather than an opportunity for self-examination. They made excuses for their untutored style and rough-and-ready grammar, but this was little more than rhetoric in the case of Ménétra, who showed scant deference to his superiors.

Ménétra littered his autobiography with classical references, and citations from the works of Jean-Jacques Rousseau, whom he had met personally. His story, however, is rambling, repetitive and episodic, like those of many lower-class writers with a limited command of narrative skills. He knew the culture of the broadside and the *bibliothèque bleue*, he knew the theatre and he had a good sense of comedy. His culture, in the words of Daniel Roche, was a 'patchwork culture', absorbing and exploiting a wide range of influences to manufacture his own version of his life.[35]

Working-class authors wrote about their personal struggle for literacy, like Thomas Tryon, born in 1634, the son of an Oxfordshire tiler. He left school at six without having learned to read, and was later taught by the Gloucestershire shepherds with whom he worked.[36] Learning to write was quite another matter, and Tryon had to seek a tutor, paying him a sheep for his trouble. A century later, as Valentin Jamerey-Duval wrote in his autobiography, he too learned to read from an illustrated volume of Aesop's *Fables* with local shepherds in Lorraine, and later treated them to recitals from the chivalric romances of the *bibliothèque bleue*.[37]

Working-class authors had various reasons for writing their life stories: they wrote to fulfil a spiritual need, to make a contribution to local history, to warn others to avoid danger and temptation or for a combination of sacred and profane motives. Writing was a way of expressing their independence and taking pride in artisan culture in general. Like the other examples discussed in this chapter, they demonstrate the rich cross-currents which flowed between popular culture and more learned literary culture in the early modern West.

7
The rise of literacy in the early modern West, c. 1600–c. 1800

In traditional societies, literacy skills were monopolised by an exclusive elite. Only the bureaucratic or clerical classes had access to written knowledge, and they wanted to keep it that way because this special attribute defined their power and status. In Europe, however, a state of 'oligoliteracy', in which literacy was manipulated by only a few, gradually gave way to universal literacy, in which almost all the population could read and write. Between the Middle Ages and the end of the nineteenth century, when mass literacy was achieved in the West, a greater number of people gained access to literacy. This chapter dissects the meaning and context of the rise of literacy up to the beginning of the nineteenth century.

The gradual democratisation of reading and writing is an essential aspect of the passage to modernity, but progress towards more widespread literacy was always inconsistent. It experienced many hiccups and was frequently interrupted. The process of widening access to writing took various routes and obeyed different rhythms in different national contexts, so that a homogeneous path to literacy cannot be assumed. What factors, then, favoured or discouraged the spread of literacy in the early modern West? Since literacy itself took on many different forms and covered many different levels of ability, what did 'being literate' really mean in any given historical context?

In Catholic countries, including France, elementary literacy was promoted by the forces of the Counter-reformation in the sixteenth and seventeenth centuries. At other times, however, literacy stagnated or declined, particularly in periods of severe and general economic crisis, such as occurred in Europe from 1690 to the 1730s. In the second half of the eighteenth century, literacy rates improved rapidly in the Western world and this trend accelerated in the nineteenth century, as the gap between men's and women's literacy was narrowed. In America, for example, Jennifer Monaghan identified the late eighteenth century as a period of major transformation, when literacy improved and elementary education developed in new directions which were more sympathetic than before to the needs of the child.[1]

Different socio-economic groups enjoyed different levels of competence in reading and writing. One of the most striking and enduring discrepancies in literacy development was the gap between male and female literacy. Access to reading and writing must therefore be understood in a multi-dimensional perspective. What we call 'literacy' has many different meanings in different social and historical circumstances. Literacy and levels of literary competence are contingent on specific occasions and specific needs. To take a contemporary example, reading or writing a letter to an absent parent is technically and culturally a completely different task from reading and understanding a life insurance policy. Literacy cannot be discussed in a social vacuum; it only has meaning in relation to particular tasks and needs. When we talk of reading ability in the seventeenth century, we may be referring to Bible-reading, reading a newspaper or reading a work of philosophy – all different tasks requiring different kinds of literacy. The concept embraces many levels of cultural competency. At the same time, there is no clear dividing line between literacy and illiteracy. The 'illiterate' always participate in written culture, even if their universe is predominantly one of oral communication. The title of this chapter suggests a broad trend towards greater access to reading and writing, but this hides many complicating factors and in what follows an absolutely precise definition of 'literacy' may prove unattainable.

What literacy rates mean: deconstructing the signature test

The geographical spread of literacy was very uneven. Whereas high rates of literacy are recorded for early modern Northern Europe, Britain and North America, progress towards universal literacy was slower in southern Europe. Many areas of Central and Eastern Europe hardly experienced a rise of literacy at all until the twentieth century. In Vas County in western Hungary, only 53 per cent of the population was literate according to the census of 1870.[2] In Russia, only 29 per cent of men and 13 per cent of women could read at the end of the nineteenth century,[3] and the Balkans were largely illiterate until the early decades of the twentieth.

Some global comparative statistics suggest (Table 7.1), in their crude way, the rise of literacy in Europe and North America between the mid-seventeenth century and the late eighteenth century:[4]

Table 7.1 Literacy rates in selected countries, 1600–1800

Country	Period	Gender	% Literacy	Period	Gender	% Literacy
Sweden	1680	both	under 50	c.1800	both	80-plus
New England	1650–70	Men	Over 60	1790	Men	90
New England	c.1650	Women	about 30?	c.1800	Women	unknown
Virginia	1690	Men	65	1790	Men	91
Virginia	1675	Women	18	1790	Women	80
Scotland	1650–70	Men	44	1760	Men	78
Scotland	1670–80	Women	13	1760	Women	23
England	1640	Men	about 33	1760–1800	Men	60
England	1640	Women	10	1760–1800	Women	40
France	1686–90	Men	29	1786–90	Men	47
France	1686–90	Women	14	1786–90	Women	27
Turin region	1710	Men	19	1790	Men	65
Turin region	1710	Women	6	1790	Women	30
Western Hungarian Peasants	18th century	Men	2.6	Early 19th century	Men	5.5

These bald figures cannot be relied on for spot-on accuracy. They say nothing at all about the quality of the literacy they measure. Some people had 'Black Letter' literacy; in other words, they could read the Gothic script, which was easier for most ordinary people than the roman-style script of the humanists. Others could read printed letters, but had difficulty making out handwriting. The figures are silent, too, about the language in which people were supposedly literate. In the seventeenth and eighteenth centuries, only a minority of French people were competent in the national language. Many other languages were used in France, like Provençal, Breton and Flemish, while regional *patois* were used in everyday speech. Even completely illiterate people could resort to a public scribe if necessary. In the seventeenth century, professional writers would gather in search of business in prominent locations in most major cities, ready for hire to compose a formal letter to the authorities, or perhaps something more personal. They put up their stalls in the Cemetery of the Innocents in Paris, and on the Square of the Old Pilgrim (Praça del Pelhourinho Velho) in Lisbon. Sixteenth-century Avila, a city with a population under 16,000, supported 10 public writers.[5] But the most significant silence of the statistics is about whether they measure the ability to read or the ability to write, or both.

The percentages in Table 7.1 would signify much more if we understand how they were compiled. Usually they are based on a signature test, and they measure an individual's ability to sign his or her name on an official document, such as a will, a marriage contract or a deposition before an ecclesiastical court. Those unable to sign made a cross or a mark. Literacy rates, however, are measured differently in each country. In Sweden, the literacy of the population was monitored by Lutheran Church examiners, who tested households on their knowledge of the Bible. So the Swedish percentages refer to a form of literacy limited to Bible-reading. Comparing them with data from other countries might be about as useful as comparing fish with bicycles. In New England, the figures are compiled on the basis of signatures on wills, while in England and France, literacy is usually measured by signatures to register or witness a marriage in the parish registers, which survive from the seventeenth century onwards. In England, a law of 1754 stipulated that the marriage register had to be signed by the groom and bride, so that from this date the information available to historians becomes more plentiful and reliable.

The value of the signature test as a measure of competence in literacy is almost continually questioned, but it remains the best source we have, and a helpful one if we do not make it say more than it possibly can. To appreciate its significance, it should be put in the context of how people gained access to written culture in early modern Europe and how they were taught the basics of reading and writing at school. In England and France, the teaching process treated reading and writing as two separate activities; they were not taught simultaneously as they are today. In many parts of Europe and America, this was the norm until well into the nineteenth century. Reading came first in the curriculum, and writing followed, if students 'graduated' to a higher level or if they stayed at school long enough to learn more than the rudiments. At a higher level still, arithmetic would be taught. The three 'Rs', then, formed a pedagogical hierarchy, with reading at the base, writing in the middle and numerical literacy at the summit.

Signing one's own name, it can be supposed, was one of the first things a student would learn to write. Given the various stages of literacy tuition, this puts the signature at a transitional moment between reading and writing. It was a skill learned only after a student had first acquired the rudiments of reading, but possibly before he or she had fully mastered the art of writing. It follows that the signature test reveals much more about reading ability than it does about writing ability. In the modern period, Furet and Sachs found a significant correlation between the signature test and reading ability, when they compared the incidence of signatures on marriage contracts with the 1866 French census, which was the first to produce data on literacy. This discovery lends credibility to the signature as an indicator of elementary reading literacy.[6]

Many, however, may have learned to read without ever learning to write their name. The signature, in this theory, represents only the 'tip of the iceberg', because it hides from view a multitude who could read but not sign. Because of the signature's transitional status, counting signatures will therefore tend to *under*estimate the number of readers, but it may *over*estimate the number who could write with competence.[7] There were many individuals in our period who could read but not write, at least not until later in life. Jamerey Duval, for example, the self-taught French shepherd boy who became librarian to the Duke of Lorraine in the eighteenth century, could read by the age of 14 but only learned to write when he was 18.[8] Shakespeare's daughter could not sign, nor could his father, but this did not mean they were unable to read.[9]

The signature test offers the important advantage of comparability. It is a benchmark which can be counted over several centuries to indicate general trends over time. Because of the quality and continuity of parish records in England and France, it allows comparisons to be made between countries, genders and social groups. The signature test's universality and comparative scope make it an invaluable resource.

There are many problems, nevertheless, associated with this form of evidence. It is clearly a crude measure which, as has already been emphasised, cannot distinguish between different levels of reading competence, and can say very little indeed about the ability to write. It simply reveals the minimum required to satisfy the needs of Church and State on official documents. It represents the 'degree zero' of writing ability. Occasionally, we actually encounter a functionally illiterate person who could nevertheless sign his name, like William Herbert, the sixteenth-century Earl of Pembroke.[10] The opposite also occurs, when a fully literate person expressly chooses to make his or her mark rather than sign. Isaac Newton's father, for example, drew a bird as his mark when writing his will.[11] Such exceptions are warnings not to take the signature test too seriously as a precise statistical measure.

The signature does not give us equally good information about reading and writing, and as has been suggested it hides many readers who could not write. Many women were readers who never crossed the writing threshold. Women were taught to read the Bible and the catechism by the Churches, but they were not encouraged to learn to write. Writing conferred a certain independence which was considered to be a male prerogative. Many women readers may thus have signed with a mark. The records of poor Irish immigrant women who arrived in Australia in the late eighteenth and early nineteenth centuries reveal just such a gap between female reading and writing abilities.[12] The signature test probably underestimates the extent of female reading.

The signature test captures literacy at a specific moment in an individual's life. It gives a snapshot of his or her ability at a certain age, either at marriage perhaps in his or her late twenties, or when he or she was close to death in the case of signatures on wills. In other words, it cannot tell us about literacy over a whole lifetime. Reading and writing ability was usually at its highest roughly between the ages of 20 and 40, declining gradually thereafter. Sometimes individuals even experienced a return to illiteracy. Hannah Matson was a young woman from Kent who got married in 1826 at the age of 19, when she wrote her own name in the parish register. She remarried in 1843 aged 36, and this time she could only make a mark.[13] Those who signed when they married, therefore, may have lost the skill later in life, while some trembling senile signatures may hide good literacy skills earlier in life. There is much about age-specific literacy on which the literacy rates are silent.

Those who signed a will, moreover, were property-owners who were not representative of society as a whole. The evidence from wills excludes the poor who had no property to bequeath. It also excludes women who, except for a few widows, very rarely had their own property to pass on. Signatures on wills, therefore, are a source which is socially selective and both age- and gender-biased. Besides, many on their deathbed were just too feeble to sign; for this reason Cressy speculates that signatures on wills may exaggerate illiteracy by as much as 25 per cent.[14]

In deconstructing the signature test, the historian must be sensitive to the circumstances in which the signature or the mark is inscribed. In fundamentally oral societies, the signature was not a significant identifier. Verbal oaths and contracts were the norm in eighteenth-century Central Europe, for instance, and for peasants a personal signature meant very little. In Moldavia, they often could not even write a cross on a document, and instead they made an inked thumbprint.[15] The age, gender and social status of the signatory must be taken into account. There may be a wide gap, too, between reading ability and writing ability. If the limitations of the signature test are appreciated, and it is regarded as an indicator of broad trends rather than precise information, then it may serve some useful purpose. Above all, it will enable us to compare different levels of reading ability across societies and classes.

The social context of literacy

The ability to read and/or write was a function of wealth, education and the specific needs of the job. The social structure of literacy was therefore a vital determining factor. LeRoy Ladurie used a municipal census to produce figures for the signature literacy of different professions in the Norman city of Caen in 1666.[16] They are summarised in Table 7.2.

Caen was a textile-producing city, and the textile merchants personified its urban elite. This also explains the prominent presence of weavers and tailors in the sample. LeRoy Ladurie only classed as literate those who provided a fluent signature, linking the letters of their name. He excluded

Table 7.2 Signature literacy by profession in Caen, 1666

Textile Merchants	over 90 per cent were literate
Tailors and Shoemakers	about 60 per cent were literate
Bakers	about 55 per cent were literate
Stonemasons and Carpenters	40 per cent were literate
Weavers	about 25 per cent were literate
Day-labourers and Porters	about 12 per cent were literate

from the figures in Table 7.2 those who either made a mark or whose signature was hesitant or clumsy and who formed the letters of their name separately, one by one. Only male signatures were registered in this survey.

The sample shows how closely literacy depended on social status. A commercial bourgeois was roughly twice as likely to be literate than an urban artisan, while only a small minority of manual workers commanded any reading or writing ability. There was considerable variety in literacy rates within the artisan trades themselves. Retail traders who dealt with the public on a daily basis, like bakers and grocers, tended to be more literate than others. They needed to take orders, keep accounts and deal with suppliers, which were all tasks requiring literacy skills. Blacksmiths and carpenters perhaps did not have such an urgent need to be literate. Some trades hardly required it at all: in seventeenth-century London, 80 per cent of thatchers were illiterate.[17] In the countryside, literacy skills were of little practical use, and illiteracy rates were higher than in urban areas. The employment of early factory workers, too, demanded no literacy skills. Economic need could be a crucial factor in determining literacy levels.

Elementary schooling: apprenticeships in reading and writing

The rise of literacy depended more on economic functions than on educational provision. Primary schooling, which we now take for granted, was not universally available to most Europeans in the early modern period, and in any case, formal education was not essential for literacy acquisition. For centuries, ordinary people became literate without ever attending school. They learned to read and write through informal networks, in the family or the workplace, from fellow artisans, a benevolent patron or a sympathetic priest. In Britain and France, mass literacy was achieved by about 1880, before either country had fully established a system of free and compulsory primary education. By the time universal primary education became available in Western Europe, the battle for literacy was already won. Formal education had responded to the demand for literacy rather than creating it. The school was simply a catalyst for universal literacy, given a local environment which had already attained a certain cultural and literary threshold.

The provision of schooling, even in the eighteenth century, was very patchy, and it depended on urbanisation, prosperity and, above all, local demand. If the local population saw no advantage in a school, then none would exist, for it was the local inhabitants who would have to support it financially. Teachers would hire themselves to local communities for fixed periods in return for bed and board. In the Alpine villages of France, they would gather in the market place, advertising their skills by putting feathers in their cap – one feather if they taught only reading, two if they taught reading and writing, and three if arithmetic was also one of their skills (hence the phrase 'a feather in one's cap'). If they knew writing as well as reading, they could double their fee.

Becoming a teacher was often a function of agricultural poverty. Teachers had no formal qualifications and their claims to expertise were often quite dubious. For many war veterans, and others who were too old and infirm to work, teaching was a last resort. They were poorly paid, and usually moonlighted as clerks, tobacconists, barrel-makers or tailors. In Hungary, Lutheran teachers were cantors and funeral assistants who saw teaching as their second or third job.[18] In France, teaching orders like the Christian Brothers (Frères de l'Ecole chrétienne) played a major role in providing elementary education for the poor. In England, many children attended a Dame School, where a local woman might teach the rudiments of reading and the Ten Commandments. In all these cases the parents paid a fee. The sexes were segregated in the classroom, and the so-called 'individual method' prevailed, in which the teacher attended to each student one by one, leaving the rest of the class to other activities or total boredom.

Learning to read consisted first of being taught to recognise and speak individual letters, then syllables, then whole words. The Bible and the catechism were the basis of reading tuition. In France up to the late eighteenth century, children were taught to read first in Latin before they learned French. Writing was another skill entirely, and required considerable technological expertise. The quill had to be sharpened, and it took some dexterity on the part of a child to manipulate it without spilling ink on the page. Afterwards, the paper had to be dried by sprinkling it with a fine powder of sand or ground shell. It was hard to teach young children how to handle the quill and to adopt the best posture for relaxed writing. It might take 5 years of continuous schooling to master the technique, but the majority of elementary school children did not attend for more than 3 years at the most. Writing was laborious and the materials expensive, so young children were first taught to write in sand-trays, and then with

Figure 7.1 An American horn book, teaching the ABC and Lord's Prayer. © Library of Congress.

a stylus on a soft wax surface. Slates came into general classroom use during the eighteenth century.

In English-speaking countries, every student had a horn book, which was a small, flat piece of wood with a short handle, with pages attached, covered in protective transparent horn (Figures 7.1 and 7.2). It contained the alphabet, the elementary syllables consisting of two letters each, and often a prayer like the Our Father. In Puritan New England, prayer books and Psalters were used to teach reading until a student was capable of handling passages from the New Testament. Until the late eighteenth century, the Puritan apprenticeship in reading was a grim business. Children were inspired by the fear of Hell and oppressed by the need to be spiritually prepared for death.

Even when a school did exist in a village, the attendance of local children was by no means guaranteed. In the early nineteenth century, fewer than 8 per cent of school-age children attended school in the Dordogne or the Gironde in south-west France.[19] In the 1770s, school attendance in Austria and western Hungary was only about 15–20 per cent of eligible children.[20] The demands of the family economy were paramount. Peasant

Figure 7.2 This horn book, dating from about 1800, was known as the 'British Battledore', in reference to the wooden racket used in the game of shuttlecock. © Mansell/Time Life/Getty Images.

parents could not afford to sacrifice the labour and earnings of their children for the sake of school attendance, except in the winter months when there was less demand for agricultural work. In Prussia, peripatetic teachers who went from home to home were actually called 'winter-teachers' (*winterschulmeister*).[21] In nineteenth-century Russia, parents would even demand that teachers pay *them* for keeping their children away from gainful employment.[22] Schooling, therefore, was not directly connected to the rise of literacy. It remained improvised and fragmented and attendance was often brief and always interrupted. As a result, no matter what children managed to learn at school, there was a high risk that in later years they would slip back into illiteracy.

Primary education was not designed to equip students for a better job nor to promote social mobility. On the contrary, it existed to maintain stability and godliness. Education reinforced the dominant culture and religion, rather than encouraging any questioning of values and institutions. The State also saw it as a valuable means of spreading the use of a national language, at the expense of local dialects and regional languages like Breton in western France or Gaelic in the Scottish highlands. In the Lutheran Nordic countries, the head of the Lutheran household was expected to play an important role as a moral leader and educator. This was especially the case in Sweden, which opted for an educational system based on home instruction rather than on established schools. According to the Lutheran ideal, the paterfamilias read aloud from a familiar book to gatherings of all family members and servants. A good example of such patriarchal reading was provided in Ingmar Bergman's partly autobiographical film *Fanny and Alexander*, in which the entire household gathered at Christmas for such a reading.

The importance of gender and religion

Until the end of the nineteenth century, as Table 7.1 showed, the rate of female literacy was customarily lower than that of males. When Sara Nalle examined the defendants who came before the Spanish Inquisition in Toledo between 1600 and 1650, she found that 62 per cent of men accused could sign their name, but only 7 per cent of females were able to do so.[23] To some extent, as I have argued above, female illiteracy was an optical illusion created by the very nature of the sources. The signature test has a habit of obscuring the extent of women's reading, because so few women were taught how to write. Writing was an autonomous and potentially critical activity which was risky to encourage, especially in a woman. Circumscribing women's literary culture within the needs of a Christian life was a way of ensuring they remained dependent and above all obedient to the Church. This did not at all mean that women were unable to read.

The scarcity of educational provision has already been emphasised, but it was even scarcer for girls. Girls attended school less frequently than boys, and when girls did receive a school education, the emphasis was on sewing and housekeeping skills rather than writing or arithmetic. The Quaker schools of Pennsylvania were exceptional in teaching girls to read and write and in having mixed-gender classrooms.[24] In upper-class circles, in contrast, where tutoring was available, women's literacy was not inferior to that of men. In large cities, too, the gap between male and female literacy rates was narrower than it was in the countryside. According to Cressy, 48 per cent of London women were literate by 1700, and London was perhaps one of the first cities in the world where a majority of women could read.[25] Women who ran a small shop or a business were, of necessity, able to read. Otherwise, women's economic roles rarely demanded that they should be literate.

The cultural priorities of Counter-reformation Catholicism thus created a situation in which women could read but not write. Religious pressures could exert a strong influence over the rise of literacy, regardless of denominational affiliation. Table 7.1 suggested high literacy rates in Lutheran Sweden, Presbyterian Scotland and Puritan New England, all uncompromisingly Protestant societies, and this has sometimes given rise to the assumption that Protestants had a natural advantage over Catholics. Certainly, by the 1670s, all the American colonies except Rhode Island had passed legislation mandating that children be taught to read, but passing a law did not guarantee a successful result.[26] The notion that radical Protestantism created a more literate society looks shaky. For one thing, Catholic literacy rates varied enormously in different countries: the Catholic minority in Prussia, for example, was far more literate than Irish or Italian Catholics. Furthermore, Scottish exceptionalism is something of a myth, as Houston has argued, because literacy levels in lowland Scotland were quite similar to those just over the border in the northern counties of England.[27] There were other factors in play and differences in social status rather than religious affiliation could be crucial. The French textile city of Nîmes, for instance, had a substantial Calvinist population, which was overall more literate than its Catholic fellow citizens. The Protestants, however, formed the social and economic elite of textile merchants, employing a workforce made up in the majority of Catholic labourers. The Protestants of Nîmes were more literate than the Catholics because of their higher social status, not because of their religion. Nevertheless, it is clear that wherever there was close rivalry between religions, the competitive urge drove the spread of elementary schooling. In Scotland, the Presbyterians made the effort because for them extirpating Popery was an imperative. In Languedoc, too, Catholics and Protestants created schools in competition with each other. As Lawrence Stone concluded, with perhaps a little exaggeration,

> The rivalry of the various Christian churches and sects for control of men's minds did more to stimulate education in the West between 1550 and 1850 than any other single factor.[28]

Even where religious influences did promote literacy, it tended to be a restricted kind of literacy, focussed primarily on scripture and catechism. In Denmark, literacy was driven by the need to recite the Lutheran catechism and commentaries upon it and, in the eighteenth century, elementary schools were inspected by local bishops to make sure the required texts were being memorised. Some reading knowledge was necessary to qualify for confirmation, and without being confirmed, no one in the Danish–Norwegian kingdom could get married, own land or enlist in the army.[29] Writing was an optional extra, for which boys had to pay (no one seems to have considered that girls needed or wanted to write).[30] Although in this context some independent reading could, and sometimes did, follow the acquisition of basic literacy skills, the Lutheran Church prioritised a conservative and limited form of reading. Religious and pietistic influences did not necessarily provide literacy skills of a modern or liberating kind.

The ecology of literacy

Reading and writing were skills more commonly found in the town rather than the countryside, and literacy rates were higher in large cities than in small ones. Large cities like London and Paris tended to be highly literate; in revolutionary Paris, 90 per cent of men and 80 per cent of women could sign their own wills.[31] Urban areas with a high population density could read and write better than dispersed hamlets. Towns had more bourgeois inhabitants, more artisans and members of the liberal professions than rural areas, and in urban agglomerations one did not have to walk several miles to get to school. In eighteenth-century Finland and Iceland, settlements were scattered and there were no urban centres to speak of. In such an environment, establishing permanent schools was impractical (but this did not apparently prevent the Icelanders from achieving mass reading literacy as early as the 1790s).[32] In more urbanised parts of Europe, some towns were more literate than others. For example, a traditional city whose economy rested on its law courts, its role as an administrative centre or as the centre of a diocese, had a more literate population than a port town or a newer industrial agglomeration. In eighteenth-century northern France, the old city and bishopric of Douai enjoyed a higher rate of literacy than the new cotton-manufacturing centre of Roubaix, just over 40 kilometres away. In fact, the new cotton-spinning towns attracted immigrant labour from the surrounding countryside, which meant effectively that they imported illiteracy. In the early years of industrialisation, the influx of illiterate peasant workers actually depressed the literacy rate in dynamic manufacturing areas such as Lancashire or Roubaix. The literacy rate could go down as well as up, and it did so if an area quickly acquired a large proletarian workforce.[33]

The crude statistics of literacy rates, taken country by country, hide many geographical variations. The further one ventures away from any metropolis, for example, the less literate the population. In the south-eastern English county of Essex, pastoral and coastal areas were far less literate than inland Essex, because the latter was closer to London and to the powerful commercial magnetism of the capital. On the other hand, the highest literacy levels in England were to be found in Cumberland, Westmoreland, Durham and Northumberland.

In 1879–80 an enterprising French school inspector, Louis Maggiolo, conducted a celebrated survey of national literacy.[34] Maggiolo's work had a clear ideological agenda: he set out to prove that the Church had done little to improve French literacy before the Revolution of 1789. In fact, the results proved inconclusive, for the rise in literacy had certainly predated the French Revolution. Maggiolo, however, put the geography of French literacy into stark perspective. France was revealed as two contrasting regions: the prosperous, educated and literate north and east, separated from the far less literate south and west by the so-called 'Maggiolo line', bisecting the country roughly from St. Malo to Geneva. This simple division can be misleading, even in its own geographical terms. It tends to ignore the urban, literate Midi, the southern crescent running east from Bordeaux and Toulouse to the Mediterranean coastline, and curving north from Provence up the valley of the Rhône. On the whole, however, the lowest but fastest-growing literacy rates in France were to be found in regions south and west of Maggiolo's imaginary line of division. For many parts of the Midi, the nineteenth century was to be a period of 'rattrapage', of catching up with the north. The west of France, in comparison, found it more difficult to 'catch up'; in fact it could be argued that even by 1914 it had failed to do so. Some Bretons, however, would prefer to interpret this failure in terms of successful resistance against the colonising impulses of the francophone state.

In spite of Maggiolo's deficiencies his findings were remarkably influential. But his extraordinary project suggested that the so-called 'Maggiolo line' was vanishing from sight, just as soon as it had been revealed. The expansion of basic literacy everywhere was obliterating historic differences in the literacy rates of France's many and diverse regional cultures.

The politics of literacy

Political pressures, too, determined literacy levels. Conservative elites wanted to restrict popular literacy. They feared that educated peasants would acquire dangerous ideas, and might have the means and desire to abandon their life of back-breaking work in the countryside to find alternative employment in the city. The landowning classes sometimes felt that teaching their social inferiors to read and write would lead to the depopulation of the countryside and a loss of essential manpower.

In the American colonies, teaching writing to black slaves was banned in South Carolina in 1740 and in Georgia in 1755. After the American Revolution, several southern states banned teaching slaves to read as well.[35] Making reading and writing more accessible might lead to ideological challenges and possibly rebellion. After the outbreak of rebellion in the Caribbean, and then the rise of the abolitionist movement in

Britain, southern slave-owners became even more sensitive on the topic of slave literacy. In 1831 the literate slave Nat Turner had with others killed 55 whites in Virginia (Turner's rebellion), and in 1829 David Walker published his provocative pamphlet entitled *Appeal to the Colored Citizens of the World*. The political climate therefore favoured further repression. As a result, Georgia, Louisiana, Virginia, Alabama and South Carolina all legislated between 1829 and 1834 to ban teaching blacks how to read and write. Slaves, however, fought for their literacy, as a form of resistance and as a way of proving they were the intellectual equals of whites. They learned from paying free blacks to teach them, from secret Bible study, or by scanning one indispensable small-format manual – Noah Webster's *Elementary Spelling Book*, which sold 20 million copies in the nineteenth century.[36] Janet D. Cornelius estimated that about 10 per cent of blacks learned to read and write during the age of slavery.[37] Often they learned from whites themselves, some of whom felt it was a Christian and a moral duty to teach slaves the Bible. Hence for black slaves, literacy learning had religious roots. Literate black men became preachers, and wanted to 'take the Bible back' or, in other words, to re-interpret it as a message for equality rather than one of subordination and resignation, not to mention the example of the Exodus of the Israelites from captivity in Egypt. Literate blacks risked severe punishment. If found with a book or with Webster's famous speller, they faced beating, whipping and the threat of having a thumb amputated. After the abolition of slavery, a huge suppressed demand for black education rose to the surface. London Freebee counted three great milestones in his life: the day he was born, the day in 1861 when, aged 12, he ran away to the Union Army to claim his freedom, and the day in 1863 when he learned the alphabet from a black minister.[38] Booker T. Washington described freed slaves as an entire nation wanting to go to school. But there was still a long way to go before black literacy rates approached that of white Americans.[39]

Similarly, in Europe upheavals like the English Civil War and the French Revolution of 1789 reinforced the upper-class fear of literacy. They preferred employees who neither asked questions nor developed unsuitable ambitions for social promotion. In the 1860s, landowners in the Cognac region of France got together and made an agreement only to accept peasants and employees who were illiterate.[40] Only late in the nineteenth century did some employers begin to see a literate workforce as an advantage in terms of order, stability and good morality.

Joseph Arch, the nineteenth-century Warwickshire labourer, recalled in sour terms how his employers were content to perpetuate lower-class docility and ignorance: 'The Gentry', he wrote in his autobiography, 'did not want him [the labourer] to know; they did not want him to think; they only wanted him to work.'[41] Arch became the founder of the National Agricultural Union, and for him, literacy was essential for personal fulfilment and workers' emancipation in general. His ancestors, however, did not hold such a positive view of the advantages of literacy. In early modern Europe, ordinary people experienced writing as an instrument of power, the means by which monarchies and bureaucracies imposed taxes, enforced military recruitment and justified their domination in law. In *Henry VI Part 2*, Shakespeare portrayed the Kentish rebellion of Jack Cade in 1450 as the revolt of oral tradition against the oppression of the written word. With some humour he has the popular revolution swearing to hang all lawyers and grammar teachers. The rebels promise their leader Cade that 'the laws of England shall come out of thy mouth', aspiring in other words to a personal and orally administered justice. 'It will be stinking law, one follower replies, for his breath stinks with eating toasted cheese'.[42] Similarly, the burning of the *terriers* (seigneurial title deeds) by the French peasantry in revolt in 1789 may be seen as the vengeance of rural illiterates against the power of written culture.

Meanwhile the state demanded greater linguistic conformity from its subjects. In France, education was designed to promote the use of French, but progress was stumbling: as late as 1867, only 61 per cent of French conscripts could speak the national language.[43] In the Danish–Norwegian kingdom, efforts were made to nationalise the Lapp and Eskimo minorities, and similar efforts were made to acculturate the indigenous populations of the eastern American seaboard. These attempts rarely succeeded unless indigenous peoples were taught in their own language, which was the case, as Monaghan describes, for the Wampanoags of Martha's Vineyard in Massachusetts and the Mohawks in what is now New York State. Here literacy acquisition went hand in hand with Christianisation.[44]

The bureaucratic state also demanded compliance with certain documentary norms. Individuals needed to be familiar with a range of documents for specific occasions, whether it was their certificate of baptism or the registration of their marriage or a parent's death. Beggars would carry a certificate of good conduct, a curriculum vitae of their moral worthiness, preferably attested by a local priest. If one came from an area infected by disease or the plague, a certificate of good health was an advantage. If one travelled, one needed a written passport, and this applied not just to travel across national frontiers, but simply from town to town. Anyone in business needed to be familiar with a range of written instruments such as bills of consignment and bills of exchange. A written licence was needed for a host of occupations, from exercising a profession to burying a corpse or emptying a public latrine. The great expansion of litigation in eighteenth-century Europe was only possible because of this greater familiarity with the documentary universe. Even humble peasants needed documentation to buy and sell land or verify title deeds.

By the end of the eighteenth century, the shift to a culture based on documentary exchange and verification was still slow. In the towns of eighteenth-century Lombardy, for instance, local councillors were not required to be literate, although the mayor at least did have to be able to read and write. Verbal contracts were not always or entirely superseded by the written word. In Lombardy–Venetia, the Austrian Civil Code of 1811 stipulated that contracts were considered valid if a deal was struck 'in voce o in iscritto' – either verbally or in writing. Not until 1865 did the national Italian Law Code refuse to accept marks and crosses as authentic signatures on legal documents.[45]

The use of writing as an instrument of government made the state more distant and impersonal. In the tiny Italian duchy of Parma, it had been possible to seek a personal audience with the ruler and present a petition with a few words in his or her presence. As Duchess of Parma, Marie-Louise, the second wife of Napoleon Bonaparte, used to grant four personal audiences a month in the late 1820s. But after 1832 this opportunity for face-to-face contact with the ruler disappeared.[46] Now petitioners had to write their requests on officially stamped paper, and the petitioner would, if he was lucky, be notified in writing of the time of his appointment with Her Majesty. Parma was a microcosm of wider trends: by the early nineteenth century, relations between the state and the citizen were increasingly mediated through writing, and the rise of literacy over the previous centuries made this possible.

The nature and progress of literacy, then, were embedded in political relationships between the powerful and their subordinates. Widespread literacy could vastly extend the grip of central governments over their subjects. When the rise of literacy went hand in hand with the spread of a single national language, it facilitated social and cultural integration. At the same time, the fact that more and more people could read and write caused anxiety for elites who feared challenges to their customary domination. In the early eighteenth century, Bernard Mandeville voiced this alarm in pithy fashion: 'Should a Horse know as much as a Man', he said, 'I should not like to be his rider.'[47] His social inferiors held a different view. Reading and writing, together with education in general, remained central to working-class aspirations for intellectual and political emancipation. By the nineteenth century, it seemed an essential precondition for personal liberation and a clearer consciousness of one's social situation. The pedagogue Paulo Freire recalled the words of an illiterate man from Recife in northern Brazil, who announced, 'I want to learn to read and write so that I can stop being the shadow of other people.'[48] Literacy on its own never saved anyone from poverty, but thousands remain convinced that it holds the key to intellectual fulfilment and full democratic participation in the modern world.

8

Censorship and the reading public in pre-revolutionary France

When the Parisian crowd stormed the Bastille on 14 July 1789, the great French Revolution had found its most enduring symbol. Inside the fortress, they found only seven inmates to liberate, but the prison contained hundreds of confiscated books, the victims of the monarchy's censorship regime. The Ancien Regime censorship system was complicated and contradictory, and it was never thoroughly applied. In fact the Regime's own officials connived at violating their own regulations. Whatever effect censorship may have had on publishers, printers and authors, it ultimately failed to stem the tide of seditious writings which stirred and excited the Parisian reading public in the pre-revolutionary years.

The influence of Enlightenment writings on the 1789 Revolution has been a hotly debated question, recently renewed by historians of reading. The enemies of the French Revolution were quick off the mark in blaming it on an intellectual conspiracy to undermine traditional religion and respect for the monarchy. The Revolution itself chose its own pantheon of intellectual ancestors, including Voltaire and Rousseau. The power of writers to bring about political change must be put into perspective. The influence of Voltaire's works, for example, must be considered in a context in which only one in two adult Frenchmen could actually read. The history of reading thus proves central to the controversy about the role of the intelligentsia. In order to disentangle the possible connections between the Enlightenment and the Revolution, we need to establish the contours of the French reading public at the end of the eighteenth century, to outline who belonged to it and to estimate how widely subversive literature may have circulated. Only then will we be in a position to address Roger Chartier's question: Do Books Cause Revolutions?

Censorship was potentially one important limitation on the reading public. Many regimes have attempted, usually in vain, to contain subversive writings and punish those who write, print and read them. In 1790, there were about 7,400 banned titles on the Papal Index and 14 per cent of them were French.[1] Burning books, the symbolic tactic of the Inquisition, was also a method adopted by the Paris Parlement in the eighteenth century. Books were sentenced to be lacerated and burned by the public executioner outside the Palais de Justice: this was the fate of Helvétius' *De l'Esprit* in 1759. Such attempts to destroy books pay a perverse tribute to their power. They also suggest that the authorities had 'a phobic conception' of eighteenth-century readers.[2]

Censorship in Ancien Regime France

The coercive powers of the monarchy should not be underestimated. The apparatus of censorship was in full expansion in the eighteenth century. There had been 41 royal censors in 1740, but there were 178 on the eve of the Revolution.[3] The growth of this repressive machinery was partly an indication of the expansion of the book trade itself, but at the same time it showed the monarchy's desire to control it. The system relied on the submission of manuscripts to the censors prior to publication, backed up by police inspections after publication to enforce the regulations. The censors themselves were unpaid officials, although long service was often rewarded with a royal pension. They were lawyers, intellectuals or librarians and they were in close touch with the writers they were censoring. Some writers like Fontenelle and Condillac acted as censors themselves, and it was common for writers to discuss their work with their censor.[4] They needed to make sure that it would not infringe the censors' rules, which were to defend religion, the monarchy and good morality (*les bonnes moeurs*). The government also maintained a network of inspectors, who made periodical visits to bookshops and print shops in Paris and the provinces to seize suspect material.

Many authors found themselves in prison, usually only for a few months at a time. Voltaire had two spells in the Bastille, and made good publicity out of it, while Diderot also did time in Vincennes in 1749. Authors were not the only ones to suffer. Over 100 people were imprisoned in the Bastille for book-trade offences every decade from the 1720s onwards, and the majority of offenders were booksellers and printers.[5] Repression was at its peak between 1750 and 1780, when book-trade violations accounted for 40 per cent of all imprisonments in the Bastille. In the 1780s, however, censorship became more lax and inefficient, as royal policy wavered between repression and tolerance.

The situation of printers and authors was complicated by the fact that the monarchy was not the only censorship authority. Both the Paris

Parlement (the highest law court in France) and the Theology Faculty of the Sorbonne also claimed and exercised powers of literary censorship. Although the monarchy, in the age of enlightened absolutism, tried to eliminate the medieval pretensions of these rivals, they could never be completely neglected. In 1758, the Parlement mounted a celebrated and successful challenge to the publication of Helvétius' *De l'Esprit*, after it had been approved by the censor Tercier. The forces of repression were especially sensitive in the aftermath of the assassination attempt on Louis XV by Damiens in 1757. On this occasion, the Parlement not only overturned the monarchy's decision, but also secured the dismissal of the unhappy censor Tercier himself. In 1762, the Parlement ordered the arrest of Jean-Jacques Rousseau after the appearance of *Emile*, which was solemnly burned. No doubt this aggravated that author's notorious persecution complex. In 1752 the great *Encyclopédie* itself was a target of multiple pressures from competing authorities.

Anything published in France needed royal authority, which was granted in the form of a *privilège*. A *privilège* gave the printer some important benefits: it conferred immunity from tax, it guaranteed his monopoly in a protected market, and it ensured there would be no official prosecution for the duration of the *privilège*, which might be for 10 or 20 years and could be renewed. The book trade was therefore a highly protected industry completely dependent on the royal pleasure. A range of pensions and sinecures were available to support writers. Voltaire himself was the beneficiary of royal favour in his position as Historiographer-Royal. The permanent secretary of the Académie Française was another coveted post, held by D'Alembert and Marmontel, which conferred a salary and very desirable fringe benefits like a flat in the Louvre. The Ancien Regime had many different ways of policing, sweetening and repressing the book trade.

In practice, this was a very centralised system, in which Parisian publishers enjoying direct access to authors and bureaucrats seized the lion's share of the *privilèges*. Provincial publishers complained bitterly that they could only pick up the crumbs discarded by their Parisian competitors. Provincial publishers were often forced to wait for Parisian *privilèges* to expire and for the works concerned to become public property, but the frequent renewal of *privilèges* frustrated them further. As a result provincial centres like Lyon or Rouen were driven into closer reliance on illegal and contraband works. Along with the Parisian publishers and foreign presses, provincial pirates provided a third important supply of books in the pre-revolutionary period.[6] A royal decree of 1777 limited the duration of a *privilège* to 10 years or the life of the author, which went some way towards placating provincial publishers as well as the liberal economists who wanted to deregulate the book trade. On the other hand, the *privilège* was now granted not to the publisher, but to the author. This completely altered the relationship between author and publisher, and fundamentally threatened the publisher's monopolistic rights. The publishers could no longer claim to own a manuscript and, after a delay of 10 years, it would fall into the public domain.

Until the French Revolution, the book trade was governed by a corporate structure. A mass of detailed regulations determined entry to the book trade, the recruitment of workers and access to the coveted mastership. Apprentices had to be Catholic and they were required to know some Latin and Greek. There was a limit on the number of apprentices allowed so that masters and *compagnons* were protected from too much competition. Most printers tried to keep their businesses within the family circle.[7] The government attempted to limit the number of working printers, and master printers generally co-operated with these restrictions because they had no desire to see a host of competitors establish themselves. The printers' community had an exclusive membership, its own autonomous structure and social life, electing its own officials on the feast of St. John the Evangelist, the patron saint of printers. The guild had its own *chambre syndicale*, where officials checked all imported books to eliminate contraband and illegal competition. The privileged members of this community justified its existence by the need to maintain typographical standards. Not only did the guild stand in the way of free competition, but it was a willing instrument of the monarchy's repressive policies. Its exclusive framework alienated a number of aspiring authors and publishers who formed a growing intellectual proletariat in the capital in the dying years of the Ancien Regime. Robert Darnton has suggested that this struggling mass of writers and publicists welcomed the Revolution and the press freedom that came with it as a long-awaited liberation.[8] At the same time, many hacks chose the other side and wrote in the service of the Counter-revolution.[9]

Evading repression

The forces of liberalisation found sympathisers in the highest positions of authority. Malesherbes, for example, presided over a significant relaxation of the censorship regime during his tenure as Director of the Book Trade (Directeur de la Librairie) between 1750 and 1763, and this was continued under his immediate successor Sartine. Malesherbes stretched the rules without overthrowing the system, which made publishing easier and further illustrated the repressive tolerance which characterised the Ancien Regime.

Malesherbes began with a candid admission of failure. It was increasingly impossible to initiate proceedings against anonymous authors who could not be found, especially when the police were themselves unreliable, and the administration had to cope with interference from the Parlement and the Jesuits. Some things, Malesherbes insisted, had to be censored, namely defamatory works, works against religion and the monarchy and obscene literature. Nevertheless, a few practical realities had to be recognised. Firstly, whatever the censors determined, undesirable literature would sooner or later reach its public one way or another.[10] Secondly, he argued, censorship harmed the French economy because banning a book in France guaranteed that it would be profitably published elsewhere. Censorship played into the hands of France's competitors in Britain, the Netherlands and Switzerland in particular. Lastly, in Malesherbes' view, it was sensible to accept that political culture had changed. The monarchy needed to do more in print in the public arena to mobilise opinion in its favour. Here, paradoxically, was a royal minister responsible for book-trade regulation who admitted rational arguments in favour of free speech. Malesherbes also wanted to protect writers from harassment by the Parlement and the Church.

Malesherbes found the system of royal *privilèges* inadequate, and he found a way to bypass it. Under Malesherbes, many works received a 'tacit permit' (*permission tacite*) or a simple police *tolérance*. Unlike a full *privilège*, the *permission tacite* did not recognise the legal status of the publication in question, so that it offered no protection against pirate editions, but it also implied that no legal action would be taken against it. Malesherbes did not invent the *permission tacite*, but he allowed the vast extension of this liberal strategy. It could apply to works published outside as well as inside the country, and it constituted a promise by the monarchy that the author, printer and bookseller would not be prosecuted. The main beneficiaries of the *permissions tacites* were new works, especially works of history, politics and novels.[11] After the 1760s, the number of *permissions tacites* granted annually equalled or even exceeded the number of official *privilèges*. In the 1780s, the *permissions* made up over 70 per cent of authorisations.[12] Even books which did not receive a *permission tacite* might nevertheless circulate under the indulgent protection (*tolérance*) of the Lieutenant de Police. The monarchy was thus engaged in flouting its own regulations, partly to avoid pressure from the Parlement; Malesherbes discreetly allowed literature to circulate but if the monarchy had not given formal permission the judiciary could not attack its decision. This was a clear demonstration of the futility of censorship and the ambiguity of the Ancien Regime's repressive mechanisms.

The 'weak repression' of Ancien Regime censorship was regularly evaded. Books were published anonymously or under false imprints. Sometimes inventing an imaginary place of publication was part of the irony and satire of the book itself. Thus anti-clerical works would purport to emanate from 'The Presses of the Vatican' and erotic literature claimed to be published allegorically in 'Cythera' or, advertising its intentions more crudely, in 'Couillopolis' ('Bollocksville').[13] The police could be circumvented by publishing sensitive works outside France and smuggling them over the border. The *Encyclopédie*, for example, was produced in Neuchâtel and Lausanne in Switzerland. Robert Darnton studied the publishing records of the Société Typographique de Neuchâtel to re-construct the clandestine networks which ensured that contraband, pornography and philosophical works reached their readers.[14] Books were carted across the mountain at night, customs officials were bribed and secret storage depots organised. Thousands of copies of Rousseau were produced in Holland, landed at Dunkirk labelled as 'furs' and taken to Rouen, which was a distribution centre for illegal books.[15] The whole business involved a vast network of organised corruption. The illegal journey from Switzerland to Paris was only achieved at a cost, and this was passed on to the reader: a smuggled book would cost its eventual purchaser at least double its original price. Avignon, as a Papal enclave, was another centre of contraband and publishing piracy. It was within the reach of the book production centres of Geneva and Lyon, and it had cheap local sources of paper. From the Papal city, prohibited books were distributed all over Languedoc and Provence, or up the river Rhône to Lyon, with a change of boat at Vienne to disguise their port of origin. Pirate editions from Avignon found it easy to undercut competitors.[16] In 1784, the author Bernardin de St. Pierre was invited to a school speech day, only to discover that one of the prizes he had to present was a pirated copy of his own *Etudes de la Nature*.[17]

The monarchy and the Enlightenment

The monarchy and the Enlightenment, therefore, were not implacably opposed forces. Instead they belonged to the same political culture. Malesherbes himself personified the complicity of the monarchy in the progress of the Enlightenment. The monarchy acted simultaneously as a target of criticism and an agent of change. The monarchy and the *philosophes*, as eighteenth-century social critics were known, articulated competing discourses while they both accepted the main reference points in the discussion. To return to one example already noted, the monarchy approved the publication of works like Helvétius's *De l'Esprit* in 1758, which the Parlement condemned. Beaumarchais, to take another case, spent five days under arrest for his *Marriage of Figaro*, which challenged the social order by portraying a witty, intelligent and resourceful servant condemned to a subordinate life by his low birth and status. Although the play was at first banned, Beaumarchais eventually triumphed in 1784 when it was at last performed, thanks to the support of courtiers and aristocrats – the very people his play satirised. Copies were even found in the possession of the Princesse de Lamballe, a close friend of the queen, and some of the greatest titled nobility of the realm begged for tickets.[18]

   The career of Charles-Joseph Panckoucke further illustrates the close connections between the monarchical establishment and the publishing industry which is too often assumed to be its enemy. Panckoucke was one of the first press magnates. He was a major impresario, who came to own 17 journals, of which seven had been created by himself. He developed the Rupert Murdoch-like technique of buying up minor journals either to absorb them, or just to make them disappear altogether.[19] His printing works were the largest in France before the era of industrialisation. He possessed 27 presses and employed a labour force of up to 200 employees, an enormous figure for the period. He published Prévost, Voltaire and Buffon and, before his involvement with the quarto edition of the *Encyclopédie* was over, he was already planning his own bigger, better and more systematic encyclopaedia. He was the 'Atlas' of the French book trade.[20]

He could not have succeeded without maintaining a good rapport with the authorities. Panckoucke exploited and manipulated the machinery of Ancien Regime regulation to maximise his own security and his profits. He was adept at pulling strings with ministers and officials. In 1777, he presented two dozen complimentary sets of the quarto edition of the *Encyclopédie* to ministers and Intendants, to encourage them to ban the sale of the rival octavo edition. He could persuade the foreign minister to open borders for him, and he was able to continue marketing titles which had been officially banned. By means of lobbying and generous 'gifts' to powerful people, Panckoucke promoted his speculative ventures regardless of the censorship system. Commercial success was quite incompatible with a crusade against the monarchy. Panckoucke was a dynamic and productive force within the Ancien Regime economy, but he remained in the traditional mould, supporting and defending the idea of a guild-controlled industry. 'To follow Panckoucke ... into the Revolution', Darnton concluded, 'is to watch a cultural system being overthrown.'[21]

The reading public in the Ancien Regime

The reading public of the late eighteenth century was expanding, but the audience for the literature of the high Enlightenment was still confined to the clergy, the aristocracy and the bourgeoisie. On the eve of the French Revolution, 47 per cent of adult men and 27 per cent of women could read in France (see Chapter 7). Literacy rates were much higher than average in Paris, where 90 per cent of men and 80 per cent of women could sign their wills. In the working-class *faubourg* St. Marcel, two-thirds of the inhabitants could read and write in 1792.[22] In the capital, then, there was a huge potential audience for revolutionary printed propaganda amongst the popular urban classes.

The presence of books of some kind was increasingly noticeable in eighteenth-century households, according to the evidence of *post-mortem* inventories. These are a limited source since not everyone was fortunate enough to have an estate to bequeath at death, and because the notaries who took the inventories tended to discard anything which had no material value. The mere possession of a library in any case does not necessarily indicate a keen reader. Some libraries are accumulated by collectors, others for decoration and others are simply inherited and then virtually ignored. One Breton nobleman who asked the French revolutionary authorities to return his confiscated library was even incapable of signing his letter of application.[23] But if enough libraries are surveyed, freaks like this illiterate aristocrat will not distort general conclusions.

In Chalons-sur-Marne, only one inventory in ten revealed the presence of books at the end of the eighteenth century, which is a warning not to overestimate the size of the book-buying public in provincial France. In Lyon, only 20 per cent of artisans owned books, but three quarters of the members of the liberal professions did so, owning ten times as many as the artisans.[24] In Grenoble, book ownership mirrored the social hierarchy in similar fashion: only 8 per cent of artisans and labourers possessed a library in the eighteenth century, but 28 per cent of the clergy, aristocracy and the professional or commercial bourgeoisie had one.[25] In Paris, once again, familiarity with literary culture was more widespread. In 1780, 35 per cent of the *post-mortem* inventories of lower-class estates contained books, and the size of individual libraries grew five times over during the eighteenth century.[26]

As one might expect, the private libraries of clergymen contained breviaries, Psalters, sermons, catechisms and some Bibles, to judge by Quéniart's study of inventories in western France. Clerical readers sometimes bought polemical works against the *philosophes* but, in this part of the country at least, they seemed isolated from modern secular literature.[27] The nobility on the other hand showed increasing interest in modern literature and history, both French and foreign. They bought Voltaire, Rousseau and occasionally the *Encyclopédie*, as well as enjoying modern novels. They read for intellectual interest and entertainment. Professional books had pride of place on the shelves of lawyers and doctors, but they were leaving more and more space for general literature and the theatre. The artisans traditionally depended on a few religious staples like the New Testament, books of hours and the lives of the saints. Even at this social level, however, tastes were changing to encompass practical and informative literature as well as entertaining fiction.

The diffusion of any literary genre was limited by the linguistic diversity of France. In the provinces, widespread ignorance of the French language obstructed the spread of enlightenment literature, just as it was also to obstruct the spread of the message of the French Revolution. According to the Abbé Grégoire in 1794, at least six million Frenchmen were ignorant of the French language, and another six million could not sustain a conversation in it (the total population of France was then about 27 million).[28] Only a minority of French men and women were exclusively French-speaking at end of the eighteenth century. French was the language of officialdom and a written language, while *patois* (regional dialects) were spoken in everyday conversation. On the borders and in large parts of the west, the centre and the south, the population used non-French languages like Flemish, German, Italian, Provençal, Occitan, Basque or Breton. The ability to use French in speech or writing was a trait which distinguished the bourgeois from the artisan or the labourer. In Bordeaux, Grégoire learned, aspiring artisans would use French as a sign of status to distinguish themselves from the Gascon populace.[29] The phenomenon of bourgeois bilingualism should not disguise the fact that it was the educated bourgeoisie and local *notables* who were the chief agents of the spread of the French language, and therefore of enlightened literature and the French Revolution's nationalist ideology.

The *Encyclopédie* as a best-seller

The *Encyclopédie* of D'Alembert and Diderot was one of the key works of the European Enlightenment. Unlike today's encyclopaedias, it did not aim for a neutral description of the current state of knowledge. It did of course include technical articles on up-to-date scientific methods, but it also provided a critique of the social and political institutions of the Ancien Regime in the spirit of rational reform. The project engaged the leading intellectuals of its day. The *Encyclopédie* was 'a publisher's dream', according to Robert Darnton, who has done more than any other historian to demonstrate that this important vehicle of enlightenment thought had a wider audience than was previously assumed.[30] In 1773, Diderot reported to the Tsarina Catherine II that 4,500 copies of the first edition had been sold at over 900 *livres* each. This produced a turnover of over four million *livres*, of which more than half was profit. Cheaper editions subsequently appeared, extending traditional production techniques to their absolute limit. Paper was still made from cloth, collected by hundreds of ragpickers, and it customarily absorbed between 60 and 75 per cent of production costs. Ink was made from a mixture of walnuts, resin and turpentine, while bread was the commonest eraser. Printing presses were wooden and hand-operated but relatively cheap: the Société Typographique de Neuchâtel paid more for a barrel of ink than for a second-hand press. Printing the *Encyclopédie* was beyond the capability of any existing print shop and the job was contracted out to two dozen different workshops. This was one of the great capitalist enterprises of the century. It involved over 150 writers and kept thousands of workers employed for a generation.

The original folio edition, published in Paris, cost 980 *livres* and comprised 17 volumes of text and 11 more of illustrations. It was subsequently reprinted in this format in Geneva and Italy. The real breakthrough came with the production of progressively cheaper editions in smaller formats (see Table 8.1). The Swiss quarto editions of 1777–79

Table 8.1 The diffusion of the *Encyclopédie*

Edition	Date	No of Vols	Subscription Price	Print run in France	Print run outside France	Extra copies	Total print run
Paris folio	1751–72	17	980 livres	2,000	2,050	175	4,225
Geneva folio	1771–76	Reprint	700–840 livres	1,000	1,000	150	2,150
Lucca folio	1758–76	Reprint	737 livres	250	2,750	?	3,000
Livorno folio	1770–78	Reprint	574 livres	?	1,500	?	1,500
Geneva-Neuchâtel in-4o	1777–79	36	240–384 livres	7,527	754	514	8,525
Lausanne-Bern in-8o	1778–82	39	225 livres	1,000	4,500	?	5,500
TOTAL				11,507	12,554	839	24,900

contained 36 volumes but the subscription price had fallen to 384 *livres*. The Lausanne and Bern octavo edition of 1778–82 made the *Encyclopédie* even more accessible. This was a 'no-frills' *Encyclopédie*, produced on second-rate paper and eliminating most of the costly engravings. It was hastily put together: print-workers left their fingerprints on the pages, there were many misprints and the pages were badly folded. It bore all the signs of a cost-cutting exercise, but in this format the work cost only 225 *livres*, less than a quarter of the price of the original folio edition. For a skilled artisan, the cost of the first folio represented over a year's wages, but the new editions were potentially affordable for more than just a wealthy and progressive elite. Darnton has demonstrated that the true circulation of the *Encyclopédie* was about 25,000, if all editions are taken into account in both France and the rest of Europe.

The *Encyclopédie* showed that the eighteenth-century Enlightenment could reach a broad public of the professional bourgeoisie, royal officials and small-town notables. In Paris and the provinces, it sold to the bourgeoisie of officials, *rentiers* and lawyers. The subscription list from the city of Besançon shows that it found its way into the libraries of *parlementaires*, army officers and administrators as well as some of the clergy and titled nobility. Half of the subscribers in Besançon came from the first and second estates, the very social groups whose privileged status would be destroyed by the Revolution. In Darnton's words, it 'did not seep into the base of society: it circulated through the middle sectors and saturated those at the top'.[31] In Europe, it was popular in the Netherlands and the Rhineland as well as northern Italy, where there were many clerical subscribers. In Livorno, sales were promoted by a priest who got 10 per cent commission on every sale. In Lucca, the clergy promised to publish a refutation, in case the Pope was thinking of banning it. In fact he did not ban it, but the Spanish Inquisition did.[32] The *Encyclopédie* was a best-seller on a European scale.

Dangerous philosophy and radical pornography

'Did books make the French Revolution?', asked Roger Chartier in his *Cultural Origins of the French Revolution*, expecting the answer 'no'.[33] The same question was asked of West German television's contribution to the revolutions in Eastern Europe in 1989, once again illustrating the political power sometimes attributed to the information media. The debate on the intellectual origins of the French Revolution was traditionally answered by reference to four great French *philosophes*: Montesquieu, Diderot, Voltaire and Rousseau. This focus on Great Thinkers was a feature of Mornet's pioneering work on the subject, which although dated remains an essential reference point.[34] Mornet saw the decisive struggles of the Enlightenment played out in mid-century, with the enlightenment intellectuals increasingly dominant after the 1760s. There are many problems with such an explanation. There was no direct or necessary link between these thinkers and the outbreak of the Revolution. For one thing, Montesquieu and Rousseau were enlisted and often quoted by the Counter-revolution as well as by revolutionaries. Furthermore, much of Diderot's work was published after the Revolution itself and could not have been known to the pre-revolutionary public. The reading public of the eighteenth century did not always see these authors as subversive; Voltaire's contemporaries, for example, valued him as a classical dramatist rather than as the author of the *Dictionnaire philosophique*.

Robert Darnton has proposed an alternative approach to traditional intellectual history, in focussing on a different group of minor and mostly forgotten authors.[35] Lesser-known writers – including Raynal, Linguet, Mercier and a host of other pamphleteers – exerted an influence on the eve of the Revolution far greater than that of the four most illustrious *philosophes*. For Darnton, the key to the question lay in the cheap, ephemeral pamphlet literature, the caricatures and broadsheets for which there was a ready market in pre-revolutionary Paris. Voltaire himself had hinted as much when he wrote to D'Alembert in 1766:

> I would like to know what harm a book costing a hundred crowns could do. Twenty folio volumes are never going to cause a revolution; those little portable books are the ones to fear.[36]

Pamphlets, *libelles* and *chroniques scandaleuses* were often pornographic, mercilessly exploiting every rumour about the king's sexual impotence, and Marie Antoinette's legendary lust for an infinite series of lovers of both genders. This, Darnton tells us, was the literature that undermined the Ancien Regime. The *chroniques scandaleuses* helped to shatter the sacred aura of monarchy, presenting a decadent and corrupt court in the final stages of moral degeneracy. If we want to know how literature eroded the credibility of monarchist ideology, we must forget the big-ticket authors and be prepared to enter the literary slums of the Parisian gutter press.

There was a very fine line between philosophical works and outright pornography, and it was often crossed. *Les Amours de Charlot et Toinette* (The Love-life of Charley and Toni), first published in 1779, opened with the queen masturbating and continued with various sexual orgies. *La Vie privée de Louis XV* (The Private Life of Louis XV) was in similar mould, getting as much mileage as possible from the rise to fame of Louis XV's mistress Madame du Barry, who was a former prostitute. The exploits of *Dom Bougre* (Friar Buggery) were another long-term success.[37] Another genre detailed the imagined sex life of cloistered nuns, constituting erotic literature and an attack on convents at the same time. The pornographic *Thérèse philosophe* had a deliberately ambiguous title, which perfectly illustrated the mixture of genres. These stories could be read in several ways: on one level they might appeal to the *voyeur* and to readers in search of erotic thrills; on another political level they satirised the monarchy and the Church.

The real influence of such literature, however, is difficult to estimate. We can never assume that readers believed everything they read. Parisian consumers were not necessarily gullible, and they were capable like every other reader of maintaining a critical distance from their texts. Readers are not passive, but have the capacity for resistance and disbelief. Even if some readers *did* believe the *chroniques scandaleuses*, it is not evident that this made them into revolutionaries. Roger Chartier expressed some scepticism about Darnton's thesis on the basis of his own conception of the reader as an active and autonomous being.[38] Chartier argued that the pornographic pamphlets of the 1780s were popular only because the public was ready for them. Public opinion was not transformed by the *libelles*; it was *already* disenchanted with religion and the monarchy. Literature did not turn readers into revolutionaries, but rather the existing climate of opinion created a strong demand for subversive literature, which the outpouring of scurrilous pamphlets supplied. Chartier thus turns the familiar and clichéd question about the intellectual causes of the French Revolution on its head. The pornographic radicalism of the Enlightenment was not the cause but the product of the de-sacralisation of the Ancien Regime, whose charismatic aura had already been dissipated by various developments including Louis XV's own excesses.

Darnton readily responded to these critical suggestions.[39] He produced a substantial list of best-selling forbidden works, now including Voltaire in the top ten alongside Mercier, Raynal and the prolific but obscure Pidansat de Mairobert. He insisted that such forbidden literature moulded public opinion as well as reflecting it. Pamphleteers turned verbal rumour into print, which gave it permanence and credibility. They also transformed urban myths into coherent narratives. In this way, the disaffection of the public was shaped and directed.[40] Darnton placed literature and its public within a context in which oral transmission was still a powerful force. He encouraged an interpretation in which verbal rumour, hearsay and gossip interacted with print within the multimedia network of the city streets.

Robert Darnton has defined an alternative canon of the Enlightenment, in which unscrupulous writers would produce anything for a quick *sou*. This unconventional view has not pleased everybody: for some it seems too much like the commodification of the Enlightenment and an overemphasis on mercenary motives in the normally more dignified domain of intellectual exchange. Daniel Gordon calls it 'The great Enlightenment massacre', parodying the title of Darnton's own book *The Great Cat*

Massacre.[41] Darnton's amicable debate with Roger Chartier has probably run its course and has little more to tell us, but it has completely renewed traditional thinking about the connection between Enlightenment and the French Revolution. It is no longer adequate to confine the subject to a few great writers honoured by posterity; nor is it possible to assume that simply reading salacious stories about Marie Antoinette turned loyal subjects into violent revolutionaries.

9
The reading fever, 1750–1830

Towards the end of the eighteenth century, many European observers expressed astonishment at the appearance of a completely new phenomenon: a reading craze had engulfed the population. One German visitor to Paris remarked,

> Everyone in Paris is reading...Everyone, but women in particular, is carrying a book around in their pocket. People read while riding in carriages or taking walks; they read at the theatre during the interval, in cafés, even when bathing. Women, children, journeymen and apprentices read in shops. On Sundays people read while seated at the front of their houses; lackeys read on their back seats, coachmen up on their boxes, and soldiers keeping guard.[1]

This writer was especially struck by the proliferation of female readers and readers from the lower classes, two developments which other commentators also found alarming. Rapid and superficial reading also worried William Wordsworth, who complained about society's 'thirst after outrageous stimulation', in which the respected classics like Shakespeare and Milton were 'driven into neglect by frantic novels, sickly and stupid German tragedies, and deluges of idle and extravagant stories in verse'.[2] The reading craze inspired furious criticism as well as stunned amazement.

Reactions to the reading fever are easy to find, but they constitute the impressions of a few individuals, and historians usually prefer more solid evidence before jumping to conclusions. They nevertheless lend support to the notion that a 'reading revolution' occurred in the Western world in the late eighteenth century. The concept of revolution is no doubt overworked, and it makes more sense when it describes a sudden and violent change rather than cultural trends which took over half a century to surface. Was there a 'Reading Revolution' in the late eighteenth and early nineteenth centuries? Not all historians would accept that a reading revolution occurred. We are on safer ground if we identify the last two decades of the century as the important moment when traditional reading styles gave way to more modern reading practices. The period examined in this chapter stretches from 1780 up to 1830, by which time technological changes were drastically changing the nature of printing and publishing (see Chapter 10).

The exponents of the 'reading revolution' of the late eighteenth century do not simply assert that people were reading more or that the reading public was growing larger. We must consider qualitative as well as quantitative changes in reading practices. In other words, people were not just reading more, but they were also reading differently. This is sometimes described as a change from traditional to modern reading, or from 'intensive' to 'extensive' modes of reading. The theory of the reading revolution has several dimensions. Reading practices, in this view, were becoming less religious and more secular; individual silent reading was supplanting communal, oral reading; readers were consuming an endless variety of texts rather than concentrating on a limited number of canonical works. The novel had an important role to play in these new reading practices. This chapter will examine what changed at the end of the eighteenth century, and will elucidate continuities as well as ruptures. At the same time, we must recognise the appearance of new forms of passionate and empathetic reading which many thought represented a dangerous addiction. The late eighteenth century was quick to deplore chain-readers just as today we disapprove of chain-smokers.

The print explosion

The French Revolution abolished the apparatus of Ancien Regime censorship, which was already dysfunctional (see Chapter 8). It swept away the corporate system which had governed the book trade and the printing industry for centuries. The result was an astonishing explosion of print. A plethora of pamphlets, journals and ephemeral literature flooded the market. In 1789 alone, 196 new newspapers appeared in Paris, and the number of active printers quadrupled as a result of deregulation. As Carla Hesse puts it, the centre of gravity of Paris publishing shifted away from erudite literature to a more democratic publishing culture of political polemics and the newspaper press.[3] The dismantling of monarchical controls between 1789 and 1791 created a deregulated market which was wide open and fiercely competitive. Many printers and booksellers could not survive the new cut-throat climate, and a number of new ventures ended in bankruptcy.

The French Revolution created a primitive form of copyright. Until the revolution, there was no royalty system, and authors sold their manuscript to their publisher once and for all. The revolution, however, strengthened the author's right to intellectual property which had been partially recognised by the law of 1777 (see Chapter 8). The law of 1793 made the written text the legal property of its author for his or her lifetime and for ten years after the author's death. This had an important consequence: the works of enlightenment authors such as Voltaire and Rousseau were now within the public domain and therefore anyone could legally publish them.

In Britain, a copyright system had existed since the Copyright Act of 1710 recognised exclusive copyright for 21 years for books already in print and for 14 years for new books. If, after 14 years, the author was still alive, his or her copyright could be extended for another 14 years. This legislation, however, was widely ignored, until, as William St. Clair emphasises, a decision taken by the House of Lords in 1774 confirmed the end of perpetual copyright and made many eighteenth-century works cheaply available. The technique of stereotyping enabled publishers to produce economic reprints of a text several times over from the same metal plates. According to the book trade's own estimate, there was a fourfold increase in output in England in the last quarter of the century. Within five years after this deregulation of the publishing market, Defoe's *Robinson Crusoe* had sold more copies than in all the 70 years since its first publication in 1719.[4]

In France, the revolution invested the printed word with a consciously militant function. The revolution's nationalist and integrating message was transmitted through print, which implicitly challenged the traditional leadership role of the clergy, and deliberately undermined the localism of non-French languages. This new politicisation of print was fully reciprocated by the revolution's enemies. The revolution suddenly made Paris the centre of the world's attention. At the beginning of 1789, the best access to French political news was through independent journals published outside the country: the *Gazette de Leyde* (Leiden Gazette), printed in the Netherlands, was a particularly reliable source. Now, however, Paris became a news production centre in its own right, and would-be journalists flocked there to make their careers. The thirst for political news about France's momentous revolution made Paris the centre of the information industry in Europe.[5]

A surge in print production was visible elsewhere, too. The annual book fair in Leipzig, where booksellers exchanged their newest wares and settled accounts, attracted interest from all over Europe. In 1765, its catalogue offered 1,384 titles. By 1785 the catalogue had almost doubled in size to include 2,713 titles, and by 1800 it offered 3,906 titles. When the Austrian Emperor Joseph II introduced press freedom in 1780, a deluge of pamphlets descended on Vienna, while elsewhere in German-speaking Europe, newspaper circulation expanded. In 1801, the *Hamburgischer Correspondent* had a circulation of over 50,000.[6] In Britain, production reached astronomic levels. Before 1700, England was producing about

1,800 book titles annually, but by 1800 the annual average was over 6,000 titles. As in the rest of Europe, growth was particularly rapid in the last two decades of the century.[7] Unlike France, where production was concentrated in Paris, Britain, Italy and Germany had many regional printing centres. In Spain, print production took off later, but here too book production tripled between the first quarter of the eighteenth century and 1790.[8] The number of new works in Castilian increased by 75 per cent in 15 years between 1775 and 1789.[9] Spain was subject to severe repression in the 1790s as the Church and the monarchy tried to isolate the country from the contagion of revolutionary doctrines. Nevertheless, Spain did not remain on the sidelines of the reading revolution for long.

Remarkably enough, this expansion occurred without any corresponding advances in the technology of production or distribution. The print explosion burst over an industry which was still operating with techniques which would have been familiar to Gutenberg. Compositors assembled the metal characters one by one for printing on hand-operated wooden presses. By increasing the number of compositors, producing double-sided sheets and working all through the night, Parisian papers could just meet the demand for a regular weekly or bi-weekly edition. If in addition they adopted smaller fonts they could produce 300 copies per hour of an 8-page in-octavo paper. The *Journal de Paris*, with a print run of about 15,000, needed half a dozen presses working in parallel to achieve this. Paper was still very expensive: printing, paper and folding absorbed about 50 per cent of a newspaper's production costs. Distribution might take up another 40 per cent and maintaining the list of subscribers another 10 per cent. Subscription in advance was still the normal sales method; selling papers in the street by individual issues was in its infancy.[10] The industry was thus expanding without experiencing any structural modernisation. As a result, print runs remained limited. Books were often produced in three volumes (the 'three-decker novel') to cater for the lending library or the *cabinet de lecture*, where readers could hire them by the hour. This was a safe and predictable market but the normal print run of a novel at the end of the eighteenth century was only 750 or 1,000 copies. The largest print runs were monopolised by catechisms and almanacs.

A media revolution

The best evidence for a wider reading public in this period lies in the growing audience for the newspaper press and in the revolutionary changes which affected the information media in the French revolutionary decade. Between 1789 and 1799, over 2,000 new newspapers appeared in Paris alone. In the high-risk atmosphere of those years, many of them did not survive more than a few editions. In the French provinces, over 1,000 new journals appeared between 1789 and 1799, and about 12,000 pamphlets were produced in the same period.[11] In England, total newspaper sales reached 16 million copies by 1790.[12] Newspapers appeared more frequently than before, sometimes twice a week or even daily instead of weekly, and they contained more political reporting.

A journalistic revolution accompanied these developments. For the first time, journalists attended political assemblies, like the Estates-General and then the National Assembly in Versailles, to report on political speeches. In England, newspapers had already won the right to publish parliamentary proceedings in the Wilkes agitation of 1771. This deliberate 'coverage' of a specific event was a complete innovation in journalism. A special shorthand was invented to supply reporters' needs. Political speeches delivered in the French revolutionary assemblies could be read just a few days later in the main provincial cities. Whereas in the Ancien Regime periodicals reported political events at a distance and often with a considerable time-lag, the French revolutionary press favoured fast and, if possible, instant reporting. The journal no longer aspired to calm, reflective detachment. Instead, it was provocative, polemical and the reporter added value by virtue of his role as an eyewitness.

The learned periodical still had a role to play, especially in an age when print runs remained small by our own standards. In the late eighteenth century, the sedate and learned monthlies satisfied an educated demand for useful knowledge, a critical curiosity about world affairs and an urge to promote social reform. They were agents of the Enlightenment, even though their subscribers were drawn from a narrow group of nobles, clergymen and the professional, administrative and commercial bourgeoisie. Jack Censer's researches into six French journals appearing between 1755 and 1789 produced a list of 2,355 known subscribers.[13] The aristocracy made up about half of them. There was a significant number of bankers and merchants but workers and craftsmen were absent from the subscriber lists. Until sale by issue became more widespread, ordinary readers could not afford the serious press.

The daily or bi-weekly newspaper was still conservative in appearance. It carried no advertisements and no loud headlines. English papers preferred a large in-folio format, but in France the octavo was far more popular, which meant that the newspaper did not clearly differentiate itself from a small book. The French revolutionary paper usually had either 8 or 16 pages and it invited the subscriber to read it like a booklet of continuous text which was hardly fragmented.

Although the newspaper looked nothing like a modern tabloid, it was nevertheless in the process of fundamental change. Radical journalism had its pre-revolutionary antecedents, most notably in Linguet's short-lived but very provocative *Annales politiques*, first launched in 1777. But now the press claimed a new kind of legitimacy: its reports would not only be sincere and truthful, but it would also act as the 'sentinel of the people'. This tribune-like function was implicit in the titles of successful papers like Brissot's *Patriote français* and Marat's *L'Ami du Peuple*. It was taken to another level in 1793–94 in Hébert's *Père Duchesne*, in which a fictional character posed as the spokesman of the *sans-culottes*, conducting fictional dialogues with enemies of the people, couched in the violent, oath-ridden language of the Parisian streets.

Camille Desmoulins, like Hébert, was a revolutionary journalist whose career ended at the guillotine. He, too, registered the transformation of the French press from the stuffy provincial calendar into the dynamic political force of the revolutionary years. He wrote in his own paper:

> In the Ancien Regime, the periodical used to give you banalities about the weather, the price of hay, the depth of the river and the time when the street-lanterns would be lit. Today, journalists fulfil a public ministry. They denounce, issue decrees, set standards, condemn or absolve. Every day they deliver harangues from their soap-box and some of them are stentorian orators who can be heard all over the 83 departments. Seats are going for only two *sous*. Newspapers rain down every morning.[14]

The 'media revolution' had a long way yet to run. In 1836, Emile de Girardin drastically reduced the price of his newspaper *La Presse*, aiming at a mass readership and greatly enhanced advertising income. In the late eighteenth century, the modern press was in its infancy but it was undergoing changes which contributed to the 'reading revolution' of this period.

The public sphere and the 'Republic of Letters'

Increasing print consumption was fundamental to the creation of a public sphere, as argued by the philosopher-historian Jürgen Habermas. Habermas saw the pre-revolutionary period as one in which a metaphorical arena was opened up where political discussion could take place in a 'public sphere' beyond the supervision of the monarchical state.[15] By a public sphere, we mean the development of a civil society free of state control, and the possibility of open and public debate conducted freely by individuals and more or less self-governing institutions. In the Ancien Regime monarchies, in contrast, political life was strictly controlled by the ruler, while the State and the Church dictated the terms of any public discussion. Government in the Ancien Regime depended on secrecy; but the growth of the public sphere aimed to expose the workings of the authorities to the harsh light of day.

As Habermas well realised, 'public opinion' had burst on the scene many times before the late eighteenth century. In moments of conflict and revolution, like the French Frondes or the English Civil War in the mid-seventeenth century, vigorous pamphlet wars erupted which the dying or defunct regime was quite incapable of silencing. In the 1760s, there were signs on both sides of the English Channel that popular participation in political life was on the rise. In England, a campaign of newspaper articles, pamphlets and broadsides attacked the King and parliamentary corruption. Such a campaign was launched to secure the re-election to the House of Commons of the controversial John Wilkes, member for Middlesex. Wilkes had been imprisoned for seditious libel and expelled from parliament, but in 1768 his Middlesex electorate of shopkeepers, small merchants and manufacturers defied the government and re-elected him anyway. The Wilkite agitation depended on print: a seditious issue of Wilkes' paper *The North Briton* in 1762 had originally led to his arrest. By the 1770s, something had been achieved in the interests of transparent government: London newspapers could at last print full reports of parliamentary debates for the first time without fear of legal action.

In France, meanwhile, Voltaire entered the fray in 1762 with a celebrated pamphlet in defence of the Protestant Jean Calas, who had been convicted by the Parlement (or provincial court) of Toulouse for murdering his own son, rather than allowing him to convert to the Catholic faith. In a furore which threatened to re-ignite the sectarian bigotry of a previous era, Voltaire defended reason and common sense in his exposé of a notorious miscarriage of justice. Furthermore, he was claiming the right of public intellectuals to scrutinise and dissent from judicial decisions and to intervene in public debate. He embodied the prototype of the engaged intellectual, who was to become a distinctive part of French life, up to Emile Zola's defence of Alfred Dreyfus and Jean-Paul Sartre's opposition to the Algerian War.

Clearly, there were plenty of antecedents for the formation of a public sphere before the end of the eighteenth century, both in Western Europe and North America. For Habermas, this period was not the beginning of the public sphere, but rather a new and very particular phase in its growth. He linked its development to the growth of a free market and the spread of commercial capitalism. This context was certainly appropriate for the early growth of newspapers, devoted to market news and anything which might affect price fluctuations of essential goods. The late eighteenth century was also a period in which culture was becoming commercialised and a consumer society was born. Books, newspapers and the theatre were all commodities in the new urban consumer culture.

In this crucial period, therefore, debate increasingly escaped state censorship and people were free to publicly criticise social and political institutions. This critical community relied on books, newspapers, clubs and cafés, constituting an independent but informal court, delivering critical judgements on public affairs. At the same time, it insisted on the vital principle of publicity and transparency of government. Public opinion was an independent tribunal to which the authorities were forced to appeal for approval.

Habermas saw the new public sphere as a specific feature of bourgeois society. 'Public opinion', therefore, really referred to the opinion of a bourgeois intellectual circle, for ordinary people were considered not yet enlightened enough to participate fully in public debate. The leading model was England, where censorship had been brought to an end with the Licensing Act of 1695 and where there was already a vigorous parliamentary life. France and Germany provided rather less developed continental variants. The 'public sphere' would be impossible to conceive without the development of print and newspaper culture. In fact, it rested on cultural institutions for which print was an important medium. In Germany, reading associations and literary circles provided a forum. In London and Paris, a dynamic coffee-house culture offered sites for relaxed male sociability which were closely associated with reading and public discussion of the news. In Germany, France, Russia and Britain, Masonic lodges thrived, representing an exclusive fraternity meeting independently of the State to discuss public affairs. According to Daniel Roche, about 5 per cent of France's adult male population may have been freemasons on the eve of the French Revolution.[16] This did not mean they were all revolutionaries, as some conspiracy theories were to claim; on the contrary, most probably leaned towards conformity.

In provincial France, the academies studied by Daniel Roche challenged the cultural hegemony of Paris to provide a social network for the educated public.[17] Over the century as a whole, the majority of provincial academicians came from the clergy and the nobility, which contradicts Habermas' notion of an exclusively bourgeois public sphere. The provincial academies, like the public sphere itself, were urban phenomena, engaging the local cultural elite of public-spirited men in a variety of scientific pursuits: they created libraries, sponsored botanical gardens and ran essay prize competitions to find the best technical solutions to everyday problems. They had their regional pride, but maintained broad cosmopolitan links through correspondence with other learned societies. They represented the best of local talent, coming together to improve society and the economy through useful and enlightened reforms.

Literary salons were another important component of the new structure of the public sphere. The salons were unique in providing a forum where both sexes communicated with each other on the political and literary agenda of the day. The legal profession made its contribution, too, as Sarah Maza has shown. In a series of celebrity trials in Ancien Regime France, lawyers appealed directly to the general public by publishing their arguments. Their *mémoires judiciaires* were officially destined only for the court, but some were sold to the public in print runs of up to 20,000.[18] The lawyers were sometimes besieged at their own homes for copies, and excerpts appeared in the European press. In publishing their trial briefs, lawyers were asserting the cardinal principle of the publicity of proceedings. They claimed in melodramatic fashion to defend the weak against the strong, and they appealed to the anonymous tribunal of public opinion as though it had the real authority to decide.

These new institutions of the public sphere defined themselves as members of what was known in France as 'the Republic of Letters'. This denoted a secular culture, and an egalitarian spirit operating within a cohesive community well aware of its international dimensions. The egalitarianism of the public sphere, however, was limited. In the cases of the freemasons, the coffee houses or the French provincial academies, it was clearly limited to men. Even in the literary salons, female participation was not necessarily welcomed on an equal basis. The real art of the *salonnière* was to put herself in the background, to facilitate discussion and to let others (i.e. male intellectuals) shine in conversation. In Germany it was said that the salon hostess was valued for her 'erotic radiance'. Perhaps the salon helped to legitimise the participation of women in intellectual life; but conventional gender expectations still prevailed. The 'Republic of Letters' was to some extent a social mixture, in the sense that aristocrats rubbed shoulders with members of the bourgeoisie. It thus implicitly embodied an alternative society to the traditional hierarchy of the Ancien Regime. Institutions like the Masonic lodges, however, were secretive and closed off from the rest of society. If such institutions represented equality, they also demonstrated exclusiveness.

Habermas' configuration requires some revision. The literary community which led the formation of a critical public was aristocratic in composition as much as it was bourgeois. Furthermore, the public sphere was still a gendered space in which intellectual men assumed the leading roles. Nevertheless, leaving aside Habermas' argument that the public sphere later disintegrated at the hands of the mass media, this concept remains useful for thinking about the cultural history of the period.

The development of print culture allowed the intellectual elite to envisage for itself a leading and influential role in society. Through the print media, it could now seriously challenge State and Church control over the supply of information and its interpretation. The formation of public opinion in Ancien Regime France was a long-term process, but in one form or another it depended on the press just as it did in Britain. Public opinion seemed a powerful safeguard against arbitrary despotism, as long as it relied on enlightened discussion amongst educated men. The culminating blow for the publicity of government was struck by the finance minister Necker, who for the first time made the crown's budget public. In 1781, his budget sold 3,000 copies on the first day of issue, and 10,000 per week immediately afterwards.[19] No doubt Necker massaged the budget figures; but it had never occurred to any of his predecessors to involve public opinion in discussion of the royal finances.

A reading public in transition

The secularisation of literary taste was an important ingredient of the reading revolution, even if its rhythm and geography were not at all uniform. In eighteenth-century France, there was an appreciable decline in the publication of religious works. At the beginning of the century, devotional and religious literature had accounted for one half of all book titles officially licensed, but by 1785, the proportion of titles in theology had fallen to only 10 per cent of total production.[20] These are official figures which do not encompass the full range of clandestine and 'tolerated' publications. They did not necessarily mean that fewer religious titles were appearing in absolute terms: the decline was relative to production in the other main categories, which in the knowledge classification system of the time were Law, History and Geography, Arts and Sciences and Belles-Lettres. There was a similar fall in the production of works in Latin: at the Leipzig fair, the 1740 catalogue listed 28 per cent of titles in Latin, but in 1800 works in Latin accounted for less than 4 per cent of the total.[21] The traditional categories of erudite literature were giving way to a new vogue for smaller-format novels.

This was not yet a universal trend. In the American colonies, David Hall has stressed the continuing importance of the traditional market for Protestant works, especially Bibles, religious tracts and sermons and he found no evidence of a reading revolution before 1790.[22] Here, if people bought more books in the eighteenth century, they still bought religious books. In the Windsor District of Vermont, put under the microscope by William J. Gilmore, reading was becoming a 'necessity of life', as novels, almanacs and especially weekly newspapers provided a more varied reading diet alongside the traditional Bibles, psalms and prayer books. The extent of book ownership itself, however, should not be overestimated. Estate inventories from the early nineteenth century show that 63 per cent of families in Windsor District had a library, but the median size of their libraries in 1816–30 was only five books each, and 22 per cent of families in the survey kept just a single book – the Bible.[23] Gilmore argues that rural New England was on the brink of modernity, but many of his findings point us in the opposite direction; they show us the centrality of the Bible and of the family as a site for reading aloud, as well as small personal libraries stocked with steady sellers like the Bible, *Pilgrim's Progress* and *Robinson Crusoe*. In rural Virginia, book ownership was rarer: 50 per cent of white people did not own any books when they died, and 25 per cent possessed only a Bible.[24] The persistence of religious publishing was not confined to the Protestant world, for in Italy, too, religious books still accounted for between 20 and 25 per cent of production at the end of the eighteenth century.[25] The proportion was comparable in Germany, where religious publishing constituted 20 per cent of the market in about 1775.[26]

This nevertheless represented a decline although outside France the relative collapse of the religious book was less sudden. Its fall should be seen in the context of the long-term decline of religious authority. Counter-reformation injunctions to attend Mass regularly particularly at Easter were obeyed, but other changes testified to the weakening hold of traditional religion in France. Recruitment for the priesthood, for example, was dropping, while preparations for death more rarely included the exhibition of the corpse and the funding of masses for the souls of the deceased, which had been common in Mediterranean France. Demographic historians emphasise the growing adoption of family limitation techniques, particularly in the 1790s. The decline of religious books was one among many signs of a profound but largely subterranean change in which French culture distanced itself from orthodox religious teaching.[27]

As religious publishing declined, so other categories boomed. In France, the number of titles in history, biography and geography remained fairly stable throughout the eighteenth century, but within this category there was an increase in profane at the expense of religious history. At the same time, there was a notable rise in the proportion of titles produced in science and the mechanical and useful arts. Mathematics, medicine and political economy were all fields of greater interest and increasingly attracted eighteenth-century readers. Recreational literature grew exponentially and the novel, above all, was the beneficiary of the changing profile of secular reading. The late-eighteenth-century French public showed a healthy appetite for fashionable English novelists, and the genre found new readers further and further down the social scale.

In America, according to Cathy Davidson, the novel was the chapbook of the eighteenth century, in the sense that it was increasingly cheap and accessible to uneducated readers who read nothing else. In 1797, the *New York Magazine* proclaimed, 'This is a novel-reading age.'[28] If Protestant New England had lagged behind the 'reading revolution' in Western Europe, America seemed ready to catch up in the final decade of the century. The Protestant clergy, meanwhile, saw its authority threatened and condemned the pernicious influence of fiction.

The rise of the novel has been for some time a staple of eighteenth-century literary history. Half a century ago, Ian Watt's much-quoted study associated its rise with the growing self-confidence of the middle class.[29] Cultural historians would generally agree and would situate novel-reading within the wider development of a consumer society in the eighteenth century. This was the moment of the commercial take-off for literature in England, where 60,000 titles were produced in the decade of the 1790s.[30] In London and Paris, the middle classes were consuming more of everything, including novels, as the growing market for tableware, furnishings and fine clothes testifies.

English novels were particularly in demand, from Fielding, Sterne and Richardson in the middle of the century, to the Gothic novels of Ann Radcliffe and 'Monk' Lewis at the end of it. There were over 470 translations of English novels into French in the eighteenth century, and most of these were after 1741, when Richardson's *Pamela* appeared in French.[31] When Daniel Mornet surveyed the contents of 500 private libraries in France, he found *Pamela* was the most popular of all English novels, while *Clarissa Harlowe* and *Tom Jones* were not far behind, and these three eclipsed all French titles except Françoise de Graffigny's *Lettres d'une péruvienne*.[32]

The British domination of the genre entered a new phase after 1818 with the appearance of Walter Scott's Waverley novels in French translation. Scott, like Richardson before him, became a best-selling writer on a truly international scale. His English-language editions alone sold more copies in this period than all other contemporary English novelists put together. By 1850, for instance, none of Jane Austen's novels had achieved sales of 8,000 – a figure that many of Scott's novels reached in the first week they appeared.[33] In Germany, too, English novels were in demand, especially the sentimental novels of Richardson, appreciated everywhere for their high moral concerns which incidentally made them more acceptable to Protestant authorities. The production of novels in Germany rose from fewer than 200 titles per year in the 1770s to over 1,400 by the end of the century. There was a ninefold increase in German novel publishing between Goethe's *The Sorrows of Young Werther* (1774) and his *Wilhelm Meister* (1796).[34]

When Ian Watt formulated his thesis on the rise of the novel, he focussed on the canon of white male authors: Defoe, Fielding and Richardson. He left out of consideration many women novelists who enjoyed a high reputation, like Marie-Jeanne Riccoboni, Fanny Burney and Sophie Cottin. Women writers participated fully in the production of fiction, but they were also prominent amongst the consumers of novels? The evidence is conflicting. Jan Fergus' study of two booksellers in the English Midlands found little evidence that women dominated the novel-reading public, or even that men and women enjoyed different, gender-specific books.[35] Fergus did, however, note that husbands often acted as purchasers or subscribers in their wives' name, so perhaps the female reading public is partly disguised by the booksellers' records. The feminisation of the reading public was plain to many commentators, most of them male and possibly alarmed because this meant a potential challenge to patriarchal control. The conventional view of gender roles demanded that women should read under male supervision. Coleridge thought that reading the *Spectator* aloud to his wife and daughters required careful handling in case it should 'offend the delicacy of female ears, and shock feminine susceptibility'.[36] 'Chaste women don't read novels' was Jean-Jacques Rousseau's warning, for the novel could arouse unrealistic expectations and stimulate erotic desire in the vulnerable female reader. The common novel, in the words of the *Lady's Magazine*, was 'the powerful engine with which the seducer attacks the female heart' and only moral novels were recommended. Novels of adultery were especially suspect, including Rousseau's own best-seller, *La Nouvelle Héloïse*. Reading novels gave enormous pleasure to women but, in Jacqueline Pearson's phrase, 'each reading pleasure is haunted by a dark double'. Behind the innocent and virtuous domestic novel lay the suggestion of sexual temptations.[37]

Women readers were supreme in one arena: as subscribers to circulating libraries. In wealthy private houses, the library was a male preserve, and its door was often locked to exclude women and children. Jane Austen, for example, had no library to retire to, but in *Pride and Prejudice* her fictional Mr. Bennett ran frequently to his library as a refuge from feminine domestic tumult. Meanwhile Darcy, another member of the library-owning classes, vowed to maintain the great library at Pemberley, the estate which he had inherited. Apart from aristocratic private libraries, an increasing number of subscription libraries appeared, formed by committees of notables who put up the original capital, set the subscription rates and ordered the books. This was the model for the 'social library' founded by Benjamin Franklin in Philadelphia in 1731, an early prototype. In Germany, too, reading clubs offered a social atmosphere and shared subscriptions to leading journals. Such institutions, however, tended to express middle-class male solidarities.

The circulating library, on the other hand, offered books on loan to a much broader public. Customers paid a yearly, half-yearly, quarterly or perhaps just a weekly fee to borrow books. Novels formed a substantial part of their stock and an even larger proportion of borrowings. In the 1760s, circulating libraries (as distinct from subscription libraries run by shareholders) started to appear in the American colonies and, by 1773, examples existed in Annapolis, Charleston, New York, Boston, Philadelphia and Baltimore. They opened daily, and welcomed female and younger borrowers. But they could not keep up with the constant demand for new books, and their stock became rapidly out of date. Few would survive the war and economic depression.[38] By the end of the eighteenth century, circulating libraries were to be found in any self-respecting English country town, and there were 112 in London alone. They were well supported by female readers. Jane Austen and her family depended on them. They bridged the gap between the relatively restricted and learned reading public of the early eighteenth century and the mass consumption of pulp fiction later in the nineteenth century.

The public, as St. Clair insists, was multi-layered. While readers with lower incomes could afford cheap reprints of the eighteenth-century canon, books by new authors remained expensive.[39] Only after a considerable time-lag did the works of the so-called 'romantic era' fall into the public domain and become more accessible. Not until the second half of the nineteenth century could readers fully discover Austen and Stendhal, Wordsworth and Coleridge. Between 1780 and 1830, the reading public was in a transitional stage. Many readers rejected the literary apparatus of a dying world, but the public was not completely ready to embrace a new world of completely secular and recreational literature. Reading for pleasure was becoming the cultural norm, but traditional reading practices would endure.

Intensive and extensive reading styles

German scholars have been the most consistent defenders of the reading revolution thesis, and none more so than Rolf Engelsing. Engelsing studied the development of middle-class reading in the northern German city of Bremen, making use of *post-mortem* inventories. He detected a change from what he defined as 'intensive reading' to 'extensive reading'.[40] In a culture of 'intensive reading', books were scarce and expensive, and readers returned repeatedly to a small number of steady-selling titles which were handed down from generation to generation. Reading was largely driven by religious or pietistic concerns and texts were frequently memorised or verbally recited. The book itself was respected both as a rare physical object and as a source of authority. In the eighteenth century, in Engelsing's argument, the German bourgeoisie turned to a culture of 'extensive reading' in which books were more readily available. They became familiar, everyday objects to be read and discarded rather than repeatedly re-visited. Reading was more secular and silent individual reading more common than reading aloud in a religious environment.

Some of these changes were not peculiar to Germany, but may have been characteristics of a Protestant style of reading encountered elsewhere. In New England, for example, commentators in the early nineteenth century looked back with nostalgia at the great cultural changes which had occurred. 'How the world has changed', wrote the American publisher and children's writer, Samuel Goodrich, as he surveyed his Connecticut childhood from the vantage point of the 1850s. In those days, he explained, books had been read with serious attention, not skimmed through and then discarded like waste paper. He described the deliberate gestures of the reader and the solemn nature of the act of reading:

> The aged sat down when they read, and drew forth their spectacles, and put them deliberately and reverently upon the nose. These instruments were not as now, little tortoise-shell hooks, attached to a ribbon, and put off and on with a jerk; but they were of silver or steel,

substantially made, and calculated to hold on with a firm and steady grasp, showing the gravity of the uses to which they were devoted. Even the young approached a book with reverence, and a newspaper with awe.[41]

In Goodrich's lifetime, books were valuable items. The scarcity of books and reverence for print were two characteristics of the traditional world of reading identified by Hall in Puritan New England, echoing Engelsing's notion of intensive reading.

As Matthew P. Brown has demonstrated, reading in early New England was characterised by scarcity rather than plenty. Reading was closely associated with Sundays and fast-days. It was chiefly directed towards devotional books, and access to any literature had to be authorised. New England readers read sometimes like pilgrims, on a spiritual journey leading to the redemption of their soul; and they read sometimes like bees, regarding their books as treasuries of wise proverbs, which they could extract like pollen for the edification of the hive.[42] Lewis Bayly's *The Practise of Pietie* typically recommended a deep or intensive reading of the Bible:

> One Chapter thus read with *understanding*, and meditated with *application*, will better feed and comfort they soule, than *five* read and run over without marking their *scope* or *sense*, or making any use thereof to thine *owne* selfe.[43]

Readers were expected to humble themselves before Holy Scripture. They were encouraged to approach it with the question: what must I do to be saved? And the answer would be buried piously and profoundly within their hearts.

Reading aloud within family groups was a frequent practice, and this, too, was an aspect of traditional literacy, now virtually lost. Reading, whether silent or aloud, took place in a religious context, either for the purposes of the education of the young or in the context of family piety. Books were so rare that the Bible might be the only book ever read by New England families. As a result, its pages were well-trodden territory and its wisdom constantly evoked. The Goodrich family Bible was read from beginning to end by Samuel's father no fewer than 13 times, over a span of a quarter of a century.[44]

The intensive style of reading which Engelsing detected in northern Germany was not specific to any place or time, although it may have been characteristic of Protestant reading cultures in general. Oral historians of early-twentieth-century Australia, for example, emphasise the importance of the family Bible. What distinguished it from every other book was the practice of recording items of family history in the blank pages inside the back or, more usually, the front cover. The family Bible registered and commemorated every landmark and rite of passage in the Christian life of succeeding generations. It was an assertion of family identity which could only be conceived within a Christian framework.[45]

Collective reading in a religious context was another survival from an age of traditional literacy. This was usually an occupation for the evening, when the whole family was together after work, led by the parents in the presence of all the children. One Australian interviewee, Laura P., recalled that collective Bible-reading was a central family institution. 'Reading the Bible', she declared, 'was part of our life.' Her father, a classics graduate and high school teacher, led family prayers and, if there were any guests for dinner, they were included in the reading. After dinner, she recalled, the family would 'read round' the Bible; in other words, each member would take a verse in turn around the table.[46] A traditional style of reading persisted in New South Wales, as in New England.

The survival in different contexts of intensive reading practices dilutes the impact of Engelsing's argument about a decisive cultural shift in the eighteenth century. So too does the appearance of new forms of intensive reading, which owed nothing to Protestant piety. A fever gripped readers of the sentimental novel in the second half of the eighteenth century, which drew them into a very close relationship with their texts. They empathised strongly with fictional characters and imagined they enjoyed an intimate and privileged relationship with their favourite authors. Three best-selling novels of the century inspired this extreme intensity: Richardson's *Clarissa Harlowe* (1747), Rousseau's *Julie, ou la Nouvelle Héloïse* (1761) and Goethe's *The Sorrows of Young Werther* (1774). These stories generated a profound emotional response and interest in the fate of their heroes and heroines. Goethe's novel of tragic love inspired suicides. Young readers donned blue tailcoats and yellow breeches to identify with the hero, and the Leipzig authorities tried to ban the outfit.[47] Readers' tears flowed profusely and they did not always seem able to distinguish fiction from real life.

The epistolary novel, reproducing the fictional correspondence of its protagonists, invited the reader to share the characters' emotions. Unlike other narrative forms, the epistolary novel did not seek to direct the reader from a position of emotional distance from the action. Rousseau's *La Nouvelle Héloïse* was such a novel, published in over 70 editions before the end of the century. It too induced tears and readers choked with sentiment through Julie's deathbed scene. One reader was so moved by it that he felt that 'at that moment I, could have faced death with pleasure ... and with Julie in her tomb, I saw only a frightening void in nature'.[48] Julie's death felt like the reader's own, and the emptiness was his own emptiness. Other readers of Rousseau illustrate this close emotional identification and remind us that it was by no means the exclusive property of female readers.[49] Readers like Jean Ranson believed Rousseau was speaking to them 'from the heart'. He wanted to meet the author and discuss his heroine. Indeed, Rousseau's tomb at Ermenonville was to become a cult pilgrimage site. Ranson named his second son Emile after one of Rousseau's novels, and adopted Jean-Jacques' advice on child-rearing. Rousseau received an intensive correspondence from readers of this novel in 1761.[50] Richardson, like Rousseau, also received correspondence from his readers, as a result of the intense response his fiction provoked. Lady Bradshaigh was one fan who could hardly endure the emotional tension of *Clarissa*. She wrote,

> Would you have me weep incessantly?...I long to read it – and yet I dare not...in Agonies would I lay down the Book, take it up again, walk about the Room, let fall a Flood of Tears, wipe my Eyes, read again...throw away the Book crying out...I cannot go on.[51]

Crying was not just a sign of emotion for such readers. It expressed a positive aesthetic judgement on the sentimental novel. This was a new form of readers' response. It was both secular and individual, but it was the opposite of the nonchalance associated with an extensive reading style.

Several objections can therefore be mounted against Engelsing's revolution in which extensive reading modes replaced intensive ones: some traditions survived long beyond the eighteenth century, and new intensive reading styles emerged in response to the novel of sensibility. In addition, to classify reading aloud as part of traditional literacy blurs the subtle differences between various forms of verbal reading. When the male head of a household read the Bible to the family, or when Coleridge, cited earlier, read the *Spectator* to his wife and daughters, there was a traditional and patriarchal element to the reading. The listeners had no choice about what they heard and the reading might be censored for their 'benefit'. Reading aloud, however, was not necessarily so hierarchical. Sometimes women read to each other and the act of reading aloud strengthened bonds between female friends or relatives. In other contexts, reading aloud could be a seduction technique. The incidence of Bible-reading should not stereotype our conception of verbal reading.

Various reading styles are encountered in the same household or even in the same reader, as the case of Anna Larpent indicates.[52] Larpent, born in 1758, was the daughter of a diplomat and the wife of a theatre censor. Her reading did not correspond to any reading stereotype. She read philosophy, history and accounts of Captain Cook's voyages. She read aloud to her children, and also in adult company, for this was a social grace highly prized in polite society. She read a stream of novels, often when out walking, preferring those written by women, but she was also a religious reader, and every day she read from the Bible, the psalms or a pious text. It would be impossible to classify her eclectic reading practices as those of either an intensive or an extensive reader: she was both at once.

The jury is still out on some aspects of the reading revolution. The rise of the newspaper press and the circulating library are indisputable. So too is the evidence for an expansion of recreational reading from the final two decades of the eighteenth century. As we have seen, however, the notion of 'extensive reading' is more problematic. Novel-reading did not necessarily turn readers into passive consumers, and reading Richardson, Rousseau or Goethe was no trivial matter.

10

The age of the mass reading public

Between the 1830s and the First World War, the entire process of literary production was industrialised and a mass reading public came into existence. A series of technological changes transformed printing and paper manufacture, and the railways created new opportunities for distribution and marketing on a national and international scale. The roles of printer, publisher and bookseller, which had previously been combined, became specialised professions. The West experienced a cultural transformation which led by the 1890s to the emergence of a mass literary culture. This transformation was driven by the press. It went hand in hand with the appearance of large-circulation daily newspapers and illustrated magazines, which attracted advertising revenue and were no longer exclusively dependent on expensive subscriptions. Until this period, the essential conditions of publication had changed very little since the age of Gutenberg. The industrialisation of production in the early nineteenth century, however, marked a watershed: in political terms, the Old Regime had ended in 1789, but the typographical Old Regime expired in the 1830s.

Writing practices were also democratised, and this will be discussed in Chapter 12. This chapter reviews the many social, economic and technological developments which contributed to the growth of a mass market for literature. How did a mass market come into existence? How did this change the way that ordinary readers found access to books and newspapers? Several developments made the transition to a mass market possible. The population grew more rapidly after the second half of the eighteenth century, and it was increasingly concentrated in cities. A dense urban population had always stimulated print communication, and it was now a major incentive for the expansion of the newspaper press. In the 1850s, New York accounted for just 2 per cent of the population of the United States, but provided 18 per cent of its newspaper circulation and generated 36 per cent of its publishing income.[1] The population of Germany, to take another example, rose from 28.8 millions in 1838 to 64.8 millions in 1910, a huge increase which frightened Germany's neighbours and seemed to threaten European stability. By then, over half the German population lived in towns with more than 5,000 inhabitants.[2] In the last quarter of the century, most of the population were enjoying an unprecedented level of prosperity, with a little disposable income to spend on meat, beer and newspapers. Meanwhile, mass literacy was achieved in the Western world by the last decades of the century. By the 1890s, over 95 per cent of the population in the advanced countries could read and write. Technological changes, then, did not in themselves drive the industrialisation of the book, which was a response to the expanding possibilities of the market. They are nevertheless fundamental, and a convenient place to begin.

New technologies, rising production

At the beginning of the nineteenth century, a number of inventions of English or German origin transformed the printing process, allowing greater quantities of sheets to be printed at a faster rate. The Stanhope press, invented in about 1800, was the first all-metal press, which had a platen large enough to print a complete folio at one pull. This was a great advantage for large-format periodicals, and the London *Times* was one of the first purchasers. After the Napoleonic War, Ambroise-Firmin Didot bought one in London, and French manufacturers started to copy it. It was in Didot's printing shop that David Séchard served his apprenticeship in Balzac's novel *Lost Illusions*.[3] Séchard returned to the sleepy town of Angoulême, where his father, a crabby and miserly traditionalist, was extremely sceptical about the newfangled Stanhopes, fearing that they would damage the characters.

The Stanhopes were in fact very powerful, but the ambitious newspaper proprietor needed something faster. Koenig's steam-driven cylindrical press, invented in 1811, promised to end the physical hard labour of printing and inking every folio. By 1820, it could produce 1,000 copies per hour.[4] A number of improvements followed in the wake of these pioneering developments. Applegarth's press enabled the *Times* to print on both sides of the paper at once. Paper could be fed into an Applegarth from four different angles to produce 4,000 impressions hourly and, by 1850, he had designed an eight-feeder machine to produce 10,000 copies per hour.[5] In the 1860s and 1870s, British and colonial printers adopted the Wharfdale, an even faster cylindrical press. Within the space of half a century, mechanisation had transformed ancient practices. The artisanal character of the printing industry was giving way to large-scale production. In Balzac's *Lost Illusions*, characters were still inked by hand using small copper balls.[6] By mid-century, this job could be done automatically by rollers on steam-driven presses.

The new hardware required considerable capital investment. The simplest Koenig press initially cost £900, which made it ten times as expensive as the Stanhope.[7] Only large circulation newspapers could afford this investment, and it was no coincidence that the London *Times* was at the forefront of new printing technology. In France, *Le Petit Journal* later achieved the circulation to make such an investment worthwhile, and in the 1870s Marinoni made a six-feeder machine for this paper.[8] In France, mechanisation was largely concentrated in the capital, but new techniques gradually spread to Germany, and later to the rest of Europe. In Spain, where restricted literacy and a limited home market made modernisation a much slower process, the first Koenig press arrived in Barcelona in 1885.[9] Here, as in the French provinces, older methods of production did not disappear but existed side by side with industrial technology.

The manufacture of paper was industrialised. The traditional method of making paper from rags was replaced by using vegetable matter – first straw and then wood pulp. As a result, the cost of paper fell dramatically. Paper had been the biggest single item of publishing expenditure, but it accounted for only 10 or 15 per cent of the production budget by 1914. Over half the paper in England was already machine-made by 1825.[10] Unfortunately, the new processes sometimes involved chemical treatment to whiten the paper. Many books produced in the 1870s and 1880s were consequently highly acidic and a century later hundreds and thousands of volumes were rotting away on library shelves.

The mechanisation of paper-cutting, folding and binding followed. Book illustration was transformed by the introduction of lithography and then of photographic techniques which opened up new possibilities, especially for children's books. Only one bottleneck remained: the labour-intensive task of composition. For centuries, compositors had assembled the type by hand, character by character. Towards the end of the century, new techniques were introduced in the United States which hugely accelerated the process. In 1884, Mergenthaler's Linotype appeared, to be followed by Lanston's Monotype in 1887–89. A single worker using Linotype could set 8,000 characters per hour, whereas the very best compositor could not improve on 1,500 using traditional methods.[11]

A surge in book production occurred, which can be measured by the increasing number of titles appearing each year. In Britain, production rose to over 5,000 in the 1850s. The volume of production reached a plateau in the 1860s, but then another rise beginning in the 1870s brought production levels to new heights. By 1909, Britain, with its lucrative overseas markets, was producing over 10,000 titles per year.[12] In France, the number of titles produced exceeded this, even though war and revolutions caused serious interruptions to economic life. The main growth spurts occurred in the Restoration period (1815–30) and in the Second Empire (1852–70). By the end of the century, France produced over 13,000 book titles annually.[13] Global production in France and Britain, however, was overshadowed by the flood of titles appearing in imperial Germany. In 1884, book production in unified Germany was running at over 15,000 titles per year. The Second Reich was a period of unprecedented growth, when publishers could reap full benefit from mechanisation, falling production costs and the creation of a single national market. By 1913, Germany produced 35,000 titles, making it the biggest world producer.[14]

In the first decade of the twentieth century production had reached a peak and the market appeared saturated. In France, production was stagnant by 1900, and it declined in the years before the First World War, which resulted in a spate of discount selling to unload surplus stock. Britain weathered the situation rather better, perhaps because its important export outlets compensated for any levelling-off in home demand. By the 1850s, Australia had overtaken India as Britain's main overseas book market. It was the largest market for British books from 1889 to 1953, and over 25 per cent of British book exports were destined for Australia between 1900 and the Second World War.[15]

These statistics are a guide to the fluctuating rhythm of production over the whole century, but they say nothing about the changing profile of the market. What kinds of books were being produced in ever-larger quantities? Two genres in particular benefited from expanding global production – novels and educational books. In France during the 1840s novels probably accounted for over 330 titles per year.[16] In the USA, the lurid sensationalism of the 'dime novels' sold millions of copies, especially to Civil War soldiers.[17] A mass market for children's books was emerging everywhere, especially after governments legislated to establish national systems of compulsory primary education. For the first time, it was possible to make a fortune specialising in school books, which is exactly the strategy chosen by Hachette in France and Thomas Nelson in Britain. Simon Eliot found that fiction and 'juvenile literature' soared, to account for 23.3 per cent of book production in Britain by the First World War.[18] Collodi's *Avventure di Pinocchio*, first published in 1886, was a best-seller in Italy before becoming a global favourite. In the English-speaking world, Lewis Carroll's *Alice's Adventures in Wonderland* (1865) and Robert Louis Stevenson's *Treasure Island* (1883) became all-time best-sellers. For young girls, Lucy Maud Montgomery's *Anne of Green Gables* (1908) and Louisa May Alcott's *Little Women* (1869) topped the popularity polls for decades in the United States and throughout the British Empire.

Religious books were still important, especially if sheer quantities are considered. In Britain, they still accounted for over 15 per cent of production at the end of the century, in spite of the drift towards more secular reading.[19] The production of religious tracts and Bibles maintained a phenomenal rhythm in the first half of the century. According to Leslie Howsam, the British and Foreign Bible Society turned out no fewer than 6.4 million cheap Bibles in a single decade (1837–47).[20] Unorthodox religious opinions would always be best-sellers, and this was the case in France for Lamennais' *Paroles d'un Croyant* (A Believer's Words), an instant success in 1833, and Ernest Renan's *Vie de Jésus* (Life of Jesus) later in the century. Lévy produced Renan's work in 70,000 copies in-octavo in 1863, followed by 80,000 more in the miniature in-32o format. The profits helped him buy a new building in the fashionable rue Auber, near the Paris Opera.[21]

Just as the nineteenth-century book trade was producing a huge number of new titles, so too print runs were increasing, although not at the same rate. At the beginning of the nineteenth century, the average print run for a novel was only 1,000 or 1,500 copies. The first edition of Stendhal's *Le Rouge et le Noir* (The Red and the Black) appeared in Paris in 1831 in only 750 copies. A second edition quickly followed, but it too had a run of only 750 copies. By the 1840s, however, some best-selling authors like Victor Hugo appeared in editions of 5,000. The scale of production changed enormously by the 1870s, when the cheapest editions of Jules Verne appeared in print runs of 30,000. In the 1850s, Harriet Beecher Stowe's *Uncle Tom's Cabin* broke all previous sales records in the English-speaking world, and revealed the existence of a market still not yet fully tested. Although its anti-slavery message provoked hostility in the American South, it sold well in the USA, and Sampson Low claimed 1.5 million copies were sold in Britain and its colonies.[22] In the early years of the twentieth century, it became common for fiction titles to achieve print runs of 100,000 copies.

At the beginning of the nineteenth century, the reading public was still restricted to an educated elite. The readers of Walter Scott, Jane Austen and even Charles Dickens were largely middle-class. According to Adeline Daumard, books were important household possessions for the Parisian bourgeoisie in the early nineteenth century. She found that 60 per cent of the professional classes left a personal library when they died, as did half of Parisian public servants and 35 per cent of the commercial bourgeoisie.[23] Later in the century, this middle-class public expanded to include a greater number of shopkeepers, artisans, office workers and even factory workers. This was a slow process, and it was not necessarily achieved by the provision of better education facilities. Conditions in nineteenth-century British classrooms, which were so powerfully attacked by Dickens, did not in any way encourage children to read books. Nevertheless, there was more leisure time available at the end of the nineteenth century, and the gradual reduction in working hours in the last quarter of the century made it possible for ordinary workers to become readers. Working-class reading will be considered more fully in the next chapter.

Smaller formats, lower prices

In post-revolutionary France, the pace of change was uneven but inescapable. Charpentier pioneered a revolution in the 1830s by producing novels in small in-18o (octodecimo) format (known as the 'in-18o Jésus'), rather than the customary larger and multi-volume in-octavo format, which had been designed for sale to *cabinets de lecture*. Charpentier made the text more compact, and reduced novels to one instead of three volumes, thereby reducing the price and expanding the clientele of purchasers. This was an important early breakthrough in the expansion of a mass reading public for cheap fiction. It was followed in 1855 by Michel Lévy's collection of contemporary novels at only one franc; and in the mid-1890s, Flammarion and Fayard priced their new series of fiction even lower. By 1913, French readers could buy classic novels for only ten cents a volume, while in Spain the one-peseta novel made fiction widely accessible from the 1870s onwards. The steady fall in production costs brought popular fiction within affordable range for more and more consumers.

In Britain, the multi-volume novel survived a little longer than in France. The three-volume novel ('three-decker') was produced for the circulating libraries so that they could hire out separate volumes of the same book to different customers simultaneously. The leading library, Mudie's, would regularly take enough copies of new releases to give publishers a secure income, which reduced their incentive to produce cheaper books. Cheap reprints and serialisation in the press, however, undermined the circulating library market, although it endured until 1894. Instead, publishers adopted a strategy of issuing titles at intervals on a descending price scale. If the best-quality five-shilling edition sold well, a cheaper edition at half the price would follow. If the market still looked promising, an even cheaper sixpenny edition was issued, on inferior paper with a larger print run. Authors did not necessarily like this treatment; for many of them, the good quality in-octavo production remained the high-prestige format they respected. Nevertheless, the demise of Mudie's assisted price-cutting.

The price of newspapers fell, too. At the beginning of the nineteenth century, the London *Times* cost seven pence, which put it out of range of workers. In 1836, the stamp tax on newspapers was reduced to one penny, which brought prices down, and the tax was abolished in 1855. In 1861, taxes on paper were also removed. By 1874, most daily newspapers in England only cost one penny. By concentrating on dailies, however, we lose sight of the Sunday paper, which became an English institution and represented the only reading of thousands of working-class families. A plethora of illustrated magazines churned out a diet of sensational melodramas, sentimental romances and thrillers set in exotic locations. One of the most successful of these was *Reynolds' Miscellany*, produced in eight-page issues in-octavo with a print run of 200,000. Others tried to raise the tone by providing more instructive reading, like Charles Knight's *Penny Magazine*, issued from 1832 to 1845, which had many imitators overseas. *Pearson's Weekly*, established in 1890, sold half a million copies per week, and in the USA the circulation of the *Ladies' Home Journal* passed the million mark in 1903.[24] Alongside the mass circulation daily, a multitude of periodicals and magazines now served the 'extensive reader'.

In the United States, the expansion of the press far outstripped population growth, and by 1900 there were 20 daily papers published for every one in circulation in 1850.[28] They still relied on subscription sales, boosted by a variety of bonuses and discounts, as enterprising proprietors offered new subscribers inducements such as packets of tomato seeds, watches, sewing kits, rifles and prize hogs.[26] By the end of the century, street sales were the norm: Randolph Hearst depended on his army of newsboys when he launched the Chicago *American* on 4 July 1900. The mass circulation daily – with its newsboys, kiosks and brash advertisements – defined city life, and its pages were a guide to its entertainments, jobs, places to live and its sleazy underworld of crime. Commuters devoured them morning and night.

As copyright law almost everywhere progressively transferred more and more classic novels and canonical works into the public domain, cheap reprints of the classics became extremely profitable. Flammarion, accordingly, launched a series of *Auteurs célèbres* at 60 centimes per volume in 1887, another series of *Meilleurs classiques français et étrangers* at 95 centimes and a *Select-Collection* which sold six million novels in four years at 50 centimes each.[27] In Germany, Reclam's *Universal Bibliothek* was launched in 1867 with a cheap edition of Goethe's *Faust*. By 1896, it had produced 3,470 items and was regarded as a national treasure.[28] The vogue for making classic literature available to all culminated in England with J.M. Dent's Everyman Library. This instantly recognisable series included hundreds of titles, all at one shilling per volume in small format and retaining high-quality production values.

Publishing by instalments, usually monthly, was a strategy adopted by many publishers in mid-century to reach readers who did not have the cash to spend on a book. Any kind of literature could be produced in this way, and it was – fiction, encyclopaedias and religious works were sold in separate episodes and reached an ever broader public. Emile Zola, Larousse's *Grand Encyclopédie Universelle* and even Karl Marx were marketed by instalments. In Spain, instalment publishing had an unusually long life. It was still popular in the early years of the twentieth century, when readers could buy episodes of *El Cuento Semanal* (The Weekly Story) at a street kiosk for 30 centimes, which was cheaper than a one-kilo loaf of bread.[29] Publishers deliberately timed the issue of each instalment to coincide with payday on Fridays.

Dickens' first title to appear in serial form was *Pickwick Papers* with Chapman and Hall in 1836, and after a slow start it achieved sales of 40,000 per episode. *Nicholas Nickleby* followed in 1839, with equal if not greater success. Altogether Dickens wrote nine novels appearing in monthly parts, costing 1 shilling each for an episode of 32 pages. As John Sutherland argues, this was a temporary phase. A single instalment was certainly cheap, but following through to buy the entire book over a year and a half was not at all economical, and it could cost the reader as much as a pound overall. By the 1860s, so many magazines carried fiction that instalment publishing was rarely profitable. Thackeray had succeeded in this form with *Vanity Fair*, but he abandoned instalment publishing in 1859 after *The Virginians* made a loss.[30] Dickens started his own magazine *Household Words* in 1850 for only two pence, followed by his *All the Year Round*. He published himself, Wilkie Collins and Elizabeth Gaskell and sold a regular 100,000 copies per month.

Magazine serialisation, like film rights today, was very profitable for authors, but it imposed a demanding rhythm of production. Novelists needed to write 20,000 words per month to keep up with the publisher's commitment to the public. Trollope mastered the discipline: he managed to produce novels while holding down a job in the post office, which makes him the Bryce Courtenay of the nineteenth century. Authors were paid by the line, which partly accounts for the interminable length of the works of successful writers like Eugène Sue, author of *Le Juif errant* (The Wandering Jew) and *Les Mystères de Paris* (The Mysteries of Paris), today almost unreadable. Sue made up his plot as he went along, and received letters from involved readers advising him on how to develop it. This was a precursor of the relationship sometimes enjoyed by television soap operas with their audiences. Authors became adept at sustaining a feeling of suspense and anticipation. Boston readers crowded the quays when the ship approached from London carrying the episode of *The Old Curiosity Shop* which would tell them the fate of Little Nell. The faithful reader of a long-running monthly serial was making an ongoing commitment and needed to be an expert in delayed gratification. He or she could not flick to the final pages of the story to preview the resolution of the mystery. A community of readers could develop, who discussed the developments of the last episode and the possible outcome of the next. Serialisation was used to good effect by Dickens, Trollope, Thackeray and Alexandre Dumas. Dumas became a writing factory, subcontracting his novels out to underling authors. The French critic Sainte-Beuve deplored such developments. In his 1839 pamphlet entitled *The Industrialisation of Literature*, he argued that great art could not be produced in such circumstances. Producing fine literature, however, was not always uppermost in publishers' minds. Some, like Pierre Larousse, had a pedagogic mission and were determined to bring knowledge to the people. Others were inspired by what Balzac diagnosed as 'la rage de gain' – the profit mania.

The publisher arrives

In 1839, when Sainte-Beuve lamented the increasing importance of money and the rising tide of mediocrity in literary life, he was most concerned about writers. He felt they were betraying their art by rattling off *feuilleton* episodes on demand. But what of the publishers, the people who were paying the mercenary authors he deplored? The publisher emerged as a specialised profession for the first time in the nineteenth century. He was now an entrepreneur, with responsibility for gathering investment funds and recruiting a stable of authors with whom he tried to establish a special relationship. Victor Hugo's complete works, for example, were so enormous that publication was just too expensive for most publishers to handle all at once. A large consortium of investors was required. In 1838, the Duriez company was formed to exploit Hugo's works, both written and unwritten, as if he were a high-yield oilfield. For a time shares in Hugo were quoted on the stock exchange.[31]

Publishing was a risky business and many in the trade lived on credit. Louis Mame went bankrupt four times between 1810 and 1837.[32] Werdet had slightly different problems. He became the publisher of Balzac, which was an interesting way of playing Russian roulette with one's career. The generous credit which Werdet extended to Balzac was one cause of his bankruptcy in 1837. In 1845, he went bankrupt again and became a travelling salesman, although he had to adopt a false name because creditors were still pursuing him in the 1850s. He died blind, unnoticed and penniless, unable to finance his own burial. Sophisticated financial management was now required for publishers to keep afloat in a world of cut-throat competition. A pioneer like Flammarion could succeed with an initial capital of only 2,000 francs and a bookstall by the Odéon theatre, but others like Charpentier, who had shown the way ahead in the 1830s, did not ultimately prosper because their financial grasp left something to be desired.[33] Publishers had a wide range of decisions to make, on the format and the retail price of a title, the terms of the contract with the author, the timing of reprints, the organisation of advertising campaigns and distribution strategies. Many of them saw themselves as intellectual leaders or as men with a responsibility to popularise knowledge and educate the masses. If they succeeded, they could become household names, like Larousse with his dictionary and Baedeker with his travel guides. In Britain, they united under the leadership of

Macmillan to impose the Net Book Agreement of 1899, which set the rules for bookselling and tried to eliminate wildcat discounting. Global recognition of copyright law gave them greater security against illegal book piracy. The international copyright convention signed in Bern in 1886 crowned a series of unilateral agreements between European states, and was an essential precondition for a global economy of the book.

In England, Macmillan, Murray, Longmans and other publishing families established themselves. Some British publishers were self-made men who had risen from very modest origins, like John Cassell, a former mill operative, temperance lecturer and tea and coffee merchant. They were inspired by a missionary zeal to educate the general public, by providing cheap encyclopaedias and magazines. In France, publishing played a prominent role in the advance of a capitalist economy. Family firms still dominated French publishing; indeed powerful dynasties emerged, like the Panckoucke-Dalloz and the Didot families. Family firms, however, did not always have the resources to remain self-financing, and they were increasingly transforming themselves into limited companies, like Paul Dupont in 1871 and Hachette in 1919. There was no income tax in nineteenth-century France, which helped to prolong the possibility of self-financing. Other publishers developed the 'vertical concentration' of the industry, buying their own paper manufactures at one end of the production process and bookshops at the other. They developed closer links with business and finance capital. They invested in land and industrial shares. The Garnier brothers, for example, made a fortune from the sale of erotic and obscene books under the July Monarchy, but they were also moneylenders and book exporters to South America. They invested massively in real estate in the Montparnasse district, and by the Third Republic they owned more than 40 Parisian apartment buildings. In fact, their income from real estate was four times greater than their profits from publishing. Similarly, after 1890, Calmann-Lévy moved his money into railways, public utilities, the Banque de France and Rio Tinto mining.[34] Publishing was now an integral part of the capitalist world. According to Christine Haynes, the publisher entered the social imagination as an 'evil genius', but he was also admired as a bold entrepreneur on a Napoleonic scale.[35]

They had to know their market, and they often began by specialising in a profitable niche. Ladvocat was the doyen of the French romantics in the 1820s, and was the model for Balzac's character Dauriat in *Lost Illusions* (as usual an excellent source). Didot on the other hand specialised in classical texts. By 1830, Louis Hachette had seen the potential of exploiting the demand for school textbooks, first at primary but subsequently also at secondary level. He produced a journal for the teaching profession (*Le Lycée*), which was his own best publicity medium. Hachette benefited from the support of Minister of Education Guizot and by the early 1840s he produced an average of 110 titles every year.[36] In the Second

Empire, he pursued the franchise on railway station bookstalls, inspired by the English example of W.H. Smith. This was a step out of educational books into general literature as well as a move towards greater control of distribution. In the decade of the 1860s, Hachette produced the huge total of 4,406 titles.[37] The Messageries Hachette became a major distribution company. Hachette was a ruthless boss with a very demanding work ethic, but when he died in 1864 he was an enormously rich example of the self-made man.

Publishers used posters, press advertisements and, above all, book reviews, to announce and promote their books. They developed a seasonal marketing strategy. Christmas began to dominate British production, and between 1850 and 1880, 30 per cent of all book titles published were issued for the Christmas season.[38] In France and Italy, collections of stories, poems and illustrations were produced as New Year gifts (*étrennes*), and everywhere the school prize market was substantial. Hetzel produced a superb full-length edition of a Jules Verne title twice a year for these markets.

The arrival of the railway brought newspapers like *Le Petit Journal* into the heart of the French countryside, and pushed the remaining *colporteurs* to the remotest rural areas. *Le Petit Journal*, founded in 1863 as a cheap, small-format daily selling for five centimes, was the first daily newspaper in France to conquer a provincial readership. By 1887, it had a print run of 950,000, which made it the largest daily in the world.[39] In contrast to its predecessors, *Le Petit Journal* had very few subscribers: it sold directly to readers through a national network of outlets. It was sold at Hachette's new railway kiosks, and distributed from depots set up in small towns. Itinerant vendors on bicycles, who were paid employees of the paper, collected it from station depots and then took it into the countryside.

Railway bookstalls were an important new departure. In 1848, W.H. Smith opened the first railway bookstall in London's Euston station. Soon, distinctive single-volume 'yellowbacks' sold to travellers were undermining the three-decker novel. Other publishers like Bentley and Routledge created their own Railway Libraries for this new market. In France, however, the right to sell at railway stations was jealously guarded by a single company. Having secured his monopoly, Louis Hachette created seven special series for the railway bookshops. Each one was cheap, relatively short, in the portable in-16o format, contained inoffensive material for a wide public and was colour-coded, including his *bibliothèque rose* (the pink library) for schoolchildren.[40] Hachette's bookstalls also sold books produced by other publishers, but at Hachette's prices. Although Flammarion wrested the franchise from Hachette in 1896, Hachette won it back again after 1903. Counterbidding from competing publishers forced up rents, but Hachette was shrewdly buying up newspaper suppliers. By the end of the century the

main business of the railway bookstalls was selling newspapers, which
accounted for three quarters of their turnover.

Libraries, reading rooms and bookshops

The growth of public lending libraries was very uneven, but they became
an essential part of the landscape in the age of mass reading. In France
they developed very late in the nineteenth century, and in Australia commercial lending libraries dominated the field until well into the twentieth.
Public lending fared better in Britain and the USA. A range of other institutions offered reading opportunities: at the end of the century, there
were lending libraries in factories and department stores, and libraries of
religious associations, political movements and trade unions. Only a few
of the possibilities are surveyed here.

In France, *cabinets de lecture* offered books for hire by the volume or
by the hour. Some were little more than kiosks, where passers-by could
hire newspapers for an hour or two. Others were offshoots of printing
shops. In Paris, a subscriber would pay about 3 francs per month and
another 15 or 20 centimes when he or she hired a book. The subscription was equivalent to a whole day's pay for a French worker, and the
clients of the *cabinets de lecture* were rather students and their girlfriends,
lawyers, doctors and respectable bourgeois. They needed little initial capital and were an attractive business proposition for a widow or a retired
soldier. Parisian *cabinets de lecture* were in their heyday in the 1830s
and the early 1840s, when there were over 200 officially authorised in
the capital, mostly in the Latin Quarter or wherever there was a passing
crowd – on the *grands boulevards*, near the theatres of the Boulevard du
Temple or in and around the Palais-Royal.[41] In other parts of Europe, the
cabinets de lecture endured much longer, because book prices did not fall
as sharply as they did in France. In Germany, some were huge businesses,
like the gargantuan Borstell and Reimarus establishment in central Berlin,
which in 1891 offered 600,000 volumes for hire on four storeys. Its pres-
tigious customers included Prince Bismarck and the historian Theodor
Mommsen.[42]

Whatever their size, reading rooms thrived because of the inadequacy
of library provision. The traditional library did not lend books. It saw
its main role as the conservation of rare objects rather than serving the
reading public. It opened only for a few hours each week, and catered for
a handful of scholars rather than the general public. In fact the librarian
might regard a reader as an unwelcome intrusion. One French librarian,
congratulated on his ability to keep readers out of the building, replied,
'Monsieur, do you think I would have accepted this position, if I was
obliged to get up constantly for the imbeciles who might come here to
read novels or poetry?'[43]

Of course provincial libraries had scant resources, and they were not staffed by professionals. Reform movements set out to change this and create lending libraries to serve the public. Public libraries, it was thought, would counteract the influence of socialist literature which had threatened society in the 1848 Revolution. For French liberals it was equally important to challenge the influence of clericalism over the masses. Lending libraries were designed to improve and edify the working classes and reduce their alcoholic excesses. In France, the Franklin Society and the Ligue de l'Enseignement (Education League) launched movements in the 1860s for the establishment of popular libraries and, by 1902, there were as many as 300 of them. We shall see in Chapter 11 what working-class readers made of them.

In Britain, legislation of 1850 enabled local councils to levy one half-penny in local taxation to finance library facilities, and this was doubled in 1855. This gave Britain its distinctively decentralised public library system. In 1902, Leeds, with a population of 400,000, boasted a central library and 14 branches open all day, together with lending and news-paper rooms.[44] Nothing on the European continent could match this, and in fact the imposing nature of public library buildings often deterred modest workers from venturing into their hallowed hallways.

In the United States, however, a mixture of local taxes and the generous philanthropy of Carnegie and others ensured a denser provision of pub-lic lending institutions, especially in Massachusetts. About 1,600 public libraries were built in the USA between 1886 and 1917 with funds provided by Andrew Carnegie, a poor Scottish migrant who became a millionaire steel manufacturer and large-scale philanthropist. Carnegie's vision of a public library was an imposing Italianate-style building, with a dome and a classical colonnade, preferably surrounded by a park. Carnegie aimed to provide books for the self-improving worker, but small-town middle-class administrators preferred their libraries situated far away from working-class neighbourhoods, and closer to churches and calm residential areas.[45] A daring plan for the library in Gainesville (Texas) in 1922 allocated a special 'negro reading room', and the local black population was expected to raise the money to stock it. It was to be situated in the basement of the building so that users would not inconvenience white readers. But the plan was too radical and was never implemented.[46] There was sometimes a tension between the elite's respect for institutions of high culture and its worthy desire to make them available to the unwashed masses. Libraries were designed in principle to bring culture to all, regardless of class, but in practice they seemed like sacred spaces, marble palaces where one dared not talk aloud, which intimidated readers instead of inviting them inside.

Book-buyers were better served than ever before. Bookshops assisted the democratisation of reading culture and promoted the acculturation of the rural masses. Like the *cabinets de lecture*, they were sometimes a sideline, run by a grocery or a hardware store. At the same time, they could be a centre for political activism. The establishment of a book-shop in a small town linked the provincial reader with metropolitan literary culture, and opened up possibilities for literary and cultural stan-dardisation all over the country. In France, in small towns with a retail bookshop, the cheap popular novels rolling off the presses in Paris were rapidly accessible to all social classes. In the mid-nineteenth century, the public library existed as yet only in embryonic form. For a brief historical moment, the retail bookshop became a vital agent of cultural uniformity, as well as a generator of publishers' and newspaper editors' profits. The creation of the national bookshop network, therefore, was a vital step in the building of a national, if not yet quite a global, village. In Germany, there was a retail bookshop on average for every 10,000 inhabitants by 1895, and the ratio was constantly improving.[47] In France, this kind of density had been achieved a little earlier in the century. Some regional dif-ferences persisted, but nationwide bookshop growth was flattening them out.[48] Capital cities were inevitably well provided with sales outlets. In Brandenburg and Berlin, there was a bookshop for every 3,700 inhabi-tants in 1913, while in Paris the corresponding ratio was already 1:2,000 in the middle of the nineteenth century.[49]

The sale of literature in the street formed another dynamic market. In France, this tended to be highly politicised, with high points for the sale of pamphlets and broadsides occurring at election time or during the controversies surrounding the Dreyfus Affair. In Spain, in contrast, street sales compensated for poor bookshop provision and for the fact that bookshops were for intellectuals and professional people and not welcoming places for the impecunious lower classes.[50] In Madrid, read-ers could buy directly from blind peddlers around the Puerta del Sol or from the occasional street kiosk, and instalment fiction episodes were even delivered to the subscriber's door. Mobile stalls in the city offered cheap and second-hand literature, especially for children. Madrid book fairs became very popular in 1930s, when booksellers sold everything at a 10 per cent discount. Republicans regarded such popular events as a very positive element of democratic culture, and the Second Republic spon-sored mobile book trucks to visit small towns. All kinds of new outlets now offered literature for sale. Books were sold in department stores, in railway platforms and on temporary stalls set up in city streets. In 1912 the German publisher Reclam even set up ten-pfennig slot machines to sell books in stations and hospitals.[51] The book was now an everyday object of mass consumption.

National markets

In Eliot's formulation, there were two stages in the industrialisation of reading.[52] The first began in the 1830s and belongs to the first half of the nineteenth century. This was the age of steam presses and the earliest railways. Alongside these icons of modernity, however, circulating libraries thrived and chapbooks were still sold by itinerant peddlers. Then, after 1870, a second transformation occurred, with the introduction of lithography, electricity, the sixpenny paperback, lending libraries, universal literacy and the mass circulation daily newspaper. This schema has a British ring to it, but the pace of development varied in other societies. The full impact of the railways was not felt in France or Germany until the last third of the century, and in some parts of Europe itinerant sellers and *cabinets de lecture* survived into the twentieth century although they had grown obsolete elsewhere. Eliot's summary gives prominence to technological changes, but in this chapter a wider range of transformations have been emphasised, including the emergence of the publisher as the forerunner of the modern capitalist entrepreneur and the development of a bookshop network.

In the last quarter of the nineteenth century, the mass circulation of cheap popular fiction brought about new cultural connections. The globalisation of mass culture started here, in the nineteenth-century mass market for fiction. The transformation of reading in the nineteenth century created integrated national markets. In eighteenth-century France, for instance, the only books which the whole country read were catechisms, prayer books and the lives of the saints. By the end of the nineteenth century, readers all over France were buying or borrowing novels like Hugo's *Notre-Dame de Paris* (The Hunchback of Notre Dame) or Dumas' *Les Trois Mousquetaires* (The Three Musketeers). A homogeneous reading public had been created, and the distinctive audiences of learned literature on one hand and the popular texts of the *bibliothèque bleue* on the other had become merged in the formation of a new mass audience. To adapt Eugen Weber's phrase, readers had become Frenchmen.[53] The creation of a national market in books was also an essential precondition for the unification of Germany. The same is true for Italy after 1861, although the growth of book production was geographically uneven, with Milan leading the way. A relatively high rate of illiteracy slowed down the development of a national reading public. Everywhere, this process required the advent of the railways to deliver books, a national banking system to make complex transactions possible, a national postal service to deliver newspapers and national systems of primary education to socialise young readers.

The role of education in all this, however, should not be exaggerated. Universal literacy was achieved in Britain and France before national systems of free, primary education had been fully established. The influence of formal education was no more than intermittent in Western countries until the 1880s. Without formal schooling, beginners used a multiplicity of extra-curricular avenues to reading and writing, starting their apprenticeship in literacy with family members, neighbours, workmates, priests and employers, to name just a few resources available. New categories of readers joined the reading public, which expanded to include firstly the lower middle class of shopkeepers, clerical workers, artisans and craftsmen, but eventually unskilled workers as well. By the end of the century, even the European peasantry was learning to use the instruments of written culture. When universal primary schooling did become established, learning to read and write moved from home to school. The access to written culture thus became divorced from the rhythms of work and family life. School-based reading created a new social and national identity which obliterated divisions of class, religion and ethnic origin to create a more standardised public culture.

11

New readers and reading cultures

The half century between the 1880s and the 1930s was the golden age of the book in the West: the first generation which acceded to mass literacy was also the last to see the book unchallenged as a communications medium either by the radio or by the electronic media of the twentieth century. The reading public had acquired several new layers and the book had reached a mass readership. It had become 'desacralised', an everyday object of consumption like soap or potatoes. This chapter will consider two important sectors of the mass reading public: women readers and workers. Women, of course, had always been part of the reading public, but they had never loomed as large as they did in the nineteenth century, or posed such acute social problems as readers. Working-class readers were another new element of the reading public and, as in the case of women, their reading was regarded by elites as problematic. More people could read than ever before but, according to French commentator Arnould Frémy writing in 1878, the book was being swamped by an ocean of triviality produced by the newspaper press. The press was encouraging rapid and superficial judgements, presenting 'an immense bazaar of facts, interests and ideas in which the most serious contemporary issues rub elbows daily with the most futile details of everyday life'.[1] Today's educators often complain that people read too little; the nineteenth-century complaint was that people read too much, too indiscriminately and too subversively. Mass reading was a new social problem.

Chapter 10 introduced some of the fundamental conditions which brought a mass literary culture into existence. This chapter focuses the spotlight directly on readers themselves. It considers what we know of the preferences and practices of women and working-class readers. Their individual responses to attempts to guide and supervise their reading must be recognised. As Jonathan Rose provocatively argued, we must 'interrogate the audience' and unearth clues to their reactions.[2] Workers and women were not passive readers, ready to be shaped and disciplined. They were active readers quite capable of either accepting or resisting the reading models urged upon them and, in spite of all the difficulties they faced, of improvising their own literary culture.

The new readers of the nineteenth century were a source of profit, but they were also a source of anxiety and unease for social elites. The 1848 Revolutions were partly blamed on the spread of subversive and socialist literature, which reached the urban worker and a new audience in the countryside. In 1858 the British novelist Wilkie Collins coined the phrase 'The Unknown Public' to describe the 'lost literary tribes' of three million lower-class readers, 'right out of the pale of literary civilisation' because they never read a book.[3] He referred to the readers of illustrated penny magazines, which offered a weekly fare of sensational stories and serials, anecdotes, readers' letters, problem pages and recipes. The readers of the penny novels included many domestic servants and shop-girls, 'the young lady classes'. According to Collins, 'the future of English fiction may rest with this Unknown Public, which is now waiting to be taught the difference between a good book and a bad'. England's new readers, who never bought a book or subscribed to a library, provided middle-class observers with a sense of discovery, tinged with fear.

The female reader: in search of a place of her own

The handicaps under which all but the wealthiest women had laboured were disappearing. The historic discrepancy between male and female literacy rates was narrowed and finally eliminated by the end of the nineteenth century (see Chapter 7). Girls' education expanded, but continued to lag behind that of boys everywhere in Europe. At the end of the eighteenth century, only 9 per cent of pupils in Russian state schools were girls, and in Navarre (Spain) in 1807 boys' schools outnumbered girls' schools by two to one. In France, the first training colleges for female schoolteachers were not established until 1842, but by 1876 over two million French girls attended school.[4] The provision of more formal schooling for girls therefore followed, rather than preceded, the feminisation of the reading public. Expanding opportunities for female employment (as teachers, shop assistants or postal clerks) and changing expectations of women did more to raise the level of female literacy. The nineteenth century witnessed the emergence of women writers and intellectuals who were the descendants of the eighteenth-century 'bluestockings'. Women writers, pilloried mercilessly by satirical journals like *Le Charivari* as a threat to domestic stability, made their mark. A few individuals like George Sand were notorious, but this should not disguise the more general contribution made by literary women everywhere in the nineteenth century. The *femme de lettres* had arrived.

The role of the female reader was traditionally that of a guardian of custom, tradition and family ritual. Pierre-Jakez Hélias, recalling his own Breton childhood at the beginning of the twentieth century, recalled that the lives of the saints had been part of his mother's trousseau:

> In the house, aside from my mother's prayer books and a few collections of hymns, there were only two large volumes. One of them, which was kept permanently on the window sill, was Monsieur Larousse's French dictionary...the other was closed into the cupboard that my mother had received as a wedding gift. It was *The Lives of the Saints*, written in Breton.[5]

This account links a series of cultural dichotomies based on religion, language and gender. The maternal wedding chest was a hoard of religious knowledge, in opposition to the Larousse, a treasure of lay wisdom. *The Lives of the Saints* (*Buhez ar zent* in Breton) represented Catholic France, while Larousse was an emblem of secular republicanism. Hélias' mother's chest was, at the same time, Breton-speaking territory, while the windowsill supporting Larousse was a kind of altar devoted to the French language. *The Lives of the Saints* was a specifically female preserve, and the traditional image of the woman reader tended to be of a religious, family-oriented reader, far removed from the concerns of public life.

The new woman readers of the nineteenth century had other, more secular tastes, and new forms of literature were designed for their consumption. Cookery manuals, like *La Cuisinière bourgeoise* in France, and Mrs. Beeton's guide in Britain were important blueprints for middle-class behaviour, and were designed to help the mistress of the house instruct her servants better. Recipes and advice on etiquette were incorporated into women's magazines alongside fashion news. The *Journal des Dames et des Modes* (Ladies' and Fashion Journal) was a pioneer which lasted from 1797 until 1837, carrying engravings and descriptions of both male and female outfits. Gradually, fashion magazines began to reach a more popular readership – a trend indicated in France when *la femme* (woman) replaced *la dame* (lady) in magazine titles. By 1866, *La Mode illustrée* (Fashion Illustrated) had a print run of 58,000, with its combination of fiction, household hints and sumptuously illustrated fashion pages.[6]

Weekly illustrated magazines flourished during the Second Empire in France, many of them based on English antecedents like the *Penny Magazine* or the *Illustrated London News*. *Le Journal illustré*, for example, was a weekly, established in 1864, with eight pages in folio format. One or two pages were taken up with an illustration, and other features included views of Paris, puzzles, some European news, society chat and theatre news. In 1864, an entire issue written by Alexandre Dumas and Gustave Doré boosted circulation to 250,000.[7] Such weeklies, costing ten centimes and sold at street kiosks, were becoming an integral part of mass urban culture. *Les Veillées des chaumières* (Evenings at the Cottage) catered specifically for female readers, and promised something more moral and uplifting than its competitors. *Les Veillées des chaumières* had two columns of text, with very few breaks except chapter headings. Only in the twentieth century did women's magazines discover the value of breaking up the text and of interspersing it with illustrated advertisements. In so doing, the magazine offered a kind of fragmented reading, more perfectly attuned to the interrupted working rhythm of a modern housewife.

Women readers and the novel

For contemporary publishers, the woman reader was above all a consumer of novels. They offered series like Werdet's *Collection des meilleurs romans français dédiés aux dames* (Collection of the best French novels dedicated to women) or fiction for *le donne gentili* (gentlewomen) offered by Stella in Milan. Such titles were making a claim to respectability, attempting to re-assure both male and female purchasers that the contents were suitable for delicate eyes. They tried to corner a particular sector of the market, but at the same time they encouraged the growth of a female reader's subculture. This development ultimately restricted, rather than expanded, sales, and the practice was rarely continued beyond the Restoration period (1815–30). Nevertheless, to create a series defined by its public, rather than its material contents, was a new development in publishing.

The novelist Stendhal emphasised the importance of the female reader. Novel-reading, he claimed, was the favourite activity of French provincial women: 'There's hardly a woman in the provinces who doesn't read her five or six volumes a month. Many read 15 or 20. And you won't find a small town without two or three reading rooms (*cabinets de lecture*).'[8] Although women were by no means the only readers of novels, they were regarded as prime targets for popular and romantic fiction. The feminisation of the novel-reader seemed to confirm dominant preconceptions about gender roles and the nature of female intelligence. Novels were held suitable for women because they were seen as creatures of the imagination, of limited intellectual capacity, both frivolous and emotional. The novel was the antithesis of practical and instructive literature. It demanded little in intellectual terms, and its sole purpose was to amuse readers with time on their hands. Above all, the novel belonged to the domain of the imagination. Newspapers, reporting on public events, were usually a male preserve; novels, dealing with the inner life, were part of the private sphere to which nineteenth-century bourgeois women were, in theory, confined.

This implied a certain danger for the nineteenth-century bourgeois husband and *paterfamilias*: the novel could excite the passions and stimulate the female imagination. It could encourage unreasonable romantic expectations; it could make erotic suggestions which threatened chastity and the stability of marriages. The nineteenth-century novel was thus associated with the (supposedly) female qualities of irrationality and emotional vulnerability. It was no coincidence that female adultery became the typical novelistic form of social transgression in the period, from Emma Bovary to Anna Karenina and Effi Briest, for seduction and the novel were closely linked. Flaubert's Emma Bovary became the archetype of a woman ruined by her reading fantasies. Emma, dissatisfied with marriage to a well-meaning but boring country doctor, devoured poetry and erotic romances which inflamed her imagination and led her into illicit affairs which were ultimately no more satisfying than her marriage. Emma Bovary's romantic reading precipitated her search for fulfilment, her disastrous adultery and descent into bankruptcy, and her eventual suicide.

Reading had an important role in female sociability at every social level. In Indiana in the 1880s, the women of the Hamilton family, studied by Barbara Sicherman, constituted a multi-generational reading club. Their reading sessions involved reading aloud, discussions of books, sewing and gossiping.[9] In pubs and *cabarets*, men discussed public affairs over a newspaper, while fiction and practical manuals, in contrast, changed hands through exclusively female networks. One Bordeaux writer commented in 1850: 'These days society is split into two great camps; on one side the men, who smoke and gamble, on the other the women and young girls, whose life is divided between reading novels and music.'[10] When readers of both genders came together, the woman was often in a position of tutelage to the male. In some Catholic families, women were forbidden to read the newspaper. More frequently, a male would read it aloud. This was a task implying a moral superiority and a duty to select or censor material.

While the man was expected to read the political and sporting news, women appropriated the sections of the newspaper devoted to *faits divers* and serialised fiction. The territory of the newspaper was thus thematically divided according to gender-based expectations. The *roman-feuilleton*, or serialised novel, was a subject of everyday conversation among women readers, and many would cut out the episodes as they were published, and paste or bind them together. The improvised novels so created could be passed on through many female hands. As a shoemaker's daughter from Provence, born in 1900, explained,

I used to cut out the serials from the journal and rebind them. We women passed them round between us. On Saturday evening, the men went to the café, and the women used to come and play cards at our house. The main thing was, that's when we swapped our serials, things like *Rocambole* or *La Porteuse de Pain*.[11]

In this way, women who might never have bought a book improvised their own library of cut-out, or re-sewn and often-shared texts.

Conventional readers and non-conformists

Oral historians who have interviewed women about their family's reading practices in the period before 1914 have become familiar with a few common attitudes. The commonest female response, looking back on a lifetime's reading, is to protest that there had never been any time for reading. For women and their mothers, 'I was too busy getting on with my duties', or 'Mother never sat down idle.' Peeling potatoes, embroidery, making bread and soap left no time for recreation in the memory of many working-class women. They recalled that as children they feared punishment if they were caught reading. Household obligations came first, and to admit to reading was tantamount to confessing neglect of the woman's family responsibilities. The idealised image of the good housekeeper seemed incompatible with reading.

Working-class women, however, *did* read, as oral historians have also discovered – magazines, fiction, recipes, sewing patterns – but they persisted in discrediting their own literary culture. Interviewees frequently described their own fiction-reading as 'trash' or 'nonsense-reading', a waste of time which offended against a rather demanding work ethic. Such women, encountered by oral historians in France and Australia, denied their own cultural competence.[12] They accepted conventional expectations of the woman as housekeeper, intellectually inferior and a limited reader. Those who violated these stereotypical patterns read in secret. For them, books provided furtive and illicit enjoyment. Lavinia Swainbank, a housemaid in an English stately home in 1925, read her employer's books, which was a common but dangerous practice. Winifred Foley, a general maid, was beaten by her 90-year-old mistress in the 1920s for reading *Uncle Tom's Cabin*.[13]

Alongside conventional readers and female readers who were in denial that they read anything at all, we find many examples of rebel readers who protested against the intellectual restrictions imposed on them. Emma Goldmann, for example, was in conflict with her father, who wanted her to marry young and responded to her refusals by throwing her French grammar onto the fire. Goldmann wrote in her autobiography:

Girls do not have to learn much! All a Jewish daughter needs to know is how to prepare *gefilte* fish, cut noodles fine, and give the man plenty of children . . . I would not listen to his schemes. I wanted to study, to know life, to travel.[14]

Through independent reading and study, women found freedom and a new sense of identity, but this could create problems and family tension. In New York in the 1890s, Rose Cohen rented books from soda-vendors to read nightly with her family. Reading helped her escape from her ghetto on the Lower East Side, but as she read more Gentile books and mixed with more Gentile people, her father felt threatened and her own loyalties appeared confused. Reading raised difficult questions for Rose Cohen about her identity as a Jew and as an American.[15]

One young girl who struggled for her independence as a reader and a woman was Margaret Penn, autobiographical author of *Manchester Fourteen Miles*. First published in 1947, the book described the author's life near the northern English city of Manchester in about 1909.[16] Margaret, or Hilda, as she called herself, had illiterate and devoutly Methodist parents. She read all the family's correspondence aloud, and she read the Bible to her parents. As a young teenager, she began to borrow novelettes from the local co-operative library. Her parents, however, objected to her reading anything except the Bible and books from Sunday school. They further wanted to confine her reading to Sunday.

Hilda, however, persuaded the local Anglican vicar to give his approval to her borrowing from the co-operative library. She read *Robinson Crusoe* and *Tess of the D'Urbervilles*, which would have shocked her parents, as would her choice of the best-selling Victorian melodrama *East Lynne*. Her parents, however, were forced to accept the advice of the vicar, but Hilda's illiterate mother remained suspicious of any book that Hilda would not read aloud. Hilda refused to go meekly into domestic service as her parents demanded. Instead, aged 13, she left for Manchester to begin work as an apprentice dressmaker. She had encountered constant attempts to prevent her from indulging in 'idle reading'. Her difficulties were severe, since her parents would at first tolerate nothing but religious reading, and insisted on oral reading as a means of supervision. Her crime was aggravated by the fact that she was a girl, who had no business thinking about education or improving herself. Hilda's father blamed reading for her refusal to accept her destiny. Perhaps it was a symptom rather than a cause of Hilda's desire for liberation.

Women of the middle or lower middle classes rarely faced such obstacles as readers. Even if they could not afford to buy books regularly, they became regular customers at public lending libraries. This was especially true in large cities. In the lending libraries of the Paris *arrondissements* in the 1880s and 1890s, there was a substantial proportion of women readers – about half the total clientele in the first and eighth *arrondissements* (the Louvre and the *faubourg* St. Honoré), and about one-third in Batignolles.[17] Unemployed women, described by librarians as *propriétaires* (property-owners) or *rentières* (living off a private income), reinforced the demand for novels and recreational reading in late-nineteenth-century lending libraries.

As never before, the female reader compelled recognition, from novelists and publishers, from librarians and parents keen to discourage time-wasting or to protect their daughters from imaginative fancy or erotic stimulation. The problem was not only what women read, but how they read. They were accused of reading in a superficial and 'desultory' way. At the end of the nineteenth century, when there was an intense collective neurosis about racial decline, women's desultory reading was condemned as one symptom of degeneracy, which emasculated and orientalised the race.[18] There was an assumption that women read in an identificatory way, that they became deeply implicated in the desire and suffering experienced by fictional characters (although there is no clear evidence that women readers identify with fictional characters any more than men do). Medical discourse underpinned common prejudices, by asserting that women's low brain-weight indicated inferior intellectual capacity, while the distinct shape of the female brain supposedly denoted greater powers of affectivity and intuition than the male could muster. Too much study was debilitating for women, and over-stimulation from novels could bring on hysteria and loss of fertility. For women, reading was considered a severe health hazard. 'I shall carry to my grave', wrote novelist George Eliot in 1839, 'the mental diseases with which [novels] have contaminated me.'[19]

Catholics, liberals and later feminists all converged to propose reading models designed to drag women away from sensational fiction. Whether the purpose was to bring women back to Church or to give them more realistic expectations of marriage, the message was the same: read some history and carefully chosen literature and do so more systematically. 'Read doggedly', as Lucy Soulsby rather charmlessly put it:

> I say to you, read doggedly; the snare of a free life is desultory reading. Make any plan of stiff reading you like, and stick to it for one year, writing out notes of what you read, and you will be fitter for real work if it comes, as come it will.[20]

Romance reading and feminist reading

No one could stem the tide of romantic fiction, represented today by Harlequin, Silhouette and Mills and Boon. Mills and Boon, whose name is synonymous with the formula romance genre in the twentieth century, was founded in 1908, and began life publishing Jack London and successes like *The Phantom of the Opera*. The company narrowly survived the Depression and started to specialise in romantic fiction from the 1930s. They pushed conventional values of marriage, domesticity and motherhood, reacting against the more racy fiction which had characterised the pre-1914 years. Mills and Boon stories were always told from the heroine's viewpoint, inviting reader identification. Their popularity rested until quite recently on maintaining a strict sexual morality – the Mills and Boon heroine was always a virgin at marriage. They relied heavily on orders from libraries and serialisation in women's magazines, and established their name long before they launched into paperback publishing. W.H. Smith's library reported in 1950 that an average Mills and Boon novel was borrowed 165 times.[21] Mills and Boon published hundreds of unknown authors, none of whom became star commodities: instead, the publisher was the brand name.

Was women's romance reading purely escapist? On one hand, it can be argued that romance fiction tranquillised women, guiding them docilely towards their domestic role. Publisher Alan Boon seemed to reinforce this interpretation when, in the 1980s, he compared the effect of reading Mills and Boon to taking valium.[22] On the other hand, romance fiction could empower female readers. Instead of accepting easy generalisations, we must interrogate the audience. Janice Radway did exactly that, interviewing a group of romance readers in the American Midwest. These romance readers felt they participated in a large and exclusively female community of readers and writers. They were critical readers who wanted heroines who were independent and intelligent and not at all passive. The women readers Radway questioned saw their romance reading not as an act of conformism which reinforced a patriarchal ideology but rather as a claim to female independence. For the romance readers of Smithton, the act of reading was in itself an assertion of the right to privacy, and a temporary refusal of their everlasting duties as wives, mothers and housekeepers. Romance reading, Radway argued, was a mild protest against the emotional demands of husbands and children.[23]

Romance reading alone does not define the female reader. From the end of the nineteenth century onwards, the feminist press promoted an alternative reading model: it addressed a putative reading community of emancipated women. In the English-speaking world, this imaginary reading community of New Women had its own genealogy, tracing its literary ancestry back to Mary Wollstonecraft, and descending through George Eliot to Olive Schreiner. Reading lists were prescribed, to draw female readers away from melodramatic fiction and to urge on them the importance of more serious reading on political issues, the extension of the franchise or the eradication of poverty. The 'new woman' was educated, independent, and not necessarily married. She was interested in politics and science, as well as art and history. She might well be a pacifist, and she was almost certainly opposed to the common male vices of drinking and gambling. She was encouraged to be a discriminating reader, not a casual or 'desultory' one. The elements of a suffragette library prescribed by *The Woman's Voice* in 1895 included works on slum housing, alcoholism, and illegitimacy.[24] It offered, with Aveling and Bebel, a brief introduction to European socialism. It promoted the ancestors of the movement in Britain, like Wollstonecraft and the examples in Charlotte Stopes' *British Freewomen*, from Boadicea onwards. The politicised woman reader was thus provided with a broadly European agenda.

Women's reading, then, was not merely escapist but could lead to greater participation in public life. Consider Adelheid Popp, born in 1869 in Vienna of Czech parentage, and deprived of a formal education when her drunken father died and she had to contribute to the family income. As a young girl, Adelheid consumed romantic and historical fiction.[25] When she claimed she was being sexually harassed by her factory boss, her illiterate mother told her dismissively that she must have been reading too many novels. When she was 15 years old, her mother threw all her novels out of the house. Looking back, Adelheid described this as a pre-socialist period, when she accepted all kinds of falsehoods. She had believed in miracles and gone on pilgrimages. She had accepted anti-semitic propaganda uncritically and took an unhealthy interest in the life of the Imperial family. Then Adelheid experienced a reading metamorphosis, which took her way from the inner world of romance literature and into public political debate. A fellow worker introduced her to the Social Democratic press and she started to borrow books from the local workers' library. When she read Social Democrat literature aloud at work, the clerical staff would say that she spoke 'like a man'.[26] In her autobiography, she described her trepidation at being the only woman present at her first political meeting, how she overcame her fear, became increasingly articulate and took up political journalism. In 1892, she became editor of *Arbeiterinnen-Zeitung*, and after the First World War she was elected to the Austrian National Assembly.

Her reading trajectory illustrates two faces of the working-class woman reader. At first, she was a very private reader of romantic and historical fiction. Her reading was subjective, solitary and it nurtured sentimental fantasies which she later rejected. In her second reading phase, Popp read socialist philosophy, history and party newspapers. She had undergone a profound reading transformation. Her reading no longer led her into an interior world of romance, imagination or religious devotion. Instead it introduced her to party meetings, where she stood up to express the viewpoint of militant women. It led to trade unionism, journalism, periods of imprisonment and election to parliament. Through her reading experience she had found a full-time career in the public arena.

Working-class readers

New readers from the lower middle classes, aspiring artisans and white-collar workers swelled the clientele of lending libraries everywhere. A gradual reduction in the working day allowed greater opportunities for reading among the working classes. In England, a 14-hour day was commonplace in the early nineteenth century, but by the 1870s London artisans normally worked a 54-hour week. In Germany, on the other hand, a reduction of daily working hours was achieved very slowly after 1870. Shortly before the First World War, the Reich Statistical Office determined that of 1.25 million workers whose conditions were regulated, 96 per cent worked fewer than 10 hours.[27] In addition, domestic lighting improved when oil-lamps started to replace candles in the 1830s, followed by paraffin lamps after mid-century and gas-lighting at the end of the century. All this made reading less painful.

These difficult conditions explain why leisure was seen principally in terms of physical recuperation, and why, when asked what they did in their leisure time, German workers almost invariably thought of Sundays. Although they enjoyed reading, according to the *Verein für Sozialpolitik*, their favourite leisure activity was going for a walk in the fresh air. According a survey of working families in Dresden carried out in 1900, 16 out of 87 families had no printed matter at home at all. But others had socialist literature, dictionaries, encyclopaedias and illustrated magazines. Half the families surveyed had some general literature in the house, and 10 per cent owned classics by authors like Goethe and Schiller. Many expressed a preference for Emile Zola's novels.[28]

More conventional readers consumed 'Penny Dreadfuls' or their American counterparts, the dime novels. Penny Dreadfuls were booklets which contained stories of horror and adventure, specialising in the heroic deeds of notorious bandits like Robin Hood or the highway robber Dick Turpin (Figure 11.1). The dime novels, pioneered by the New York publishers, Erastus and Irwin Beadle, were usually short paperbacks (about 35,000 words), and had a lurid cover (Figure 11.2). By definition, they only cost ten cents and were available in news-stands all over the country. Between their covers, cowboys and Indians competed for the attention of the worker or adolescent in search of literary excitement. The Western genre, specialising in stories of frontier violence and often featuring Buffalo Bill, was very popular in the 1870s and 1880s, but the dime novels were not all about the Wild West. They also included romances and adventures at sea, and they developed urban settings in detective stories like the Nick Carter series. The term 'dime novel' was soon being used to describe all forms of cheap fiction, published between 1860 and 1915, and destined as entertainment for the masses. The dime novel went into decline in the 1890s and completely lost its popularity after the First World War. By

Figure 11.1   The Penny Dreadful.
Note: This American 'Good News' series provided a sensational illustrated story each week. © Library of Congress.

then, consumers had turned to other forms of entertainment, like motion pictures, radio and pulp fiction magazines.

Lending libraries and the worker

The movement to make public libraries more accessible was inspired by a desire to direct workers' reading away from such sensational material and into safe channels. Chapter 10 introduced the Carnegie libraries, but

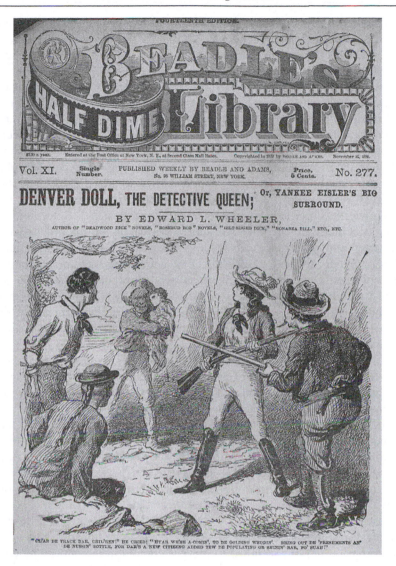

Figure 11.2 The dime novel.
Note: The dime novel was pioneered by Beadles. Their half-dime library issued stories in only 5c instalments. © Library of Congress.

here we concentrate on the relationship between the public library and working-class readers. Public lending libraries had a philanthropic and a political purpose. Like factory schools, they were envisaged as instruments of social control, designed to incorporate a sober working-class elite into the value system of the dominant classes. Charles Dickens, opening the Manchester Library in 1852, saw libraries as a guarantee of social harmony. Books, Dickens proclaimed to great applause, would give the worker self-respect, and teach him that capital and labour were mutually dependent.[29] Correctly designed workers' reading, it was hoped, could neutralise class conflict in the industrial age.

There was considerable reader resistance, however, to the libraries' attempts to provide moral and edifying literature. Lending libraries in France and Britain had some difficulty in recruiting large numbers of working-class readers. The evidence from late-nineteenth-century France suggests there were four main categories of lending library users, although the proportions of each varied according to their demographic environments. Firstly, there were property-owners and those living from an investment income. These included many women borrowers and amounted to 20 per cent of readers in Paris and Rouen.[30] A second category was made up of office workers, who usually composed between a quarter and a third of the lending libraries' customers. Secondary school students formed a third category, which was very prominent in the provinces. Lastly came the workers, who only made up between 10 and 15 per cent of library users in Paris in the 1890s, although the percentage would rise to about a quarter in other cities. In Manchester, the proportion may have been as high as a third.[31] Workers were always in a minority amongst library borrowers.

Libraries were very suspicious of working-class readers. The imposing neoclassical architecture of many civic buildings in provincial Britain constituted what Hewitt calls a kind of 'architectural intimidation' for the visitor. All would-be users in Manchester needed to present a reference and the names of two guarantors who would make good any damage or lost books.[32] Elsewhere, too, public libraries did not offer a welcoming environment. In Spain, remarked Domingo Fernandez Area in 1864, 'they do not serve the people in any way...poor people in their boots and damp, torn clothes don't venture into these imposing halls.'[33] If they did venture inside, they were likely to encounter a police presence to discourage disorderly conduct and deter tramps and drunks looking for somewhere warm to sleep. In England, libraries had book disinfection apparatus installed to prevent contagion introduced by contaminated readers. The floor plan of many libraries would enable a supervisor to watch several reading rooms at once. The librarian at the desk could observe the entries and movements of any reader, according to a surveillance model common in prisons as Michel Foucault emphasised.[34]

The problem was that readers demanded fiction. Instead of the improving and informative literature which public libraries and the British Mechanics' Institutes provided, the customers overwhelmingly borrowed recreational literature. In German workers' libraries, for example, there was a wide discrepancy between the actual tastes of readers and the expectations of the Social Democratic Party. Of almost 1.1 million borrowings from German workers' libraries recorded between 1908 and 1914, 63 per cent were in the *belles-lettres* category.[35] In the 1880s and 1890s, more than half the borrowings from Parisian municipal libraries were of novels.[36] Many librarians became very frustrated at the tendency of readers to refuse what was good for them. They tolerated the situation at first, on the grounds that once a reader was enticed into using the library, he or she would eventually 'graduate' to higher and more improving literature. This was the 'landings' theory, in which the reader entered on the ground floor, but could be persuaded to climb the staircase to discover history, philosophy and useful knowledge on higher landings. The need to censor library materials, however, suggests that this notion was a fallacy. Reading habits could easily go from bad to worse and needed to be disciplined. In Manchester, *Moll Flanders* was removed and neither Boccaccio's *Decameron* nor Casanova's *Memoirs* survived for long in a library catalogue anywhere. In France, a library commission rejected Macchiavelli's *The Prince*, Anatole France and much of Balzac. In the 1880s, *Anna Karenina*, Ibsen and Thomas Hardy were not considered suitable for French public libraries, either.[37]

The popular reader, patronisingly known in France as 'le grand enfant' (the big child), had a mind of his or her own. A lithographer, Girard, set up a 'popular library' in the third *arrondissement* of Paris and tried to evade municipal surveillance for as long as possible. At Le Creusot in 1869, one 28-year-old worker, Dumay, formed a 'democratic library' which organised support for a republican candidate in 1869, and for a 'no' vote in the 1870 plebiscite on Napoleon III's regime.[38] In Britain, the working-class readers enthusiastically chronicled by Jonathan Rose had an extraordinary reverence for canonical texts.[39] It was common to find self-taught British workers who cited Shakespeare and the romantic poets. The proletarian canon was a conservative one, and Rose's readers worshipped the classics. The working-class intelligentsia resisted contemporary modernism and preferred books by dead white males. Series like Dent's Everyman Library gave them the Great Books they demanded at prices they could afford. But this did not mean they were subservient readers. On the contrary, they took from their 'Hundred Great Books' exactly what they wanted, testing them against their own sense of realism and notions of social justice. They detested the condescension of T.S. Eliot and Virginia Woolf, but novelists who had a sense of justice and who understood the poor, like Charles Dickens and Victor Hugo for instance, got the seal of approval. *Robinson Crusoe* was read on one level as a tale of shipwreck and adventure. It was also read as a fable of individualism, of man free to fashion his life using his manual skill, independent of God and social hierarchies.[40] The self-taught reader was no blind follower of orthodoxy.

Reading and self-improvement

Self-educated and self-improving workers formed a distinctive interpretive community of readers. In the nineteenth century, they fought
grinding poverty and material handicaps to improvise a literary culture. They were both poor and lacking in educational qualifications. The
self-taught worker, deficient in both inherited and acquired cultural capital, was forced to accumulate it through his or her own efforts and
by unorthodox means. Excluded from the kinds of cultural consumption enjoyed by the well-off, the autodidact inevitably became a usurper
of cultural property. He or she was an interloper who had been denied
access to an envied cultural world.

Self-improvement – material, moral and intellectual – was a very
demanding objective. It required serious application and self-abnegation.
Time had to be set aside for the acquisition of knowledge, money had to
be saved for the purchase of books, sleep was sacrificed, health dete-
riorated, friendships were put at risk by the fervent determination to
read and to know. The goal of self-improvement was often inspired by
a non-conformist Protestant faith, and often went hand in hand with
taking the 'pledge' to abstain from alcohol. Temperance and Protestant non-conformity were expressions of a common *habitus*. Planning
a personal budget in order to save money for future needs and the purposeful use of leisure time, together with the choice of books and the
consumption of food and drink, were all cultural practices generated by
a shared aesthetic. This aesthetic valued the work ethic and the post-
ponement of personal satisfactions. It could be seen as a strategy aimed
at distinguishing the self-improver from other workers.

Young men working as clerks in the shops and offices of nineteenth-
century Boston and New York wrote self-improving diaries, in which
they charted the difficulties of forging a life of their own away from
home, and reinforced their determination to maintain moral discipline in
a materialistic and amoral world. The clerks analysed by Thomas Augst
read useful and profitable works, went to lectures and borrowed books
from the New York Mercantile Library.[41] The discipline of regular writing was important to maintain their ties with home, and it strengthened
the will to resist the sin and temptation of the city. Moreover, writing
improved their handwriting, which was an essential professional skill and
also a source of pride and achievement.

Reading, for those working-class autobiographers intent on self-
improvement, was an earnest and difficult task. Their reading was
concentrated and purposeful. It was, in many ways, an 'intensive' mode
of reading, relying heavily on repetition, recitation and oralisation as
aids to memory. Autodidacts had a specifically ardent and determined
relationship with their texts. One characteristic feature of the self-
taught intellectual was the extremely demanding course of reading he

(only a tiny minority were women) set himself. At a certain point the reader would be struck by the revelation that his reading had been desultory, indiscriminate and poorly directed. He determined to pursue a more purposeful reading plan in future. This turning point has been effectively described by Nöé Richter as 'the conversion of the bad reader', when the autodidact resolved to renounce his 'bad' reading habits.[42]

'Bad' reading habits meant reading too much idle fiction and recreational literature. Novels were condemned as futile amusements which should be discarded for more serious reading. The readers' aim was self-instruction, and they were contemptuous of recreational reading purely for its own sake. When they did turn to fiction, they looked for novels which spoke to them of their own hardships, and which had some serious social comment to make. They compared fictional worlds to their own, and judged them according to their own standards of realism. It was on these terms that British workers appropriated the work of writers like Victor Hugo and Charles Dickens. What Dickens imparted to George Roberts, a new Labour Member of the House of Commons in 1906, was 'a deep and abiding sympathy with the poor and suffering'.[43] Similarly, what the Chartist William Lovett appreciated most about Dickens were his heart-piercing exposures of hypocrisy and callousness, especially the attack on bureaucracy in the description of the Circumlocution Office in *Little Dorrit*.[44]

Ned Peters, who wrote a very detailed account of his reading on the Australian goldfields in the 1850s, was an exemplary member of this community of self-improvers.[45] Like the group of workers already mentioned, he made a conscious decision in 1833 to fight temptation and to improve his mind. He read non-fiction for his own edification, relying chiefly on Chambers' *Papers for the People*. Much of his reading was Protestant in flavour, including Paxton Hood and Oliver Goldsmith. He approved of a few novels, provided they were, in his words, 'founded on fact'. Over half of the titles Peters read fell into the categories of travel, geography, political biography and history.[46] He relied heavily on the exemplary biography, often used as an educational model by writers of advice books like Samuel Smiles (*Self-Help*) and George Craik (*The Pursuit of Knowledge Under Difficulties*).

There was a regular rhythm to Peters' reading. It was predominantly a Sunday activity: in 1855, 41 per cent of his diary entries about reading were on a Sunday. But Peters seemed to weary of the regular reading discipline he had imposed on himself. On one Sunday in November 1855, he confessed that his dutiful reading of Chambers' *Papers* 'became irksome'.[47] The life of the German philosopher Fichte left Ned 'tired and careless about reading'. Peters' diary hints at the conflicts and difficulties created by the disciplined and highly structured reading regimes of self-improving readers.

Acquiring self-culture was a collective enterprise. In Florida, immigrant cigar workers employed a reader to read aloud books and pamphlets of their choice as they worked. Sometimes the employer was only too happy to find such a way of keeping his or her workers quiet, and of helping them to concentrate throughout their monotonous day. When Elizabeth Flynn visited such a factory in Tampa in 1913, she heard a radical reading of a pamphlet on birth control.[48] Workers pooled their efforts in Mutual Improvement Societies, which made learning into a co-operative venture. In the Cheviot Hills, shepherds left books for each other in the crannies of stone boundary walls.[49] In London, a radical group of policemen (not necessarily a contradiction in terms) clubbed together to share readings of Proust, Gibbon and Tom Paine, and to go to promenade concerts. This seething working-class literary and musical culture was underpinned by the enthusiasm for personal emancipation. In Rose's bubbling compendium of the British working-class intelligentsia, we find worker-poets, artisan botanists and Lancashire construction workers reciting Tennyson. There are brass bands, Welsh male voice choirs and the Hallelujah chorus drowning out the throbbing of the looms in a Blackburn cotton mill. Rose further analysed the libraries of Welsh miners, finding that 'the miners' institutes of South Wales were one of the greatest networks of cultural institutions created by working people anywhere in the world'. By the Second World War, the Workmen's Institute of Tredegar circulated 100,000 volumes per year, and boasted an 800-seat cinema. Here the influence of Methodism, combined with a sense of Welsh cultural independence and the solidarity of close-knit mining communities, helped to establish a thriving working-class literary culture in the 'underground university' of Glamorgan.

The Victorian earnestness on which the culture of self-improvement was based now seems to belong to another planet. The pits started to close and the collection of the Tredegar Workmen's Institute was broken up in the 1960s. Universal education made the autodidact an extinct species and the growth of commercialised leisure industries dethroned print culture. For a short period at the end of the nineteenth and beginning of the twentieth centuries, it had reigned supreme as a source both of entertainment and of self-liberation.

12

The democratisation of writing, 1800 to the present

Alongside the expansion of the reading public and the increasing accessibility of books, a parallel transformation was taking place: the West was learning to write. Even people of quite humble origins made extensive use of writing in the nineteenth century, and this includes the peasant societies of Europe which had not yet become fully literate. The writings of the poor do not always fit into accepted literary genres like autobiography or the private diary; these were predominantly, but not exclusively, middle- and upper-class genres of writing. It would be a mistake, however, to assume that the illiterate cannot speak to us because they left no written traces. As this chapter will show, the traces are there if we take the trouble to look for them.

The gradual democratisation of writing is an essential aspect of the passage to modernity, although the process followed different rhythms in different national contexts. A deterministic approach to cultural modernisation would be inappropriate; the widening access to writing took various routes and a homogeneous process is not assumed here. In France, for example, this period of transitional literacy stretched from the Guizot Education Law of 1833 up to the writing frenzy of the First World War. In Italy, we need to focus the microscope on a slightly later period, from unification in 1861 up to at least 1918. In Spain, universal literacy was only achieved in the 1960s. In different ways and divergent contexts, ordinary people grappled with writing technology, and appropriated it for their own everyday uses.

What, then, were the functions of everyday writings in the nineteenth century? Writing was an essential part of middle-class culture. Nineteenth-century men and women of the bourgeoisie were prolific writers of letters, private journals and diaries. Love letters, family correspondence and *journaux intimes* indicate the multiple uses of personal writing in the past. This chapter will begin by considering the importance and some of the many purposes of *écritures intimes* or, as Dutch and German scholars prefer to call them, 'ego-documents'.

The private journal

Personal diaries take many different forms: sometimes they are an accumulation of short notes recorded at odd moments, like the ideas Stendhal scribbled on his braces; in other cases, they are more reflective and the result of considerable re-copying and editing by the author. They are a hybrid genre displaying varying degrees of privacy and secrecy. Some writers used codes to make sure intruders could not decipher their innermost thoughts: in his Charenton journal, for example, De Sade signalled a sexual experience by the symbol Ø; while Victor Hugo's troubled daughter Adèle disguised her thoughts in a form of *verlan*, a code in which letters, syllables and entire words are inverted (*verlan* = an inversion of 'à l'envers' or backwards).[1]

The personal diary, however, was not always private. It was customary in the nineteenth century for husbands to read their wives' diaries, and sometimes write entries in them, as the poet Percy Shelley did for his wife Mary. According to some theorists, the author does not write for himself or herself alone. The writer of a journal always consciously or sub-consciously addresses a real or imaginary reader, perhaps the ideal mother or a dead friend. Diaries may thus contain an element of posturing, and in Lynn Bloom's phrase, there may be 'an audience hovering on the edge of the page'.[2]

Feminist scholars have analysed personal diaries in order to retrieve and validate women's voices, and to argue that women's journal writing deserves better than to be classified as a minor literary genre.[3] Clearly, gender differences may determine not only writing practices but also the content, nature and structure of personal narratives. According to J.-P. Albert, twice as many French women keep a private journal as do men, and their writing practices differ markedly.[4] Most female writers abandon their diary before the age of 20, whereas journal-writing for men is more likely to be an activity of adulthood and middle age. The *journal intime* was a place where notions of female subjectivity could be defined. In some cases, the journal was a refuge for a woman's stifled emotions, a withdrawal into a private space where she allowed herself to express the feelings (erotic, resentful, disloyal) she dared not utter publicly.

The private journal was an instrument in the formation of a personal identity, and assisted the growth of female individuality in a patriarchal environment which made this problematic. The private journal, however, had many other purposes besides identity construction. When Philippe Lejeune advertised in 1988 in the *Magazine littéraire* for journal-writers willing to talk about their journals, he received over 40 responses. They showed that developing a personal identity is only one part of the story. Writers kept a journal to leave something for their children, or they wrote as a member of a group or for professional purposes.[5] Several of Lejeune's correspondents did not necessarily see their journal as intimate, and they envisaged other readers of their work in the present or future. Some simply wrote for pleasure. Others were afraid of death and the cruel passage of time, and they wanted to capture something of their life on paper while they could still do so.

We should consider private diaries in terms of multiple functions. There were travel diaries, dream journals and philosophical journals. There were adolescent diaries which may have had a masturbatory function. There were working journals, like those kept by the painter Ingres, or by Dostoevsky, who conducted a private written discussion of *The Idiot* in parallel to his work on the novel itself. And here we have only considered canonised authors and eminent artists.

For young Catholic girls, writing a diary was an important part of their religious education. In their spiritual diaries, they spoke to God, recorded comments on their edifying reading and conducted a daily examination of their innermost thoughts and moral conduct. For Eugénie de Guérin, who wrote one of the best-known models of a spiritual diary, her journal was an instrument of redemption and a way of mourning her brother.[6] For Eugénie and others like her, the process of journal-writing involved an intense process of self-reflection. As Béatrice Didier has suggested, we might see the nineteenth-century journal as a secularised version of the obligatory *examen de conscience*, playing a confessional role and containing self-criticism which once might have been voiced in prayer or to a priest.[7] Journal-writing was thus an essential instrument in the moral education of young girls. They were often given diaries as presents to encourage them to use them for this purpose. A tutor, usually their mother, watched over the activity, insisting on regular entries and probably reading over what the young girl had written. This supervision was particularly intense in the period leading up to First Communion, an important moment of spiritual initiation.

Contemporary French adolescents tell us that they feel an absolutely imperative need to write. According to Marie-Claude Penloup, 'children and adolescents need writing in order to function just as their bodies need an active nervous system'.[8] The Rouennais students she interviewed wrote lists, songs, jokes and stories, and devoted hours to leisure-time copying, even to the extent of copying out entire novels. The majority of such writers were female. We can find nineteenth-century adolescent girls, too, for whom writing was a necessity of existence. Philippe Lejeune reports that the pre-nuptial years from 15 to 20 are the optimum age for journal writers.[9] A sense of vulnerability or the onset of severe emotional stress were often reasons for starting a diary. Coming to terms with marriage was a major theme in the diaries of middle-class adolescent girls, and self-writing helped to prepare them for the ordeal. After the wedding, maintaining a private journal could seem quite incompatible with married life. The common destruction of private diaries at marriage suggests they were, particularly for girls, a rite of passage between adolescence and maturity.

In Caroline Brame's journal, for example, the young author attempted to come to terms with the anguish of her impending marriage.[10] Caroline was the daughter of a high-ranking public servant living in Paris in the *faubourg* St. Germain in the early 1860s, and keen to make an advantageous marriage. Not only had she seen her friends' marriages decimate her network of female companions, but now she herself faced an arranged marriage to the man she knew only as 'Monsieur Ernest'. Caroline was probably in love with Albert Dumont, the brother of a friend, but her family ordained that her husband would be Ernest Orville, ten years her elder, whom she did marry less than three months after being introduced to him. The diary, interrupted by Caroline's marriage, was a way of both expressing and controlling her personal feelings and frustrations. It signified her realisation that there were some emotions she was duty-bound to keep to herself. For Caroline, her personal journal was a means of controlling her 'egoism', whenever it came into conflict with her allotted destiny.[11]

The example of Caroline Brame may give the impression that anguished adolescent journals are the special domain of rich well-educated Catholic girls. If so, the impression is largely correct. But we may achieve some perspective and balance by briefly citing a counter-example: the journal of the young and lonely Pyrenean shepherd, Jean-Pierre Baylac.[12] Before his death from pleurisy in 1920 at the age of only 20, Baylac filled 60 handwritten notebooks, containing about 20,000 pages in all. He commented on his reading, which included Michelet, Proudhon, Lamartine and the popular novelist Ponson du Terrail, all borrowed from the local schoolteacher's library. The journal contained all his adolescent longings, masturbations, sexual desire and experiences, jealousies, sex with sheep on his lonely hillside (he called it *le crime*) and magical invocations. He recorded the punishments he inflicted on himself when he gave in to sexual temptations. He covered the front page with melancholy mottos: 'Naître, pleurer, aimer, lutter, chanter, souffrir, et mourir' (Be born, weep, love, struggle, sing, suffer and die), and 'Le génie ne fleurit que sur la terre des douleurs' (Genius only flourishes in the soil of grief). Baylac was eaten up by love, desire and guilt. In spite of his humble status, he had mastered the power of writing for the most intimate purposes.

Personal writings also had 'literary' qualities. Intimate writers among contemporary French adolescents were attracted by what Penloup has called the 'literary temptation'.[13] Private diaries often exhibit formal literary characteristics, such as alliteration, rhyme, balance, the insertion of unusual words. Writing clearly gave these teenagers pleasure. Even for the most humble authors, it seems, writing has some non-utilitarian value. Writing was seen as something which had to be polished and improved, as a struggle with words, a construction with materials carefully chosen or borrowed. The act of writing imposed its own little rituals and sensual satisfactions, as this 40-year-old French schoolteacher told Philippe Lejeune:

> Every morning, I come back to my diary.
> A rendezvous I can't miss. A pleasure I can't miss, which gives me heart to continue working at it.
> Before I even open it, I caress the cover – one that I have chosen for its texture and colour. My fingers linger over the threadbare areas, over the stains, those marks of time.
> Then I play it like an accordion, which opens and closes, with its fan of gaudily-coloured pages.[14]

Writing, then, is a physical pleasure, and an absolute necessity, as testimony and as an unavoidable means of existence.

Correspondence and family networks

Personal or intimate correspondence only formed a small proportion of the mounting body of letters mailed in the nineteenth century. A random sample of 608 letters in the French Postal Museum, dating from between 1830 and 1864, suggests that only 15 per cent of letters sent from Paris were personal, and this includes many formal announcements of births, marriages and deaths.[15] Of the 158 million postal items franked in France in 1849, personal as opposed to business correspondence accounted for little more than 10 per cent of the total.[16] Although the volume of postal items went on rising, there is no reason to suppose that the proportion of personal letters increased.

Sending a letter was an expensive operation, but the introduction of the Penny Post in Britain in 1840 potentially transformed writing practices. A flat postage rate, and the novel idea that payment would be made in advance by the sender instead of on delivery by the recipient, was to revolutionise personal and business communications. The reality was that posting letters remained a luxury in Britain for at least another generation, but cheaper and more efficient rail transport made possible a huge increase in the volume of mail in circulation. In 1849, following the British example of the Penny Post, France introduced a postal rate of 20 centimes, fixed regardless of distance and payable in advance. This encouraged the use of letter-mail, even if for many years writers often declined to pre-pay, believing the post office would take better care of their letters if there was money to be collected on delivery. The Paris basin dominated the geography of French letter-writing. With little over 3 per cent of the nation's population, Paris received 27 per cent of France's mail, according to the postal enquiry of 1847.[17]

International comparisons put French letter-writing into perspective beside the prolific epistolary culture of English-speaking countries. In 1891, the average number of letters generated per capita in France was just 19. This was considerably fewer than the 52 letters posted annually per inhabitant in New South Wales, according to the Postmaster-General's estimates at the end of the century, and even further behind Britain, where, by 1900, the postal service provided 60 deliveries of letters and postcards per capita, surely the highest rate anywhere in the world.[18] In 1900, Milan generated 20 letters per head, and Rome only 10.[19] These variations indicate different stages of popular acculturation, and different degrees of integration into national and international commercial networks.

New practices and new gestures had to be developed – streets had to be named and houses numbered, mailboxes invented and post offices set up. The users needed education in standard epistolary practices, like how to use an envelope, how to address it and how to seal it. Within a very short time, lobby groups like the Anti-Corn Law League in Britain had seen the possibility of mailed propaganda. By the 1860s, the mail-order catalogue was established, while Christmas cards grew in popularity from the 1860s and 1870s.

Surviving letters provide historians with valuable archaeological evidence, in the forms of the criss-crossed correspondence of nineteenth-century lovers, eager to fill every space on the page, the letters of friends, cousins and acquaintances, the black-edged letters of death, the announcements of pregnancies, miscarriages, births, weddings, illnesses and accidents. They include more ephemeral communications, such as the Valentine cards and the mountain of postcards produced since the early years of the twentieth century. They include even the imaginary letters, never sent, which Annabella Boswell, for one, nevertheless copied into her 'letter-book' as a young girl.[20]

We are accustomed to think of personal correspondence as a very intimate medium of written communication. The notion of correspondence, however, as a private dialogue between absent individuals is not always appropriate, given the collective nature of much letter-writing, and attempts by parents and husbands to supervise it. In 1790, the French Revolutionary National Assembly, keen to defend individual rights, decreed the inviolable confidentiality of correspondence. Such measures prevented postal workers from reading mail, and they were based on emerging ideas about private property, which made letters the property of their addressee.[21] Nevertheless, prefects could intercept and confiscate mail until the Third Republic. French fathers claimed a right of surveillance over the correspondence of their wives and children, but this right was increasingly contested in the wife's case at the end of the century. We may speculate that many women destroyed their letters in order to avoid detection by male family members.

Courting rituals and family solidarities often prevented love letters from being privately written or received. Letters written between a courting couple were customarily overseen by the girl's mother, and they had to pass through her hands. Personal intimacies could only be exchanged within the demands of existing group and family networks. In the voluminous correspondence of the Mertzdorff family, spanning from 1795 to 1933, there are shared letters with multiple authors, each family member adding a little in their own handwriting, as well as letters which are dictated to a third party, letters addressed to several recipients at once and letters designed to be copied and passed on to other members of the group. We know that even letters between the Mertzdorff spouses were read aloud on receipt *en famille*, because on one occasion Charles specifically wrote a paragraph to his wife Eugénie asking that it should NOT be read out.[22] Amongst the lower classes, the concept of individual privacy was probably even less respected. In many rural areas of France, the postman's job was not only to deliver the mail, but to read it out aloud.

Correspondence kept families together, defined their internal dynamics and guaranteed the cohesion of the familial community. About half of the letters in the Mertzdorff correspondence were exchanged between parents and children. About 10 per cent were letters between spouses, who normally corresponded with each other daily when temporarily separated by a business trip, a holiday or exceptional events like war or the siege of Paris. Another 10 per cent of letters were written or received by brothers and sisters, and another 10 per cent were between girlfriends (who were often cousins).[23] A dense fabric of relationships within bourgeois families was strengthened and perpetuated by regular and energetic letter-writing. The rhythm was dutifully maintained over generations. In the Mertzdorff family, women would write in bed or when they were about to dress or be undressed.[24] In other words, women would establish an intimate décor for the act of writing, while men would retreat to the study.

The dynamism of the family network was sustained by the rhythm of reciprocal exchange. The language may be discreet, but we must remember that the real recipient is not the private individual but the family itself. In the Mertzdorff family, Caroline thanked her friend in February 1858 for writing a less intimate letter than before, because her latest letter could be 'shown and read *in familias* which produced the best effect in the world'.[25] Of course there were strict limits to the publicity of correspondence: collective rituals like reading family letters were designed to exclude as much as to include. They defined the family group by shielding it from intruders from the outside world. Family letters would discuss health, social visits, forthcoming marriages and births, occasionally local politics and the maidservant problem. They would never discuss romance or open up about family dramas, and they rarely mentioned anything happening outside the family.

Correspondence is a highly coded form of writing, obeying generally accepted conventions, applying and adapting unspoken formulas. These formulas are the expression of shared rituals and clearly defined networks of sociability. Correspondence fills an absence, and constitutes a ritual of separation. It is further based on the mutual exchange of pleasure given by the letters and on sacrifices undergone to write and send them. Any exchange of correspondence relies on an implicit agreement about the rules to be observed. This is the 'epistolary pact', a contract to which the correspondents tacitly subscribe.

The length of letters was one delicate point of negotiation. The 'epistolary pact' demanded that a long letter should receive a letter of equal length. Most commonly, writers used a folded sheet, giving them four pages to fill. Often they overflowed into the cross-writing characteristic of letter-writing in the period between friends, lovers and close relatives. If time and inspiration were available, the writer took another sheet to add another four pages.

Specific forms of address and farewell define the tone of the relationship, encouraging familiarity or establishing distance. The spouses of the Mertzdorff family addressed each other as 'mon bon petit mari' (my good little husband) or 'ma chère petite femme' (my dear little wife). Charles called his wife 'ma chère amie'.[26] The final formula, which late-nineteenth-century etiquette manuals prescribed in minute detail, was perhaps the most important part of any letter. In Léon Gambetta's secret correspondence with his lover Léonie Léon, which generated 6,000 letters over 10 years before the politician's death in 1882, the couple were rather more amorous than Charles Mertzdorff. Gambetta called Léonie his 'gracieuse et tendre nini' or his 'chère mignonne adorée' (dear adored darling). But when Charles Mertzdorff called his wife 'his dear friend', he was suggesting a partnership based on equality. In the Gambetta–Léon correspondence, as Susan Foley points out, Gambetta called Léonie 'tu', while she addressed him with the more respectful 'vous', implying a more unequal relationship between the senior republican politician and his lover.[27]

This should not disguise the fact that personal contact in the nineteenth century tended to become, in its written forms, more expressive and more effusive. In spite of Léonie's reserve, *tutoiement* (the use of the familiar 'tu') became normal and appropriate, and words of affection could expand into hyperbolic extremes, offering 'a thousand tendernesses' (*mille tendresses*) or 'a million kisses' (*un million de baisers*), or into phrases like this one from a disappointed lover cited by Marie-Claire Grassi: 'Your long silence has quite tortured me, you have apparently forgotten the colour of my imagination.'[28]

Many authors of love letters fantasised about their happiness in a future home. As well as this *lieu de rêve*, the love letter had its shared memories, and its sacred site where the lovers first met and declared their feelings for each other. Personal anniversaries were recorded and celebrated by corresponding lovers. A certain fetishism was also apparent in the exchange of personal objects like locks of hair, a ritual sometimes reproduced today when photographs are enclosed. The love letter itself could become a fetish-object, and could be re-read, kissed and carried on one's person. All these strategies were common elements of the reception and practice of intimate writing.

'Ordinary Writings', extraordinary authors

Antonietta Procura was a tobacco worker in Trento in north-eastern Italy, born in Verona in 1888. Caught in the war zone in 1915, Antonietta was forced to evacuate her family home and took her belongings with her in a wooden trunk. In the course of this exile, she wrote a memoir of her life in pencil on the inside of the trunk, now in the Italian Historical War Museum. The trunk 'contained' her life in exile, its story written mainly in Trentino dialect and full of grammatical errors.[29] The improvised nature of Antonietta's autobiographical trunk is characteristic of the writing of the poor and uneducated. Their texts are close to oral speech and dialect, and their authors have some difficulty in keeping a straight line and in observing the rules of syntax and correct spelling. Above all, they challenge the myth that the illiterate or the semi-literate have been silent throughout history, as historians perhaps too easily assume. The voices of the poor and the uneducated may take improbable forms but they are waiting to be discovered.

Some forms of ordinary writing are obvious and well-used historical sources, such as autobiography or private correspondence. But there were many other forms, too, including memoirs of exceptional events, like Defoe's plague journal. There were *livres de famille*, which chronicled the family, its economic life, assets, debts and creditors. There were commonplace books, miscellanies and *zibaldoni*, that is, the anthologies or notebooks in which Italian peasants wrote addresses, prayers, accounts of the vintage, wills and contracts. The Finnish peasant woman Kaisa Juhantytär took up her pen to write defiantly 'I can sing Hallelujah, no matter what the world says' – an early example of feminist hymnwriting.[30] In addition, Finland had a long tradition of handwritten newspapers, produced by individual workers or perhaps by several anonymous contributors. There were life stories produced under duress, solicited by confessors or by the Inquisition. There was travel writing by journeymen, pilgrims and conquistadors. In the nineteenth century, the mass of spontaneous or ephemeral writings was swollen by the addition of birthday cards, Valentine cards, Christmas cards, holiday postcards, letters of congratulation or of condolence, and the standardised letters to announce births, marriages and deaths. These communications were important not for what they said, but simply because they had been sent.

Graffiti, too, have proliferated from ancient Rome to the present-day flourishing of urban frescos and the graffiti festivals which emerged in Europe in tandem with the rebellious culture of rap and hip hop. Mural writing decorates the ghettos of New York, and a notable explosion of display writing covered the urban territory of Paris in May 1968. At all times graffiti have ridiculed prominent figures, recorded an individual's presence for posterity or, in the contemporary city, made a violent attempt to appropriate prohibited space. In July 1917, Parisian railway inspectors at the Gare du Nord carefully recorded all the graffiti scrawled over the troop trains bringing soldiers back from the front. They took down 189 inscriptions from 43 trains, preserving all the original spelling mistakes, suggesting the depth of mutinous protest behind the front as well as in the trenches where a real mutiny occurred.[31]

Ordinary people have always experienced writing as an instrument of power, the means by which monarchies and bureaucracies impose taxes, enforce military recruitment and justify their domination in law. For example, the burning of the *terriers* (seigneurial title deeds) by the French peasantry in revolt in 1789 may be seen as the vengeance of rural illiterates against the power of written culture.

When Judy Kalman observed the professional writers working at their stalls on the Plaza San Domingo in Mexico City, she frequently came face to face with the political realities of writing.[32] The scribes working on the Plaza were literacy brokers, needed by the poor (and not-so-poor) in a society where literary competence was very unequally distributed. Kalman reported that scribes were often asked to produce legal documents, applications to local government bodies, tax returns and a range of official letters which clients knew had to be written well if they were to negotiate successfully with the authorities. They knew they needed a typed letter, they believed in its authority, they knew there was a certain formula to use when addressing the municipal authorities, and they feared the consequences of ignoring these necessities.

Two momentous events changed the cultural world of the European peasantry between the mid-nineteenth and early twentieth century: the Great Migration to the Americas and the First World War. Both generated an unprecedented quantity of writing. This was writing of absence and desire, as semi-literate workers and peasants struggled to communicate with loved ones from whom they were separated by exceptional circumstances. Letters to and from migrants were usually public property, read aloud in a family group or, as in Scotland, read from the pulpit by the local minister. Migrants' letters could sustain an imagined community linking home and diaspora with ties of culture, language and religion. Polish emigrants to the USA and South America at the end of the nineteenth century imagined themselves returning home. 'Dear Parents', wrote Ignatius Kalinowski in 1891, following a common formula, 'We step across your threshold and we greet you and we kiss your hands and feet.'[33] Such letters tried to make absence disappear and because of their very particular form of greeting they are known as 'bowing letters'. Normally, the first letters written home after departure were the longest and were sent at a faster rhythm. In time, the new life ceased to be a novelty and became a routine, a new family was established, letters became shorter and the intervals between them longer, to the extent sometimes of losing contact with one's family of origin.

The First World War also produced a massive outpouring of letter-writing, by peasants whose literary capacity has often been underestimated. Italy, during 3½ years of war, produced 4,000 million items, in spite of the fact that 35 per cent of Italians were officially illiterate on the eve of the war.[34] France produced about 10,000 million postal items, and Germany at least 30,000 million during the First World War. The years of 1914–18 engendered 'a sudden and irrepressible bulimia' of letter-writing, an absolutely diluvian outpouring which defied all attempts at administrative control.[35] The war spawned a massive and possibly unique corpus of popular literature which could not be contained in spite of the attempts of postal censors and administrators.

In their writings peasants and soldiers struggled to construct order out of chaos and to organise the confusing experience of exceptional upheavals like the war. They wrote to retrace a journey, real or metaphorical, and to discover some meaning in it. Italian soldiers immersed in the mud of Serbian trenches filled notebooks with nostalgic memories of home, family and their *paese*. They expressed a heightened sense of religiosity, imagining themselves as Christ on the via Dolorosa, or claiming the protection of the Madonna. One or two had literary pretensions, like the peasant Sebastiano Leonardi, a reader of Dante, who described his own very personal descent into Hell.[36]

In addition, ordinary writings were addressed to God. Churches and pilgrimage sites were, and some still are, covered in graffiti, and receive written prayers addressed to Jesus, the Blessed Virgin, saints or intercessors. In Lourdes, tiny written messages are stuck into every crevice of the grotto where the miracle is said to have occurred. In other churches, like St. Rita's in a working-class district of northern Paris, anthropologists obtained access to the written messages furtively delivered to a favourite saint. In some cases, they appeal for help in a family trauma, or beg for a cure to save a terminally ill parent or spouse. Or, like this message written by a redundant salesman to the Virgin Mary in the Daurade Church in Toulouse in 1987, they ask for a job: 'You know my wish: to get my job back in Mammouth [a department store], preferably in the sportswear section.'[37] If the prayer is unanswered and the situation does not improve, the author may return to repeat the message. Saints are human after all, and they have human weaknesses. They may forget to respond to the original prayer, in which case they need to be tactfully reminded of it; or perhaps they have so many requests on their hands that they need a special reason to deal with this one urgently. Such supplications were written along these lines: 'You remember me, Gesù mio, full of mercy, I'm the one who wrote you the note on green paper about my mother who is dying of cancer, if you could see your way to helping me in my trouble', and so on.

Writing, it seems, has a lasting power which lends efficacy and intimacy to communication with God and the saints. The mounting quantity of mail directed heavenwards in the twentieth century is a massive archive of human anxiety, suffering and maladjustment. It also suggests the importance of the written word in our time, and the unexpected range of its applications in daily life.

Mediated literacy

In the transition to full literacy, various forms of mediation and assistance were required. One strategy for the semi-literate was to refer to a third party or a public writer. George Blakers, cutting timber near Port Stephens in New South Wales in the 1850s, acted as a scribe for a 'neighbour' who, aware of Blakers' reputation for literacy, rode nine miles to ask him to write a letter.[38] In the First World War, a certain number of soldiers' letters were composed by dictation to third parties, but it was probably even more common for them to be read by an intermediary at their rural destination. One illiterate Spanish emigrant to America saved all the letters he received from his sister and niece, although he could not read them until he found another migrant who could do so for him. Tragically, his family interpreted the absence of news from him as a sign that he had died.[39] Public writers could be hired to compose official documents and private letters. Such intermediaries have always existed to cater for those on the margins of functional literacy. Sometimes the intermediary is found within the family. In the late nineteenth century, for example, children of school age were given responsibility for writing and reading aloud by older generations, and similar patterns have been observed in immigrant families with school-age children.

French peasants in the nineteenth century frequently referred to intermediaries in their village to write letters to higher authorities. For instance, when in 1855 a policeman's widow from Loupiac (Gironde) wanted to exempt her son from paying school fees, she approached the mayor to draft the necessary petition.[40] Rural schoolteachers too were often involved in such extra-curricular activities, acting as town clerks, giving advice about mortgages and wills and writing letters for local inhabitants. Recourse to scribes has always been a necessity for the semi-literate in periods where the bureaucratic needs of the state were expanding. When public authorities require increasingly technical responses to tax demands, judicial processes or other administrative necessities, the demand for public writers is likely to increase.

Enlisting a scribe was risky: a third party tended to recycle a small stock of conventional phrases, and to deliberately omit uncomfortable expressions of emotion. When Antoine Sylvère wrote for his family to his father, who was away from home sawing wood, he was just not prepared to transcribe all the insults that his mother wanted to heap on her husband.[41] The power of the scribe and the vulnerability of the author were well illustrated in the film *Central do Brasil*, whose principal character is a public writer who puts up her stall in the main railway station of Rio de Janeiro. The illiterate is at her mercy; for one thing, she can censor the text, and for another, she never posts her clients' letters, although she is paid to do so.

Letter-writing manuals, or advice about correspondence in etiquette books, are another kind of mediating influence. In Europe as a whole, the benchmarks in the art of correspondence were the letters of Madame de Sévigné, Jean-Jacques Rousseau or Erasmus; for Spain, add Philip II and Saint Teresa de Jésus; for Britain, add Charlotte Bronte and Charles Lamb. For centuries, epistolary manuals had been destined for a cultured elite, and they continued to be based on models inherited from courtly culture until, in the late nineteenth century, they began to adopt more democratic forms. Later their value went into a slow decline, as schools taught children how to compose a letter, and school textbooks began to reproduce model letters.[42]

The manuals provided model letters to be adopted, and they advised on the most respectable methods of using the page, in which the amount of blank space at the beginning and the close was in direct proportion to the desired dignity and formality of the correspondence. Thus *Beeton's Complete Letter-Writer for Gentlemen* advised that 'the body of the letter begin about one-third from the top of the page'.[43] The form of the letter of course differed by gender: in the manuals produced in Spain in the early twentieth century, men were only supposed to use white paper and either black or blue ink; whereas women could use any colour of paper and different inks too.[44] A single woman took a risk in writing a letter to anyone but a child or another woman. According to Dymock's *Letter-Writer*, published in Sydney in the first years of the twentieth century, a married woman would always enclose her card to indicate her married status.[45] The quality of the paper had to be chosen carefully depending on the social status of the sender and of the recipient. Postcards (according to Dymock's again) should not be used to call in a debt. Lined paper clearly denotes a weak level of writing competence (as perhaps does the habit of writing only in capital letters). Manuals incorporate a sense of hierarchy and unspoken social values. Like conduct books generally, they helped to formulate a gendered identity.

Conduct books were directed at readers and writers with an incomplete mastery of writing skills. Members of this target audience were literate, but did not feel confident enough to write to a lover, a prospective employer or a distant relative without assistance. These readers aspired to gentility, but were apparently likely to leave ink blots or make grammatical errors, since they were frequently admonished on these matters. They were told to order their thoughts and to be prudent and discreet. There remains an inherent problem in letter-writing manuals: simply using them as a resource to copy out model letters mechanically would not help anyone to confront a blank page in future. In addition, there was a grave risk that the recipient would realise that the letter had been copied from a manual.

The uses of personal writings were thus many and various. Private journals might constitute a form of psychotherapy. They might aid a mourning process, as in the case of Eugénie de Guérin, or assist anger management, as in the case of George Sand, when De Musset had left her. They offered pious exercises for the young and obedient. They pacified the pre-nuptial angst of young women about to enter unknown sexual territory in a marriage not of their own choosing.

'Ordinary Writing' embraces a wide range of genres or 'ego-documents', some familiar to the historian like diaries, correspondence and autobiography. It also includes the trivial and ephemeral writings which give order to our existence (like account books), aim to seduce (Valentine cards) or make a protest (graffiti). Its proliferation demonstrates the broadening access to writing by the semi-literate and illiterate. Sometimes they used third parties and scribes who entered a dynamic and collaborative, if not always equal, relationship with authors; occasionally they may have referred to letter-writing manuals, and slowly they came to terms with the new postal services of the second half of the nineteenth century.

Ordinary writings belong to an 'amphibious culture', in Marina Roggero's phrase, moving between the oral and the literate.[46] Multiple connections existed between orality and literacy in societies which were in the process of becoming fully literate. Studying ordinary writings and ego-documents leads into some fundamental issues in nineteenth-century cultural history: these include the history of death and mourning, of marriage and of gender relations in general; the history of the dynamics of the family, its tensions and solidarities. Writing, furthermore, had enormous power as an instrument in forging a personal identity. Finally, the study of personal writings can illuminate the development of the notion of privacy. Writing, like reading, was vital to social and cultural relations in the nineteenth-century West. It had become a significant everyday resource, not only for the middle classes of Europe and America, but also for ordinary people, peasants and the barely literate.

13
Readers and writers in the digital age

Whatever significance historians may attach to Gutenberg's so-called 'printing revolution' in the fifteenth century, there can be little doubt about the revolutionary impact of the twentieth-century computer revolution on reading. Nor can we doubt the bewildering speed of the electronic revolution itself. 'I think there is a world market for about five computers', said Thomas J. Watson, chairman of IBM in 1943, strangely lacking in the foresight we might have expected from that great company. In 1949, *Popular Mechanics* magazine, forecasting the relentless march of science, predicted that 'Computers in the future may weigh no more than 15 tons.' That prediction at least had the virtue of being correct. More recently, in 1977, Ken Olsen, then president of Digital Corp, assured the world that 'There is no reason for any individual to have a computer in their home.'[1] Computerisation has overtaken every prediction and has brought about a fast and far-reaching transformation of the way we transmit, consume and interact with texts.

It has imposed its own style of reading, which approximates more and more to the browsing methods we use to explore the Internet. The Western reader of 2009 is a 'surfer' of texts; he or she indulges in 'zapping' rapidly from one short magazine extract to another, in the kind of 'interstitial reading' referred to by Jeanette Gilfedder in her study of developments in Italian publishing in the 1990s.[2] The regulated working day allows only short fragments of reading time, which must be seized in the interstices between home and work, between work and sleep, in lunch breaks, on commuter trains, between the electric iron and the vacuum cleaner.

Yet at the same time, there are remarkable parallels between some of the reactions to the electronic revolution and reactions to the invention of printing over five hundred years ago. There are the same extravagant forecasts about the power of technology to change the world and provide a better future for all. Meanwhile, the panic caused by the printing press is echoed in contemporary fears about unlimited access to dangerous Internet sites, and the difficulties faced by national governments in policing the distribution of information. Historians of the book have heard this all before, but they are well positioned to know that the advent of the digital age has constituted a more cataclysmic 'information revolution' than the one achieved by Johannes Gutenberg. It represents the last of the great turning points in reading history foreshadowed in Chapter 1, and it is the most significant of the developments discussed in this chapter.

Pulp fiction in the twentieth century

The book-trade recovered very slowly after the First World War, and in most countries, production levels struggled in vain to match those of the pre-war boom. The rapid expansion of the reading public experienced in the nineteenth-century would never be equalled. The price of paper was no longer on a downward spiral as it had been before 1914, and the wages of printers and compositors were rising; in fact they multiplied nine times over in Paris between 1911 and 1936.[3] At the same time, reading books had to compete with a range of new leisure activities, including the radio, the cinema and the newspaper press. Only much later, when the book learned to work in tandem with the electronic media instead of competing with them would it find a new market: J.K. Rowling's Harry Potter series is a good example, in which the books, films and television repeats all reinforced the impact of each other, and at the same time they boosted, and were boosted by, the sale of related merchandise.

Important changes, however, were taking place in the first half of the twentieth century which affected the way readers received their texts. Linotype and Monotype mechanised the composition process, and the use of high-quality photographic illustration opened up new possibilities. New genres appeared, like the cartoon book, later to develop into the fully-fledged graphic novel. By the mid-1970s, the popular Astérix books had sold 40 million copies in 17 years.[4] As a result, the twentieth-century reading experience was different from that of pre-war readers. For one thing, the development of primary and secondary education made the reading public better educated than ever before. For another, the books in readers' hands were now industrialised consumer products. They were industrially bound, with attractive coloured covers, produced in familiar typefaces chosen from a narrowing range as production became increasingly standardised. Only in children's books would the young reader find more extravagant uses of fonts and more imaginative relationships between text and image. The books the public read were advertised in the press, in posters or on the radio. Publicity techniques entered a new dimension: for the first time there were book launches, publicity campaigns, complimentary copies for the press and inspection copies for educators. The twentieth-century reader was less likely to find his or her book in a bookshop than had previously been the case. Other outlets were increasingly important, including book clubs, schools for the expanding educational book market, supermarkets, drugstores and news agencies. British readers, like their German counterparts, are more inclined to buy from traditional outlets like W.H. Smith's or Waterstone's, whereas French readers buy more of their books in supermarkets and Spanish and Italian book-buyers rely more on street kiosks.[5] In the English-speaking world, the system of public lending libraries was well developed, and they opened special children's sections for the first time. This was the age of comics and of W.E. Johns' *Biggles*, Enid Blyton's *Famous Five* and Richmal Crompton's *Just William*.

The interwar period had its best-sellers: among them was *Gone with the Wind* (1936), which the successful film version helped to turn into a perennial hit. In England, Edgar Wallace thrillers, produced in Hodder and Stoughton's glaring Yellow-Jacket series, achieved colossal success. The Yellow Jacket's fame was linked to the greatest symbol of British prestige, the Empire. Its second season was heralded as the '1000 title list that spans the Empire/The List upon which the sun never sets'.[6] A 1934 publicity cartoon showed massed ranks of stick figures, all wearing yellow shirts with the Hodder and Stoughton emblem on their chest and with their right arms raised in a fascist salute. To reinforce the picture's message it had the caption 'Yellow Jackets: the Dictatorship that is Popular'. Edgar Wallace alone sold 9½ million books in 20 years. Wallace was a pre-eminent but by no means solitary example. Pulp fiction, including romances, thrillers, Westerns and adventure fiction flooded the market. In Germany, according to Reuveni, the middle class was reduced to a state of shock and dismay at the progress of rampant and tasteless consumerism.[7] One librarian from a sedate southern English village poetically declared, soon after the Second World War, 'The quiet lawns of literature are trampled by impatient feet.'[8] Publishers knew that in a world of cut-throat competition they had to provide novelty at all costs and that a few blockbusters would finance more literary and more experimental titles. As the French publisher Gaston Gallimard jokingly said, 'if I can publish poetry that no-one understands, it's thanks to my series of detective novels'.[9] The industry struggled through two world wars, the Depression and, in many European countries, Nazi occupation and bomb damage caused by one side or another and sometimes both. And yet it appeared as though hardship fed an insatiable desire to read and escape into a fictional dream world.

In Europe, comics and pulp fiction aided the spread of American cultural influences, which even the fascist regimes were unable to resist. Alongside Zane Grey's Westerns, readers all over the English-speaking world read *Tarzan*, *Blondie* and *The Katzenjammer Kids*.

Figure 13.1 The Western.
Note: The popularity of the Western in the 1920s and 1930s owed much to its leading exponent, Zane Grey. This title was published in 1923.

Local intellectuals denounced this American invasion to no effect. At the same time, more literary American influences, like Steinbeck, Faulkner and Hemingway were popular with European publishers of the 1930s, such as Mondadori. This trend continued after the war: Mondadori's

Oscar series of pocket editions was launched in 1965, suitably enough with Hemingway's *Farewell to Arms* (set in Italy in 1917). It sold 4.8 million copies in its first year of publication.[10]

Reading under the dictatorships

Reading and book production under the fascist dictatorships were strictly controlled, and Nazi book-burnings are notorious. After 1940, German newly-weds were obliged to receive Hitler's *Mein Kampf* as an official wedding gift. Jewish publishers and authors, like Marx, Freud and Kafka, were proscribed. School textbooks were put under government control, and in Germany and Italy the dictatorships used them to promote an aggressive brand of nationalism. Most publishers drew the obvious conclusion that their survival depended on a close alliance with the regime. In Italy, after all, the government could be generous to its friends and was prepared to help them export Italian literary classics. The school market was also very lucrative: in 1935, the Italian publisher Mondadori sought and secured the national monopoly on the production of compulsory elementary school texts.[11] In Ray Bradbury's *Fahrenheit 451* (1953), resistors against tyranny each memorise one canonical book so that it will never die. But this was science-fiction fantasy. With very few exceptions, book publishing under fascism did not assist critics of the regimes. The favourite media of the resistance were the radio and the clandestine pamphlet.

In the Soviet Union, a huge official effort was made to increase the basic literacy of the population. The literacy campaign had a political objective: it was designed to nurture citizens of a socialist society. Literacy campaigners ritually cited Lenin's statement that 'an illiterate person stands outside politics', and strove to 're-educate' peasants whose culture seemed steeped in a remote pre-political past. The campaign enjoyed mixed success. Many peasants failed to understand the books and newspapers they were encouraged to read, but found them good for rolling cigarettes or other more intimate uses. Once again, readers stubbornly refused to be moulded by literature prescribed by the intelligentsia. By 1939, however, the literacy rate had increased to 95 per cent for men and 79 per cent for women.[12]

Soviet readers were treated to cheap editions of selected classics, and Pushkin, Gogol and Tolstoy were produced in enormous quantities, as were non-Russian authors who carried a positive message about the power of science and progress. Thus the USSR's publishing policy was largely responsible for making Jules Verne the most-translated author in the world, in terms of the number of translated copies of his works produced in foreign countries.[13] Although private publishers survived until 1930, production was highly regulated. Library contents were purged, while the Communist Party protected ideological orthodoxy in print. Party propaganda consistently idealised the serious-minded proletarian reader.

By the 1960s, the Soviet public had grown more literate, better educated and more sophisticated and varied in its tastes. The paperback revolution, however, had not happened in the USSR, and supply still lagged behind demand (the same could be said for consumer goods in general). The gap was partially bridged by a thriving black market in books in the 1970s and 1980s. The works of authors known in the West as 'dissidents' circulated secretly in the form of self-published *samizdat* – privately roneo-ed texts which bring to mind the role of scribal publication in the seventeenth century. Alexander Solzhenitsyn, regarded in the West as the greatest living Soviet writer, was eventually forced to leave the USSR, where it was impossible for him to get published.

In the *perestroika* period of the late 1980s, censorship was relaxed, book pricing became more flexible and private publishing houses revived. There was a publishing explosion, and a brief rush to read the previously forbidden fruit of Rybakov's *Children of the Arbat*, Solzhenitsyn and Pasternak's *Dr. Zhivago*. It soon became clear, however, that Soviet readers, like the mass of Western readers, preferred fantasy literature, detective novels, fiction about the Second World War and Barbara Cartland.[14] Russian readers were no longer ideal figures in which the state placed a huge symbolic investment; they had become ordinary consumers of print.

The paperback revolution

After the 1950s, the paperback revolution, which had been initiated before the war, gathered steam. Allen Lane had launched Penguin Books in 1935, providing the English market with its distinctive, cheap but high-quality paperbacks. They were sold at sixpence each in austere colour-coded series: orange for fiction, green for crime, purple for travel and blue for biography. They could be bought at a range of shops, including the popular high-street chain stores Woolworth's and Marks & Spencer. The first 50 titles of the series sold three million copies.[15] The Penguin series appealed to the educated reader, and its phenomenal success relied on the increasing proportion of the population with a secondary and/or university education. The Penguins and their fellow seabirds (Puffins and Pelicans) commanded a huge loyalty following and, as Richard Hoggart later recalled, they spoke to the young generation of the 1930s with political ideas and intellectual aspirations.[16] Twentieth-century English authors like G.B. Shaw, H.G. Wells and D.H. Lawrence achieved sales of over a million each in the Penguin format. On the other hand, there were probably very few working-class Penguin readers. By the mid-1950s, however, Penguins were selling 11 million copies annually, while their more downmarket imitators Pan sold 8 million and Corgi, established in 1953, about 4 million. Hachette's *Livres de poche* in France and Bantam, Signet and Mentor in the USA also developed the mass paperback market.

In post-war Europe, re-construction and the boom of the 1960s produced a market ready for the paperback revolution. In countries like Italy and Spain, illiteracy finally disappeared, while the spread of television brought the national language into ordinary homes. In this period of the 'economic miracle', the reading public was relatively prosperous and well educated, and it embraced illustrated magazines and cheap pocket editions, just as it embraced other entertainment media.

In the 1990s, Marcello Baraghini's series of mini-books took the paperback revolution one step further.[17] The Millelire Series, published by Stampa Alternativa, was, as its name explains, defined by its price of a thousand lire. These small books had a standard format of 64 pages, and they were designed for the commuter market. They cost less than a cup of coffee and if you caught the train at Bologna, you could finish one by the time you reached Florence. Baraghini claimed he would democratise and 'defetishise' the book. There was no glamorous packaging, because the covers were made of recycled paper and only had two colours. The series contained absolutely no critical commentary and no information on the author; many authors were unknowns, recruited by Baraghini and sometimes induced to forgo royalties. These rather exceptional conditions ensured low prices and, because other publishers were forced to compete for the attention of the reading commuter, Italy's paperback industry experienced rapid expansion. By 1995, the *supereconomici* (books costing less than 5,000 lire) held 20 per cent of the Italian paperback market. The boom did not last: rising paper costs made it impossible to maintain the price formula, booksellers were reluctant to stock an item which offered very small profit margins, and there is quite simply a natural limit to the number of texts that can be produced within 64 pages. The mini-book, however, like the free commuter newspaper, was well adapted to the contemporary urban reading environment. Reading is increasingly fragmented and discontinuous, fitted into short intervals between domestic chores or on the train to work or standing in queues (especially in Soviet Eastern Europe). Together with the walkman, it fills the gaps of our daily lives.

Book clubs and reading groups

The emergence of mail-order book clubs, followed by a variety of informal clubs and reading circles, bypassed traditional booksellers. The ancestor of commercial book clubs was The Book-of-the-Month Club, founded by Harry Scherman in New York in 1926. Until the decline of the club in the 1980s and 1990s, its formula was remarkably success-ful. By 1929, it already had 110,000 members and the Great Depression failed to obstruct its advance. It still had about one million members when Janice Radway researched it in the 1980s.[18] Many of them had been captured by a form of inertia selling. When the club was first estab-lished, subscribers automatically received their monthly book selection, but they could return it to the club if they wished. As the system devel-oped, they could choose the 'negative option'; in other words, they could decline to take the main book choice, and select one of the alternatives on offer. In this way, the Book-of-the-Month Club gave its members a limited freedom of choice.

The Club catered for the 'middlebrow' reading public of the interwar period and the years after the Second World War. The imprimatur of the club's selection committee gave the customers a guarantee that they were buying culture, whether it was to give away as a present, to fill a shelf with 'cultural furniture' or actually to read. The club's members respected books as prestige items and, significantly, the club provided them in durable hard covers. They wanted to buy the accoutrements of cultural status. Many of them came from the new managerial and professional classes; the majority had a university or college education, between a half and two-thirds of them were women and they were prob-ably overwhelmingly white.[19] They were 'middlebrow' readers in the sense that they wanted to distinguish themselves from the mass of con-sumers of 'trashy' fiction, and to identify themselves as serious readers who appreciated books for their literary quality as well as instruments of self-improvement. They read to understand a complex world but, at the same time, they were not attracted to books which were too technical, too specialised or otherwise too demanding. Thus when the Book-of-the-Month Club selection committee recommended Isabelle Allende's *House of the Spirits* as 'accessible magic realism', it was making several reveal-ing assumptions about its middlebrow readers: firstly, that they already had some idea about what magic realism was; secondly, that they found exponents of it like García Marquez too difficult; and thirdly, they were prepared to take their monthly book on trust from an expert.[20]

The middlebrow reader wanted books both for pleasure and for self-education. He or she enjoyed identifying with fictional characters, and they would read books like Toni Morrison's *Beloved* for the pleasure of being moved by literature. The editors who chose the books aimed at readers who were prepared for a totally engaging reading experi-ence. They spoke of 'inhaling' a book, about being 'mugged', 'swept away' and 'immersed' by a book.[21] The club's readers also read history, biography, popular science and works presenting an insight into topical issues. Thus the club read William Shirer's *The Rise and Fall of the Third*

Reich, which gave the post-war generation an accessible view of Hitler's regime, in spite of its gargantuan length; while Alan Paton's novel *Cry, the Beloved Country* (1948) introduced them to the racial question in South Africa, and Harper Lee's *To Kill a Mockingbird* (1960) dealt with white bigotry in the American South, albeit from the perspective of a white, liberal male.

The Book-of-the-Month Club responded to a social moment between the 1920s and the 1960s, when it appealed to upwardly mobile readers with cultural aspirations. That moment passed, and mail-order selling faded as the rapid growth of electronic media introduced new cultural intermediaries to the reading public. Today, television celebrities play this role. In France in the 1970s and 1980s, Bernard Pivot had a weekly television audience of up to five million for his book show *Apostrophes*. When President Hugo Chavez of Venezuela spoke to the United Nations in September 2000, he held up a copy of Noam Chomsky's *Hegemony or Survival*, and advised Americans to read it instead of watching Superman. Such was the impact of this item of television news that within 48 hours the book climbed from 26,000th place on Amazon.com's best-selling lists to number 3, and its publisher Henry Holt rushed through an emergency reprint of 25,000 copies.[22]

Perhaps the most influential of all book mediators, however, is television host Oprah Winfrey. Her influence is legendary, and it is said that her personal endorsements can make authors into millionaires.[23] The Oprah Winfrey Book Club, launched in 1996, addresses occasional readers or those who may not normally think of buying a book. Winfrey makes an eclectic choice of fiction, popular autobiography and a wide range of 'lifestyle' books on diet, cooking, how to stay young or how to cope with infidelity. Her influence, like that of the Book-of-the-Month Club before her, has been criticised for dictating the shape of the market and for contributing to the standardisation and mediocrity of mass culture. It should be remembered, however, that she has been prepared to address topical issues such as global environmental problems and that her recommendations have included modern or nineteenth-century classics such as Tolstoy's *Anna Karenina* (in 2004) and García Marquez's *Love in the Time of Cholera* (in 2007).

Winfrey's Book Club has a mass audience and remains solidly within the American cultural mainstream, but it makes a point of promoting positive images of black people. It draws attention to race issues, whether they are treated by black or white authors. Just like the Book-of-the-Month Club, Winfrey has strongly endorsed Toni Morrison's work, together with the perennial *To Kill a Mockingbird* and Paton's *Cry, the Beloved Country*. The book club's website informs us that Winfrey's favourite book is Steinbeck's *Grapes of Wrath*.[24]

The development of informal reading groups, some virtual but many 'face-to-face', has been a surprising phenomenon of the 1990s and early twenty-first century. Jenny Hartley surveyed 350 such reading groups in Britain, well aware that she was brushing the tip of an iceberg.[25] She encountered special identity groups such as gay reading groups or feminist reading groups, Jewish reading groups, teenage reading groups, blind reading groups and many workplace reading groups. Some are devoted to a particular genre and others to a single author, like the Marcel Proust Support Group. By far the most common, however, is the small neighbourhood reading group of six or eight members, meeting in an individual's home each month to discuss a book and enjoy some food and wine. Occasionally, the meeting is a little more imaginative and it can take the form of a literary pilgrimage, as with the group which (exhibiting some inverted logic) met in a windmill to discuss *Don Quixote* and another which went to Lyme Regis to talk about Jane Austen's *Persuasion* on location. One group devoted its time to reading nineteenth-century novels in monthly instalments, just as they were first issued.

Clearly, reading is not the only activity promoted in such settings. Collective reading groups answer a need for female sociability. The majority of members are female, and two out of three groups are specifically all-female and intend to stay that way. Some groups ban husbands from joining. Like Radway's romance readers, they seek briefly to defy the demands of everyday housekeeping and maternal chores.[26] Inevitably, there is a girls' night out aspect to some groups, and it is interesting that when Oprah Winfrey gives advice on how to form a reading group, she includes some handy recipes.

Reading groups, however, do not simply exist for the sake of a regular gossip in friendly company. They appeal to women who want to stretch themselves intellectually and who feel that their maternal roles tend to smother opportunities for a stimulating challenge. Reading groups are active and critical readers, keen to interact both with realistic fictional characters and also with themselves. They specifically do not wish to replicate the ambiance of a school classroom. On the contrary, a non-competitive environment and a relatively unstructured discussion are essential to success. There is no need, for example, to reach any conclusions. Reading groups are democratic institutions: unlike the subscribers to the Book-of-the-Month Club, they do not readily abandon their choice of reading to a committee of experts, although some may take advice from a librarian or a bookseller.

In the informal reading groups of well-educated Texan women investigated by Elizabeth Long, the choice of titles was crucial to the group's sense of identity. Many groups placed certain genres off-limits, refusing to read romances, detective stories or opaque postmodernist fiction. Many reading groups, like their earnest nineteenth-century predecessors, focus on women and do not appreciate books which seem to marginalise or portray them superficially. Readers were prepared to defer to advisors with some cultural legitimacy, like university scholars, but ultimately the choice would be made on the basis of the book's availability and as a result of consensus.[27] The decision about what to read is made collectively, even if agreement may be difficult and one group member compared it to electing the Pope.[28]

The choices made by reading groups do not automatically replicate the best-seller lists. Fiction with a firm historical context is popular, including Sebastian Faulks' *Birdsong* and Charles Frazier's *Cold Mountain*. Books with interesting cultural contexts also reach a wide audience in reading groups, such as *Memoirs of a Geisha* and Arundhati Roy's *The God of Small Things*. As in the latter case, it helps if the book is short. The two favourite novels in British reading groups offer a strong basis for emotional identification with the characters: *Captain Corelli's Mandolin* and *Angela's Ashes*.

Reading and writing in a digital age

The electronic revolution has inspired some extreme responses – an anxious nostalgia for the old, mingled with a dose of panic on one hand and a naïve enthusiasm about the promise of the future on the other. History shows us that technology has no inevitable consequences. The significance of the electronic revolution is contingent, as always, on who owns the means of production and who uses them. The result could be to widen the distance between owners and consumers, between practitioners of the new media and those excluded from the world of written culture; on the other hand, a vast and more critical reading public might be created.

In Borges' story, *The Library of Babel*, the author imagined a library containing all possible books, consisting of all possible combinations of the letters of the alphabet.[29] This dream of the universal library has often recurred in the Western imagination, and theoretically it now seems nearer fulfilment. The numerisation of texts abolishes distance and brings the virtual planetary library one step closer. In the virtual library of all numerised knowledge, the scholar will face new problems: we will soon have no excuses for not reading absolutely everything on our subject.

The computer revolutionises our relationship with texts because it removes its traditional supporting material – paper – which some would argue defines the very nature of a book. The screen supplants the codex which has reigned supreme for 15 centuries. On screen, one computerised text is not materially different from any other, in the way that a quarto volume is a different object from a duodecimo or a tabloid newspaper. The digital revolution gives all texts a homogeneous form.

On screen, the text is easily manipulated by the reader, which constitutes another revolution. Apart from being able to search a text more rapidly than is ever possible with a codex, a reader may now delete, edit and re-arrange what is read at will. Anyone can indeed produce their own newsletters, posters and even books, with images embedded within them. Desktop publishing means that every reader is his or her own printer.[30] The text is thus more unstable and liable to mutate than before. The reader has increased power to enter the text and adapt it. Although the on-screen text appears perfectly spaced, justified and complete, it is nevertheless always provisional and permanently modifiable. The computer has created interactive reading so that the very distinction between author and reader has become blurred. The Wikipedia is just one example of an online text written by web users themselves.

The new fluidity of the texts we read creates problems for the laws of copyright. Authors are particularly concerned that the unlimited global availability of Internet access will weaken their defence against plagiarism and publishing piracy. Perhaps the laws of copyright which developed in the eighteenth century, and which we have come to regard as universal, were a specific feature of the age of print culture and ill-adapted to contemporary conditions of textual communication.

The Internet is a mixed blessing. It has no memory and a huge amount of material disappears without being archived. The computer scientist Jeff Rothenberg joked, 'Digital documents last for ever – or five years, whichever comes first.'[31] In fact 70 per cent of all web pages have a life of less than four months.[32] Hardware and software rapidly become obsolete, so that data recorded on a 5¼-inch disk (the ones which really were 'floppy') may now be definitively irretrievable. Historians, incidentally, have to date been reluctant to accept responsibility for digital archiving: this looks like somebody else's problem, and it will certainly involve somebody else's money. The Internet produces a surplus of ephemeral trivia dominated by 'presentism' – the need to be new and up-to-date. Although its reach is instant and global, it threatens to entrench a new form of illiteracy, discriminating not between those who can and cannot read, but between those who have access or not to its tentacular web of communication.

The Internet encourages a kind of fragmented reading in which the reader rushes distractedly from one short item to another. This is a complete reversal of normative school-based reading styles, which encourage intensive engagement and expect the student to read a book from beginning to end without getting distracted. In *Comme un Roman*, Daniel Pennac encouraged this form of desacralisation of the text. He urged parents and teachers to allow adolescents to read for pleasure in their own way. His ten 'inalienable rights of the reader' include the right to skip pages, the right not to finish a book and, above all, the right to browse (*grappiller*).[33]

Technology has transformed writing as well as reading. The steel pens of the second half of the nineteenth century gave way to re-loadable ink cartridges, first patented by Waterman in 1884 and Parker in 1889. Then, in 1943, the biro, named after its inventor Laszlo Biro, a Hungarian-born immigrant to the USA, made handwriting easier and cleaner for all, while at the same time homogenising individual graphic styles. Within three years, Biro's invention had sold eight million ballpoint pens.[34] Half a century earlier, the typewriter was introduced. This began a process of mechanisation which gradually pushed handwriting into the realm of the personal, and created greater distance between the writer and the text. In the 1840s, Herman Melville could not get a job in Manhattan because his handwriting was too poor; now speed at the keyboard and familiarity with computer software have made good handwriting an irrelevant professional asset.[35]

The first Remington appeared in 1872, with a pedal action modelled on the company's sewing machines. Until 1878, the Remington only printed upper-case characters. Until 1900, the carriage was covered and the writer could not immediately see the printed text. The typewriter, however, produced texts faster, more legibly and in several carbon copies. It greatly reduced, for example, the time spent in publishing firms by compositors trying to make out an author's difficult handwriting. The typewriter distanced the writer from the text and depersonalised the act of writing. The typed text was even and uniform, ruling out the quirky characteristics of handwriting. It produced text much closer to its final printed version. German author Hermann Hesse bought his first type-writer in 1908 and was disturbed by the immediate confrontation with his own writing in print, noting that

> the coldness of type, which starts to look like printer's proofs, means that you come face to face with yourself in a severe, critical, ironic, even hostile way. Your writing turns you into something alien and forces you to make a critical judgement.[36]

Some writers saw romance in the machine, calling it a 'literary piano', while others enjoyed its noisy clatter, including French novelist Françoise Sagan, who compared her writing action to jazz rhythms.[37] Some creative writers felt the typewriter encouraged fluency and spontaneity. The Australian Nancy Cato said, 'When I get to the typewriter, it just comes straight out through my fingers.'[38] On his deathbed, Henry James called for his Remington.

The typewriter created new opportunities for female employment. Although the image of the 'typing pool' has connotations of mechanical drudgery and subordination, the machine could sometimes be empowering for women. In Christina Stead's novel *I'm Dying Laughing*, the main character Emily Wilkes has such an intimate relationship with her typewriter that her husband becomes jealous. After one social gathering, Emily 'had to go upstairs and work on the typewriter. It calmed her and made her feel worthwhile and fit.'[39] Many female secretaries have perhaps felt encouraged and affirmed by observing incompetent male one-finger typists.

The typewriter is now a museum piece; its main contribution, in hindsight, was to provide an apprenticeship in the use of the keyboard, which was invaluable to those entering the computer age. Both the typewriter and the computer have relegated handwriting to the most personal and domestic tasks. Sociological research reveals the obvious – there is a range of unseen domestic handwriting devoted to accounts, family budgets, lists of things to do or to buy. What is not so obvious is the gendered division of scribal labour, which operates within working-class families. In Lyon, Bernard Lehire's team discovered that women were 'family writing machines', for the purposes of organising the family and conducting relations with the outside world. The only specifically masculine writing task was filling in the annual tax return.[40] When women take charge of the paperwork, however, it is seen as a banal activity, as just another part of their daily work like cleaning and washing up. But when a man does it, it is regarded as something which demands superior competence and as something responsible which demonstrates his domestic authority.[41] In immigrant families, parents very often leave writing tasks to their daughters. Kahina, the educated daughter of illiterate Algerian parents, developed some expertise in administrative documents, and typically protested – 'But I'm the family secretary!' – when her brother asked her to write something.

Non-readers and global illiteracy

Reading surveys proliferate in Europe and they suggest that there exists a hard but diminishing core of dedicated regular readers who have good educational qualifications and comparatively high social status and who buy books, borrow from libraries and may be TV-phobic. At the other end of the spectrum is a similarly diminishing proportion of 'non-readers', amounting to about 25 per cent of the whole. In between, there are a large number of occasional readers, like the man from Languedoc whose daughter bought him a book for Christmas. 'Why on earth are you giving me a book', he said, 'I've already got one!'[42] These surveys are deceptive. Most of them rely on statements made by interviewees about their own reading, which are inherently untrustworthy. Some respondents may exaggerate their investment in book culture in order to impress, while others, especially teenage boys, will not identify themselves as readers if this does not reinforce a macho image.

Furthermore, reading surveys tend to regard the only reading that counts as book-reading, and thus their questionnaires advance an implicitly normative view of reading. The group of 'non-readers' mentioned above is nothing of the kind if we regard their magazine and newspaper reading as legitimate. According to French surveys, retired or elderly people and people living in the country are likely to rely on the local newspaper, and gardening or do-it-yourself magazines, and unlikely to read a book. Women in the Paris suburbs may not be book readers either, but they are very interested in the TV magazine. Women continue to read more than men as long as they can overcome residual guilt about neglecting home duties. One French housewife and a mother of three clearly had done so, when she told an interviewer that

> If the book's really involving, I have to keep going, my kids may be crying, they may be hungry, it gets them nowhere, or else I just do them a fried egg and I quickly go back to my reading. Listen, I could read with a bomb sitting next to me.[43]

Young people, so often denigrated as readers, have never actually stopped reading. They simply read differently from previous generations. They surf, they zap, they read while listening to the walkman. When they read a book, they are no longer entering a temple of culture, but enjoying one among many possible entertainment activities. One French survey found adolescent readers were deterred, not encouraged, by scholastic imperatives to read, and that reading was ranked fifth on their list of popular leisure pursuits, a long way behind listening to music.[44] Conventional wisdom blames television for a decline in reading. Surveys, however, do not show such a negative correlation. The main rivals to reading books appear to be not television but the daily newspaper and the i-Pod.

Traditional print culture is far from extinct. It still rules supreme in the educational sphere. Newspapers and magazines boast expanding readerships. World consumption of paper is reaching astronomical heights. Book production is rising everywhere. 40,000 titles are produced annually in Japan, constituting the densest concentration of readers in the world, in a society better known for its miniaturised computers. If there is a crisis of the book, it should be seen in a global perspective. Most anxiety about its survival emanates from the most literate, book-conscious parts of the world, namely North America and Europe. Nervous questions about the death of print literacy are a Western problem, rarely heard in Africa or South America.

Questions of literacy have to be viewed in world terms. Illiteracy in sub-Saharan Africa, for example, is running at what a European might call medieval proportions. In the West African state of Burkina Faso, according to UNESCO calculations of illiteracy rates over the age of 15, the 1995 illiteracy rate was over 80 per cent.[45] In Mali it was 69 per cent and in Niger 86 per cent. Are these perhaps societies which will accede directly to the electronic media without passing through the stage of book literacy so familiar to the peoples of the West? Hardly so if one considers the state of the media in Eritrea, where, again according to UNESCO, there is just 1 television set per 3,300 inhabitants. For millions, poverty prevents access to *any* form of communications medium. Literacy rates are also very depressed in Moslem Asia, where ideological and religious factors work against female literacy in particular. In 1995, for instance, 74 per cent of Bangladeshi women, 75 per cent of Pakistani women and 85 per cent of Afghan women were illiterate.

Perhaps this is a disappearing problem, which the inevitable march of progress will eventually eradicate, like beriberi or leprosy? Not so, for while the Western world debates the semiology of hypertext or the regulation of Internet pornography, the number of illiterates in the world is actually on the increase. According to UNESCO, there were 133.3 million illiterates over the age of 15 in Africa in 1995. This represented a *rise* in the total number of illiterates of 2.7 per cent over the five years since 1990. Concerted efforts to change this situation have rarely succeeded. They require massive coercion and the involvement of entire societies, like the relatively successful campaigns to improve literacy in Stalinist Russia, communist Vietnam or China after 1949. The great divide between the literate and the illiterate worlds still largely reflects the gap between developed or developing countries on one side and the poorest nations on the planet on the other, between 'north' and 'south'.

While we discuss the appropriateness of the Western literary canon, deplore the dangers of postmodern styles of reading and design our *bibliothèques, grandes bibliothèques* and even *très grandes bibliothèques*, it is just as well to recall sometimes that the struggle for fundamental literacy still has many mountains to climb.

Notes

1 What is the history of reading and writing?

1. Jonathan Rose, conference address to SHARP (Society for the History of Authorship, Reading and Publishing), Cambridge, UK, 1997.
2. Richard Hoggart, *The Uses of Literacy: Aspects of Working-class Life*, Harmondsworth, UK (Penguin), 1958, pp. 238–41.
3. Carlo Ginzburg, 'L'historien et l'avocat du diable: entretien avec Charles Illouz et Laurent Vidal', *Genèses*, 53, 2003, p. 116.
4. Wolfgang Iser, *The Implied Reader: Patterns of Communication in Prose Fiction from Bunyan to Beckett*, Baltimore (Johns Hopkins UP), 1974; Victor Brombert, *The Hidden Reader: Stendhal, Balzac, Hugo, Baudelaire, Flaubert*, Cambridge: MA (HUP), 1988.
5. Janice Radway, *Reading the Romance: Women, Patriarchy and Popular Literature*, London (Verso), 1987, p. 5.
6. For the RED, visit http://www.open.ac.uk/Arts/RED/index.html; and for 'What Middletown Read' consult (when it becomes available) http://www.bsu.edu.middletown/wmr/.
7. Michel de Certeau, *L'Invention du Quotidien –1. Arts de Faire*, Paris (Gallimard), 1990, ch. 12 [English translation entitled *The Practice of Everyday Life*].
8. Ibid., p. 255.
9. Pierre Bourdieu, *La Distinction: critique sociale du jugement*, Paris (Eds. de Minuit), 1979.
10. Stanley Fish, *Is There a Text in This Class? The Authority of Interpretive Communities*, Cambridge, MA (HUP), 1980.
11. James Smith Allen, *In the Public Eye: A History of Reading in Modern France, 1800–1940*, Princeton, NJ (PUP), 1991.
12. Robert Darnton, *The Forbidden Best-Sellers of Pre-Revolutionary France*, New York (Norton), 1995, p. 186.
13. Louisa Anne (Mrs. Charles) Meredith, *Notes and Sketches of New South Wales During a Residence in That Colony from 1839 to 1844*, London (John Murray), 1844, p. 30; and the same author's *My Home in Tasmania or Nine Years in Australia*, New York (Bunce and Brother), 1853, pp. 171 & 292–93.

14. Robert Darnton, 'What Is the History of Books?' in David Finkelstein & Alistair McCleery, eds., *The Book History Reader*, London & New York (Routledge), 2002, ch. 2; also published in Darnton, *The Kiss of Lamourette: Reflections in Cultural History*, New York (Norton), 1990, pp. 107–36.

15. See the critique by Thomas R. Adams & Nicolas Barker, 'A New Model for the Study of the Book', in N. Barker, ed., *A Potencie of Life: Books in Society*, London (British Library), 1993, pp. 5–43.

16. Roger E. Stoddard, 'Morphology and the Book from an American Perspective', *Printing History*, 17, 1987, pp. 2–14.

17. Fernand Braudel, *The Mediterranean and the Mediterranean World in the Age of Philip II*, Glasgow (Fontana-Collins), 1975, p. 1236.

18. Carlos Alberto González Sánchez, 'Discursos y representaciones de la cultura escrita en el mundo hispánico de los siglos XVI y XVII', *Cultura Escrita y Sociedad*, 2, 2006, pp. 35–36.

2   Reading and writing in the ancient and medieval world

1. Jack Goody, ed., *Literacy in Traditional Societies*, Cambridge (CUP), 1968; Jack Goody, *The Logic of Writing and the Organization of Society*, Cambridge (CUP), 1986; for a more nuanced view, see Jack Goody, *The Domestication of the Savage Mind*, Cambridge (CUP), 1977; Walter J. Ong, *Orality and Literacy: The Technologizing of the Word*, London (Methuen), 1982.

2. Goody, *Literacy in Traditional Societies*, pp. 11–24.

3. Pascal Vernus, 'Les lieux de l'écrit dans l'Egypte ancienne', in *Le Grand Atlas des Littératures*, Paris (Encyclopaedia Universalis), 1998, p. 338.

4. Jack Goody and Ian Watt, 'The Consequences of Literacy', in Goody, *Literacy in Traditional Societies*, pp. 27–68.

5. Goody, *The Logic of Writing*, p. 5.

6. David R. Olson, *The World on Paper: The Conceptual and Cognitive Implications of Writing and Reading*, Cambridge (CUP), 1994, p. 66; Jack Goody, *The Interface between the Written and the Oral*, Cambridge (CUP), 1987, pp. 62–64.

7. Luciano Canfora, 'Lire à Athènes et à Rome', *AESC*, 44:4, 1989, p. 930.

8. Rosalind Thomas, *Oral Tradition and Written Record in Classical Athens*, Cambridge (CUP), 1989, pp. 30–31.

9. Joseph Needham, *Science and Civilization in China*, Cambridge (CUP), 1954–59.

10. Ong, *Orality and Literacy*, pp. 32–67.

11. Ibid., pp. 68–69.

12. William Eggington, 'From Oral to Literate Culture: An Australian Aboriginal Experience', in Fraida Dubin & Natalie A. Kuhlmann, eds., *Cross-Cultural Literacy: Global Perspectives on Reading and Writing*, Englewood Cliffs, NJ (Prentice Hall), 1992, p. 82.

13. D.F. McKenzie, 'The Sociology of a Text: Orality, Literacy and Print in Early New Zealand', in David Finkelstein & Alistair McCreery, eds., *The Book History Reader*, London & New York (Routledge), 2002, ch. 13 at p. 206.
14. Jacques Dournes, 'Oralité et mémoire collective', in *Grand Atlas des Littératures*, p. 86.
15. Jesper Svenbro, 'Archaic and Classical Greece: The Invention of Silent Reading', in *HORW*, pp. 45–46.
16. Thomas, *Oral Tradition and Written Record*, p. 33.
17. Rosalind Thomas, *Literacy and Orality in Ancient Greece*, Cambridge (CUP), 1992, p. 125.
18. Ibid., p. 83.
19. Thomas, *Oral Tradition and Written Record*, p. 80.
20. Guglielmo Cavallo, 'La Alfabetización en Grecia y Roma', in Antonio Castillo Gómez, ed., *Historia de la cultura escrita del Próximo Oriente Antiguo a la sociedad informatizada*, Gijón (Trea), 2002, p. 77.
21. Paul Zumthor, 'Littératures de la voix', *Grand Atlas des Littératures*, p. 70.
22. Bernard M.W. Knox, 'Silent Reading in Antiquity', *Greek, Roman and Byzantine Studies*, 9:4, 1968, pp. 421–35.
23. Nicholas Howe, 'The Cultural Construction of Reading in Anglo-Saxon England', in Jonathan Boyarin, ed., *The Ethnography of Reading*, Berkeley, CA (UCP), 1993, pp. 59–60.
24. Paul Saenger, 'Silent Reading: Its impact on Late Medieval Script and Society', *Viator: Medieval and Renaissance Studies*, 13, 1982, pp. 383–84.
25. Paul Saenger, *Space Between Words: The Origins of Silent Reading*, Stanford, CA (Stanford UP), 1998.
26. Ibid, p. 98.
27. Ibid., pp. 210 & 239.
28. Saenger, 'Silent Reading', p. 403.
29. Michael T. Clanchy, *From Memory to Written Record: England 1066–1307*, London (Edward Arnold), 1979, and Oxford (Blackwell), 2nd ed., 1993, pp. 120–21.
30. Armando Petrucci, *Writers and Readers in Medieval Italy: Studies in the History of Written Culture*, New Haven, CT (YUP), 1995, pp. 178–79.
31. Henri-Jean Martin, *The History and Power of Writing*, Chicago (Chicago UP), 1994, pp. 56–59.
32. Antonio Castillo Gómez, *Entre la pluma y la pared: una historia social de la escritura en los siglos de oro*, Madrid (AKAL), 2006, cit. p. 7.
33. Clanchy, *From Memory to Written Record*.
34. Ibid., 1979 edition, p. 214.
35. Ibid., 1979 edition, p. 219.
36. Ibid., 1979 edition, p. 210.
37. Ibid., 1979 edition, p. 214.
38. R.M. Thomson, 'The Norman Conquest and English Libraries', in Peter Ganz, ed., *The Role of the Book in Medieval Culture*, Tournhout (Brepols), 1986, part 2, pp. 27–40.
39. Clanchy, *From Memory to Written Record*, 1979 edition, p. 42.
40. Luis Casado de Otaola, 'Escribir y leer en la Alta Edad Media', in Castillo Gómez, *Historia de la cultura escrita*, p. 114.

41. Antonio Castillo Gómez, 'Entre la necesidad y el placer. La Formación de una nueva sociedad del escrito, siglos XII-XV', in his *Historia de la cultura escrita*, p. 209.

3   Was there a printing revolution?

1. Elizabeth L. Eisenstein, *The Printing Press as an Agent of Change: Communications and Global Transformations in Early Modern Europe*, Cambridge, UK (CUP), 1979.
2. Marshall McLuhan, *The Gutenberg Galaxy:The Making of Typographical Man*, Toronto (Toronto UP), 1962.
3. Guy Bechtel, *Gutenberg et l'invention de l'imprimerie: une enquête*, Paris (Fayard), 1992, p. 20; Lucien Febvre & Henri-Jean Martin, *L'Apparition du Livre*, Paris (Albin Michel), 1958 & 1971, p. 74.
4. Albert Kapr, *Johann Gutenberg: The Man and His Invention*, trans. D. Martin, Aldershot, UK (Scolar Press), 1996, p. 286.
5. Ibid., p. 286; Jean-Daniel Schöpflin, *Vindiciae Typographicae*, Strasbourg, 1760.
6. Henri-Jean Martin, 'Le Sacre de Gutenberg', *Revue de Synthèse*, 4th series, nos. 1–2, janvier–juin 1992, pp. 23–24.
7. I owe this phrase to my colleague David Miller, who would regard the full title of Dava Sobel's book as a good illustration of the phenomenon – *Longitude: The True Story of a Lone Genius who Solved the Greatest Scientific Problem of His Time*, New York (Walker), 1995.
8. Anon, *Gutenberg erfinder der buch*, Strasbourg, 1840 (Bibliothèque Nationale Ln27.9448).
9. Henri-Jean Martin, *The History and Power of Writing*, Chicago (Chicago UP), 1994, ch. 5.
10. Bechtel, *Gutenberg*, pp. 39–40.
11. Anacharsis Cloots, *Oeuvres, tome 3, Ecrits et discours de la période révolutionnaire*, Munich (Klaus reprint) & Paris (EDHIS), 1980, *Discours prononcé à la barre de l'Assemblée Nationale au nom des imprimeurs, 9 septembre 1792*; E. Eisenstein, *Grub Street Abroad: Aspects of the French Cosmopolitan Press from the Age of Louis XIV to the French Revolution (Lyell Lectures 1989–90)*, Oxford (Clarendon), 1992, p. 158.
12. Kai-Wing Chow, 'Reinventing Gutenberg: Woodblock and Movable-type Printing in Europe and China', in Sabrina Alcorn Baron, Eric N. Lindquist & Eleanor F. Shevlin, eds., *Agent of Change: Print Culture Studies after Elizabeth L. Eisenstein*, Amherst, MA (Massachusetts UP), 2007, pp. 186–89.
13. Febvre & Martin, *L'Apparition du Livre*, p. 262 and following.
14. Henri-Jean Martin & Jeanne-Marie Dureau, 'Années de transition, 1500–1530', *HEF1*, p. 217.
15. Martin, *History and Power of Writing*, pp. 244 & 249.
16. Bruno Blasselle, *A Pleines Pages: Histoire du Livre, vol.1*, Paris (Gallimard Découvertes), 1997, p. 50.
17. Martin, *History and Power of Writing*, p. 238.

18. Andrew G. Johnston, 'Printing and the Reformation in the Low Countries, 1520–c.1555', in Jean-François Gilmont, ed., *The Reformation and the Book*, Aldershot, UK (Ashgate), 1998, p. 164.
19. Febvre & Martin, *L'Apparition du Livre*, p. 196.
20. Eisenstein, *Printing Press as an Agent of Change*, pp. 567–68.
21. Ibid., pp. 516–17.
22. Martin, *History & Power of Writing*, p. 347.
23. Roger Chartier, 'Reading Matter and Popular Reading: From the Renaissance to the 17th Century', *HORW*, p. 270.
24. Carlo Ginzburg, 'High and Low: The Theme of Forbidden Knowledge in the 16th & 17th Centuries', *P&P*, 73, 1976, pp. 28–41.
25. Harold Love, *Scribal Publication in Seventeenth-Century England*, Oxford (Clarendon), 1993, pp. 4, 59 & 180–90.
26. Dominique Coq, 'Les incunables: textes anciens, textes nouveaux', *HEF1*, p. 177.
27. David N. Bell, 'Monastic Libraries, 1400–1557', *CHBB 3*, p. 245.
28. Love, *Scribal Culture*; Manuel Sánchez Mariana, 'El manuscrito y su producción en la época del libro impreso', *HELE*, pp. 23–28.
29. Rudolph Hirsch, 'Stampa e lettura fra il 1450 e il 1550', in Armando Petrucci, ed., *Libri, editori e pubblico nell'Europea moderna*, Bari (Laterza), 1977, pp. 3–50.
30. Julia Boffey & A.S.G. Edwards, 'Literary Texts', *CHBB 3*, p. 561.
31. Martin Lowry, *The World of Aldus Manutius: Business and Scholarship in Renaissance Venice*, Ithaca, NY (Cornell UP), 1979.
32. Henri-Jean Martin, 'Lectures et mises en texte', in Roger Chartier, ed., *Histoires de la Lecture: un bilan des recherches*, Paris (IMEC), 1995, pp. 249–59.
33. Adrian Johns, *The Nature of the Book: Print and Knowledge in the Making*, Chicago (Chicago UP), 1998.
34. Ibid., pp. 22–23.
35. Ibid., p. 31.
36. Ibid., p. 91.
37. Ibid., p. 162.
38. Ibid., p. 457.
39. Benedict Anderson, *Imagined Communities: Reflections on the Origins and Spread of Nationalism*, London (Verso), 1983, pp. 47–49.
40. Uffe Østergård, 'Language and National Identity in the Danish Nation-State in the 19th Century', *History of European Ideas*, 16:1–3, 1993, pp. 213–18.
41. 'How Revolutionary Was the Print Revolution?' *AmHistRev* forum, 107:1, 2002, pp. 84–128 (debate between Elizabeth Eisenstein and Adrian Johns).
42. Stephan Füssel, *Gutenberg and the Impact of Printing*, trans. D. Martin, Aldershot, UK (Scolar Press), 2003, p. 111.

4   Print and the Protestant Reformation

1. Patrick Collinson, Arnold Hunt & Alexandra Walsham, 'Religious Publishing in England, 1557–1640', *CHBB 4*, pp. 36–37.

2. Rolf Engelsing, *Der Bürger als Leser. Lesergeschichte in Deutschland, 1500–1800*, Stuttgart (Metzler), 1974, p. 37.
3. Jean-François Gilmont, 'Protestant Reformations and Reading', *HORW*, p. 224.
4. Natalie Zemon Davis, 'Strikes and Salvation at Lyon', in her *Society and Culture in Early Modern France*, London (Duckworth), 1975, pp. 1–16.
5. John L. Flood, 'The Book in Reformation Germany', in Jean-François Gilmont, ed., *The Reformation and the Book*, Aldershot, UK (Ashgate), 1998, pp. 69–71.
6. Stephan Füssel, *Gutenberg and the Impact of Printing*, Aldershot, UK (Scolar Press), 2003, p. 163.
7. Ian Green, *Print and Protestantism in Early Modern England*, Oxford (OUP), 2000, p. 51.
8. Ibid., p. 95.
9. Gilmont, 'Protestant Reformations and Reading', p. 219.
10. Ibid., p. 216; Richard Gawthrop & Gerald Strauss, 'Protestantism and Literacy in Early Modern Germany', *P&P*, 104, 1984, p. 40.
11. Gawthrop & Strauss, 'Protestantism and Literacy', p. 40.
12. Gilmont, 'Protestant Reformations and Reading', pp. 227–28.
13. Flood, 'The Book in Reformation Germany', p. 43.
14. Miriam Usher Chrisman, *Lay Culture, Learned Culture: Books and Social Change in Strasbourg, 1480–1599*, New Haven, CT (YUP), 1982, ch. 10.
15. Ibid., ch. 7.
16. Lotte Hellinga & J.B. Trapp, 'Introduction', *CHBB 3*, pp. 17–19.
17. Green, *Print and Protestantism*, p. 248.
18. R.W. Scribner, *For the Sake of Simple Folk: Popular Propaganda for the German Reformation*, Cambridge, UK (CUP), 1981, pp. 243–44.
19. Flood, 'The Book in Reformation Germany', p. 26.
20. Ibid., pp. 52–55.
21. Ibid., p. 86.
22. Andrew G. Johnston, 'Printing and the Reformation in the Low Countries, c.1520–c.1555', in Gilmont, *The Reformation and the Book*, p. 181.
23. Scribner, *For the Sake of Simple Folk*, p. 22.
24. R.W. Scribner, 'Incombustible Luther: The Image of the Reformer in Early Modern Germany', *P&P*, 110, 1986, pp. 38–68, for this section.
25. Gawthrop & Strauss, 'Protestantism and Literacy', p. 34.
26. Gilmont, 'Protestant Reformations and Reading', p. 221.
27. Gawthrop & Strauss, 'Protestantism and Literacy', p. 35.
28. Dominique Julia, 'Reading and the Counter-Reformation', *HORW*, p. 242.
29. Francis Higman, 'Le levain de l'Evangile', *HEF1*, pp. 320–21.
30. Denis Pallier, 'Les réponses catholiques', *HEF1*, pp. 328–29.
31. Nieves Baranda, 'Las lecturas femeninas', *HELE*, p. 164.
32. Denis Pallier, 'Les réponses catholiques', *HEF1*, p. 328.
33. Francisco M. Gimeno Blay, *Quemar libros…¡qué extraño placer!*, Eutopías, 2a época, 104, 1995, pp. 1–32.
34. Cervantes, *Don Quixote*, part 1, ch. 6.
35. Sara T. Nalle, 'Literacy and Culture in Early Modern Castile', *P&P*, 125, 1989, pp. 65–96.

36. Silvana Seidel Menchi, *Erasmo in Italia*, 1520–80, Turin (Bollati Boringhieri), 1987, p. 289.
37. John M. King, 'The Book-trade Under Edward VI and Mary I', *CHBB 3*, p. 170.
38. Bernard Barbiche, 'Le régime de l'édition', *HEF1*, p. 369.
39. Menchi, *Erasmo in Italia*, p. 350.
40. Kevin Sharpe, 'Reading Revelations: Prophecy, Hermeneutics and Politics in Early Modern Britain', in Kevin Sharpe & Steven N. Zwicker, eds., *Reading, Society and Politics in Early Modern England*, Cambridge, UK (CUP), 2003, pp. 122–63.
41. Menchi, *Erasmo in Italia*, pp. 317–21.
42. Roger Chartier, *The Order of Books: Readers, Authors and Libraries in Europe Between the Fourteenth and the Eighteenth Centuries*, Cambridge, UK (Polity), 1994, ch. 1.
43. Collinson, Hunt & Walsham, 'Religious Publishing in England', *CHBB 4*, p. 59.
44. Pamela Neville-Sington, 'Press, Politics and Religion', *CHBB 3*, cit. p. 605.

5   Renaissance books and humanist readers

1. Henri-Jean Martin, *The History and Power of Writing*, Chicago (Chicago UP), 1994, p. 363.
2. Anthony Grafton, 'The Humanist as Reader', *HORW*, pp. 179–80.
3. Rudolf Hirsch, *Printing, Selling and Reading, 1450–1550*, Wiesbaden (Harrasowitz), 1974, p. 144.
4. Brian Richardson, *Print Culture in Renaissance Italy: The Editor and the Vernacular Text, 1470–1600*, Cambridge, UK (CUP), 1994, for example pp. 33 & 74.
5. Miriam Usher Chrisman, *Lay Culture, Learned Culture: Books and Social Change in Strasbourg, 1480–1599*, New Haven, CT (YUP), 1982, ch. 10.
6. Henri-Jean Martin, 'Classements et conjonctures', *HEF1*, pp. 445–46.
7. Françoise Waquet, *Latin or the Empire of a Sign from the 16th to the 20th centuries*, London (Verso), 2001, pp. 160–61.
8. Rudolph Hirsch, 'Stampa e Lettura fra il 1450 e il 1550', in Armando Petrucci, ed., *Libri, editori e pubblico nell'Europa moderna: guida storica e critica*, Bari (Laterza), 1977, p. 17.
9. Ibid., p. 18.
10. Roger Chartier, 'El concepto de lector moderno', *HELE*, p. 146.
11. Victor Navarro Brotóns, 'La lectura científica, técnica y humanística', *HELE*, p. 214.
12. Waquet, *Latin*, pp. 8–9.
13. Ibid., pp. 20–21 & 35.
14. Elisabeth Leedham-Green & David McKitterick, 'Ownership and Public Libraries', *CHBB 4*, p. 324.
15. Anna-Giulia Cavagna, paper on book culture in seventeenth-century Lombardy delivered to the SHARP conference in Cambridge, UK, in July 1997.

16. Waquet, *Latin*, p. 159.

17. Primo Levi, *The Truce*, trans. Stuart Woolf, London (Abacus), 1998, pp. 222–23.

18. Henri-Jean Martin, *Print, Power and the People in 17th-Century France*, Metuchen, NJ (Scarecrow), 1993, pp. 334–44 & 609.

19. Leedham-Green & McKitterick, 'Ownership and Public Libraries', p. 327.

20. Maureen Bell, 'Women writing and Women Written', *CHBB* 4, ch. 20; Carol M. Meale & Julia Boffey, 'Gentlewomen's Reading', *CHBB* 3, pp. 538–40.

21. Lisa Jardine & Anthony Grafton, 'Studied for Action: How Gabriel Harvey Read His Livy', *P&P*, 129, 1990, pp. 30–78.

22. Grafton, 'The Humanist as Reader', p. 197.

23. Ann Blair, 'Humanist Methods in Natural Philosophy: The Commonplace Book', *Journal of the History of Ideas*, 53:4, 1992, pp. 541–51.

24. Kevin Sharpe, *Reading Revolutions. The Politics of Reading in Early Modern England*, New Haven, CT (YUP), 2000, chs. 2 & 4.

25. Anthony Grafton, *Commerce with the Classics: Ancient Books and Renaissance Readers*, Ann Arbor (Michigan UP), 1997, pp. 67 & 88–89.

26. Grafton, 'The Humanist as Reader', p. 208.

27. Armando Petrucci, *Libri, Scrittura e Pubblico nel Rinascimento*, Rome (Laterza), 1979, pp. 137–56.

28. Grafton, 'The Humanist as Reader', pp. 187–88.

29. Richardson, *Print Culture in Renaissance Italy*, p. 48; Martin Lowry, *The World of Aldus Manutius: Business and Scholarship in Renaissance Venice*, Ithaca, NY (Cornell UP), 1979.

30. Hirsch, *Stampa e lettura*, p. 9.

31. Michel Pastoureau, 'L'Illustration du livre: comprendre ou rêver?' *HEF1*, pp. 501–29; Roger Laufer, 'L'Espace visuel du livre ancien', *HEF1*, pp. 479–97.

32. Grafton, *Commerce with the Classics*, pp. 19–35.

33. Roger Chartier, *The Order of Books: Readers, Authors and Libraries in Europe Between the Fourteenth and Eighteenth Centuries*, Cambridge, UK (Polity), 1994.

34. Leedham-Green & McKitterick, 'Ownership and Public Libraries', pp. 334–35.

6 Print and popular culture

1. Roger Chartier, 'Lectures paysannes: la bibliothèque de l'enquête Grégoire', *Dix-huitième siècle*, 18, 1986, p. 54; Michel de Certeau, Dominique Julia & Jacques Revel, *Une politique de la langue. La Révolution française et les patois, l'enquête de Grégoire*, Paris (Gallimard), 1975.

2. Cervantes, *Don Quixote*, trans. J.M. Cohen, Harmondsworth, UK (Penguin), 1950, part 1, ch. XXXII, p. 277.

3. David Cressy, 'Books at Totems in 17th-Century England and New England', *Journal of Library History*, 21:1, 1986, p. 99.

4. Antonio Gramsci, 'Osservazioni sul folclore', in his *Opere*, 7 vols., Turin (Einaudi), 1947–50, see vol. 6, pp. 215–18.

5. Peter Burke, *Popular Culture in Early Modern Europe*, London (Temple Smith), 1979, pp. 24–28.
6. Jean-François Botrel, *Libros, Prensa y Lectura en la España del siglo XIX*, Madrid (Fundación Germán Sánchez Ruipérez), 1993, pp. 123–33.
7. Geneviève Bollème, ed., *La Bible bleue: anthologie d'une littérature populaire*, Paris (Flammarion), 1975, pp. 64–65.
8. Robert Mandrou, *De la culture populaire aux 17e et 18e siècles: la bibliothèque bleue de Troyes*, Paris (Stock), 1964 & 1975.
9. Martyn Lyons, *Reading Culture and Writing Practices in 19th-Century France*, Toronto (Toronto UP), 2008, ch. 7.
10. Margaret Spufford, *Small Books and Pleasant Histories: Popular Fiction and Its Readership in 17th-Century England*, Cambridge (CUP), 1985, pp. 136–67; R.C. Simmons, 'ABCs, almanacs, ballads, chapbooks, popular piety and textbooks', *CHBB 4*, pp. 504–13; Lynette Hunter, 'Books for Daily Life: Household, Husbandry, Behaviour', *CHBB 4*, pp. 514–32; Jeffrey Brooks, *When Russia Learned to Read: Literacy and Popular Literature, 1861–1917*, Princeton, NJ (PUP), 1985; Niall Ó Ciosáin, *Print and Popular Culture in Ireland, 1750–1850*, Basingstoke, UK (Macmillan) and New York (St. Martin's), 1997.
11. Geneviève Bollème, *La Bibliothèque bleue: littérature populaire en France du 17e au 19e siècle*, Paris (Julliard), 1971, pp. 132–60.
12. Roger Chartier, *The Cultural Uses of Print in Early Modern France*, trans. Lydia G. Cochrane, Princeton, NJ (PUP), 1987, p. 253.
13. Ibid., pp. 292–309.
14. Mikhail Bakhtin, *Rabelais and His World*, trans. H. Iswolsky, Cambridge, MA (MIT Press), 1968.
15. Geneviève Bollème, *Les Almanachs populaires aux 17e et 18e siècles: essai d'histoire sociale*, Paris-The Hague (Ecole pratique des Hautes Etudes), 1969, p. 14.
16. Spufford, *Small Books*, p. 100.
17. Suzanne Tardieu, *La Vie domestique dans le Mâconnais rural pré-industriel*, Paris (Institut d'ethnologie), 1964, pp. 232, 358 & annexes.
18. Lodovica Braida, *Le Guide del Tempo: produzione, contenuti e forme degli almanacchi piemontesi nel Settecento*, Turin (Deputazione Subalpina di Storia Patria), 1989, p. 150.
19. Bollème, *Les Almanachs populaires*, pp. 73–76.
20. Bernard Capp, *Astrology and the Popular Press: English Almanacs, 1500–1800*, London (Faber & Faber), p. 79.
21. Maureen Perkins, *Visions of the Future: Almanacs, Time and Cultural Change*, Oxford (Clarendon), 1996, p. 126.
22. Capp, *Astrology and the Popular Press*, pp. 60 & 89.
23. Braida, *Le Guide del Tempo*, pp. 97–98 & 220–21.
24. Carlo Ginzburg, *The Cheese and the Worms: The Cosmos of a 16th-Century Miller*, trans. J. & A. Tedeschi, London (RKP), 1981, for all this section.
25. Ibid., p. xxiii.
26. Robert Darnton, 'Peasants Tell Tales: The Meaning of Mother Goose', in his *The Great Cat Massacre and Other Episodes in French Cultural History*, London (Allen Lane), 1984.

27. Marc Soriano, *Les Contes de Perrault: culture savante et traditions populaires*, Paris (Gallimard), 1968, pp. 127, 142–45 & 156. I have not followed the more extravagant Freudian interpretations discussed by Soriano and promoted by Bruno Bettelheim, *The Uses of Enchantment: The Meaning and Importance of Fairy Tales*, Harmondsworth, UK (Penguin), 1978.

28. Catherine Velay-Vallantin, 'Le Miroir de Contes: Perrault dans les bibliothèques bleues', in Roger Chartier, ed., *Les Usages de l'imprimé*, Paris (Fayard), 1987, p. 168.

29. John M. Ellis, *One Fairy Story Too Many: The Brothers Grimm and Their Tales*, Chicago (Chicago UP), 1985, ch. 3.

30. Ibid., pp. 72–75.

31. Ibid., pp. 176ff. & 193.

32. James S. Amelang, *The Flight of Icarus: Artisan Autobiography in Early Modern Europe*, Stanford, CA (Stanford UP), 1998, see p. 76 for Ruiz.

33. Ibid., ch. 4 & pp. 145–48.

34. Jacques-Louis Ménétra, *Journal de ma vie*, ed., Daniel Roche, Paris (Montalba), 1982.

35. Daniel Roche, 'Jacques-Louis Ménétra: Une manière de vivre au XVIIIe siècle', in J.-L. Ménétra, *Journal de ma vie*, Paris (Albin Michel), 1998, pp. 300–02.

36. Margaret Spufford, 'First Steps in Literacy: The Reading and Writing Experiences of the Humblest 17th-Century Spiritual Autobiographers', *Social History*, 4:3, 1979, p. 416.

37. Jean Hébrard, 'Comment Valentin Jamerey-Duval apprit-il à lire? L'autodidaxie exemplaire', in Roger Chartier, ed., *Pratiques de la lecture*, Marseille (Rivages), 1985, pp. 23–60.

7   The rise of literacy in the early modern West, c. 1600–c. 1800

1. E. Jennifer Monaghan, *Learning to Read and Write in Colonial America*, Amherst, MA (Massachusetts UP), 2005, pp. 303–04.

2. István György Tóth, *Literacy and Written Culture in Early Modern Central Europe*, Budapest (Central European UP), 2000, pp. 193–96.

3. Jeffrey Brooks, *When Russia Learned to Read: Literacy and Popular Literature, 1861–1917*, Princeton, NJ (PUP), 1985, pp. 3–30.

4. Statistics are deduced from Egil Johanson, 'The History of Literacy in Sweden', in Harvey Graff, ed., *Literacy and Social Development in the West: A reader*, Cambridge (CUP), 1981, p. 180; Kenneth A. Lockridge, *Literacy in Colonial New England: An Enquiry into the Social Context of Literacy in the Early Modern West*, New York (Norton), 1974; Monaghan, *Learning to Read and Write*, pp. 384–85; Rab Houston, 'The Literacy Myth?: Illiteracy in Scotland, 1630–1760', *P&P*, 96, 1982, pp. 86–90; Roger S. Schofield, 'Dimensions of Illiteracy in England, 1750–1850', in Graff, ed., *Literacy and Social Development*, pp. 201–13; David Cressy, *Literacy and the Social Order: Reading and Writing in Tudor and Stuart England*, Cambridge (CUP), 1980; M. Fleury & P. Valmary, 'Les Progrès de l'instruction élémentaire de Louis XIV à Napoléon III, d'après l'enquête de Louis Maggiolo,

1877–79', *Population*, 12, 1957, pp. 71–92; R. Duglio, 'Alfabetismo e società a Torino nel secolo XVIII', *Quaderni storici*, 17, 1971, pp. 485–509; Tóth, *Literacy and Written Culture*, pp. 48–52.

5. Jean-Paul Le Flem, 'Instruction, lecture et écriture en vieille Castille et Extremadure aux XVIe–XVIIe siècles', in Joseph Perez et al, eds., *De l'alphabétisation aux circuits du livre en Espagne, XVIe–XIXe siècles*, Paris (CNRS), 1987, pp. 30 & 36.

6. François Furet & W. Sachs, 'La Croissance de l'alphabétisation en France, XVIIIe-XIXe siècles', *AESC*, 29, 1974, pp. 714–37.

7. R.S. Schofield, 'The Measurement of Literacy in Pre-Industrial England', in Jack Goody, ed., *Literacy in Traditional Societies*, Cambridge (CUP), 1968, pp. 311–25.

8. Jean Hébrard, 'Comment Valentin Jamerey-Duval apprit-il à lire? L'autodidaxie exemplaire', in Roger Chartier, ed., *Pratiques de la lecture*, Marseille (Rivages), 1985, pp. 24–60.

9. Barry Reay, *Popular Cultures in England, 1550–1750*, London (Longman), 1998, p. 44.

10. Cressy, *Literacy and the Social Order*, pp. 55–56.

11. Keith Thomas, 'The Meaning of Literacy in Early Modern England', in Gerd Baumann, ed., *The Written Word: Literacy in Transition*, Oxford (Clarendon), 1986, p. 103.

12. Deborah Oxley, *Convict Maids: The Forced Migration of Women to Australia*, Cambridge (CUP), p. 142.

13. Barry Reay, 'The Context and Meaning of Popular Literacy: Some Evidence from Nineteenth-Century Rural England', *P&P*, 131, 1991, p. 111.

14. Cressy, *Literacy and the Social Order*, p. 108.

15. Tóth, *Literacy and Written Culture*, pp. 47–48, 59 & 68.

16. Emmanuel Leroy Ladurie, ed., *Histoire de la France urbaine, vol.3, La ville classique de la Renaissance aux Révolutions* (general editor Georges Duby), Paris (Seuil), 1981, pp. 268–69. There were 5,257 signatures in the sample.

17. Cressy, *Literacy and the Social Order*, ch. 6.

18. Tóth, *Literacy and Written Culture*, pp. 5–6.

19. P. Butel & G. Mandon, 'Alphabétisation et scolarisation en Aquitaine du 18e siècle au début du 19e siècle', in François Furet & Jacques Ozouf, eds., *Lire et écrire: l'alphabétisation des français de Calvin à Jules Ferry*, Paris (Editions de Minuit), 1977, tome 2, pp. 14–15 (English version: *Reading and Writing: Literacy in France from Calvin to Jules Ferry*, Cambridge, UK (CUP/MSH), 1982).

20. Tóth, *Literacy and Written Culture*, pp. 21 & 36–37.

21. Ibid., p. 42.

22. Brooks, *When Russia Learned to Read*, p. 3.

23. Sara T. Nalle, 'Literacy and Culture in Early Modern Castile', *P&P*, 125, 1989, pp. 65–96.

24. Monaghan, *Learning to Read and Write*, p. 194.

25. Cressy, *Literacy and the Social Order*, p. 129.

26. Monaghan, *Learning to Read and Write*, pp. 31–34.

27. Houston, 'The Literacy Myth?' pp. 98–99.

28. Lawrence Stone, 'Literacy and Education in England, 1640–1900', *P&P*, 42, 1969, p. 81.

29. Loftur Guttormson, 'The Development of Popular Religious Literacy in the 17th and 18th Centuries', *Scandinavian Journal of History*, 15:1, 1990, pp. 19–21.
30. Thomas Munck, 'Literacy, Educational Reform and the Use of Print in Eighteenth-Century Denmark', *EHQ*, 34:3, 2004, pp. 275–303.
31. Daniel Roche, *The People of Paris: An Essay in Popular Culture in the 18th Century*, Leamington Spa, UK (Berg), 1987, p. 199.
32. Guttormson, 'The Development of Popular Religious Literacy', pp. 22 & 31.
33. François Furet & Jacques Ozouf, 'Literacy and Industrialisation: The Case of the Département du Nord in France', *Journal of European Economic History*, 5:1, 1976, pp. 5–44; Michael Sanderson, 'Literacy and Social Mobility in the Industrial Revolution in England', *P&P*, 56, 1972, pp. 75–104.
34. Fleury & Valmary, 'Les Progrès de l'instruction élémentaire'; Roger Chartier, Dominique Julia & M.-M. Compère, *L'Education en France du XVIe au XVIIIe siècle*, Paris (SEDES), 1976, pp. 87–88.
35. Monaghan, *Learning to Read and Write*, pp. 242–43 & 301.
36. Janet Duitsman Cornelius, *'When I Can Read My Title Clear': Literacy, Slavery and Religion in the Antebellum South*, Columbia, SC (South Carolina UP), 1991, p. 69.
37. Ibid., p. 9.
38. Heather Andrea Williams, *Self-Taught: African American Education in Slavery and Freedom*, Chapel Hill, NC (North Carolina UP), 2005, p. 138.
39. Carl F. Kaestle et al, *Literacy in the United States: Readers and Reading Since 1880*, New Haven, CT (YUP), 1991, p. 31.
40. Nöé Richter, *Les Bibliothèques populaires*, Le Mans (Plein Chant), 1977, p. 6.
41. Joseph Arch, *The Story of His Life, told by himself*, London (Hutchinson), 1898, pp. 25–27.
42. 2 *Henry VI*, Act 4, Scenes 2 & 7.
43. Furet & Ozouf, *Reading and Writing*, p. 282.
44. Monaghan, *Learning to Read and Write*, chs. 2 & 6.
45. Daniele Marchesini, *Il bisogno di scrivere: usi della scrittura nell'Italia moderna*, Rome (Laterza), 1992, pp. 29–30, 44–46 & 55.
46. Ibid., p. 138.
47. Stone, 'Literacy and Education', p. 85.
48. Paulo Freire, 'The Adult Literacy Process as Cultural Action for Freedom and Education and *Conscientização*', in Eugene R. Kintgen, Barry M. Kroll & Mike Rose, eds., *Perspectives on Literacy*, Carbondale, IL (South Illinois UP), 1988, p. 405.

8   Censorship and the reading public in pre-revolutionary France

1. Gérard Dufour, 'El libro y la Inquisición', *HELE*, pp. 286.
2. Alexandra Halasz, *The Marketplace of Print: Pamphlets and the Public Sphere in Early Modern England*, Cambridge, UK (CUP), 1997, p. 12.

3. Nicole Herrmann-Mascard, *La Censure des livres à Paris à la fin de l'Ancien Régime, 1750–1789*, Paris (PUF), 1968, p. 42.

4. Madeleine Cerf, 'La Censure royale à la fin du 18e siècle', *Communications*, 9, 1967, p. 23.

5. Daniel Roche, 'Censorship and the Publishing Industry', in R. Darnton & D. Roche, eds., *Revolution in Print: The Press in France, 1775–1800*, Berkeley, CA (UCP), 1989, p. 24.

6. Jean-Dominique Mellot, 'Counterfeit Printing as an Agent of Diffusion and Change: The French Book Privilege System and its Contradictions, 1498–1790', in Sabrina Alcorn Baron et al, eds., *Agent of Change: Print Culture Studies After Elizabeth L. Eisenstein*, Amherst, MA (Massachusetts UP), 2007, pp. 42–66.

7. Robert Darnton, 'Reading, Writing and Publishing in 18th-Century France', in his *The Literary Underground of the Old Regime*, Cambridge, MA (HUP), 1982, pp. 167–210.

8. Robert Darnton, 'The High Enlightenment and the Low-Life of Literature', in *Literary Underground*, pp. 1–40.

9. Darrin M. McMahon, 'The Counter-Enlightenment and the Low-Life of Literature in Pre-Revolutionary France', *P&P*, 159, 1998, pp. 77–112.

10. Lamoignon de Malesherbes, *Mémoires sur la librairie et sur la liberté de la presse*, ed. Roger Chartier, Paris (Imprimerie Nationale), 1994, pp. 19, 63, 83 & 86.

11. François Furet, 'La "Librairie" du royaume de France au 18e siècle', in F. Furet & A. Dupront, eds., *Livre et Société dans la France du 18 siècle*, Paris/The Hague (Mouton), 2 vols., 1965, vol. 1, pp. 3–32.

12. Herrmann-Mascard, *La Censure des livres*, p. 115.

13. Jean-Marie Goulemot, *Forbidden Texts: Erotic Literature and Its Readers in Eighteenth-Century France*, Cambridge (Polity), 1994, pp. 84–85 & 104–05.

14. Robert Darnton, 'Le Livre français à la fin de l'Ancen Régime', *AESC*, 28, 1973, pp. 735–44; Robert Darnton, 'Trade in the Taboo: The Life of a Clandestine Book Dealer in Pre-revolutionary France', in P.J. Korshin, ed., *The Widening Circle: Essays on the Circulation of Literature in 18th Century Europe*, Philadelphia (Pennsylvania UP), 1976, and in *Literary Underground*, pp. 122–47.

15. Jean Quéniart, *L'Imprimerie et la librairie à Rouen au 18e siècle*, Paris (Institut armoricain de recherches historiques de Rennes), 1969, pp. 192–204.

16. René Moulinas, *L'Imprimerie, la librairie et la presse à Avignon au 18e siècle*, Grenoble (Presses universitaires de Grenoble), 1974, pp. 37–46.

17. John Lough, *Writer and Public in France from the Middle Ages to the present day*, Oxford (Clarendon), 1978, pp. 193–94.

18. Daniel Mornet, *Les Origines Intellectuelles de la Révolution française, 1715–1787*, Lyon (La Manufacture), 1989, pp. 293–95. First published in Paris (Armand Colin), 1933.

19. Suzanne Tucoo-Chala, 'Capitalisme et lumières au 18e siècle: la double réussite du libraire Ch.-J. Panckoucke, 1736–98', *Revue française d'histoire du livre*, 13, 1976, pp. 646–47.

20. George B. Watts, 'Charles-Joseph Panckoucke, "l'Atlas" de la librairie française', *Studies on Voltaire and the 18th Century*, 68, 1969, pp. 67–205;

Robert Darnton, *The Business of Enlightenment: A Publishing History of the Encyclopédie, 1775–1800*, Cambridge, MA (Belknap), 1979, pp. 66–75.

21. Darnton, *Business of Enlightenment*, p. 541.

22. Daniel Roche, *Le Peuple de Paris, essai sur la culture populaire au 18e siècle*, Paris (Aubier), 1981, pp. 206–11.

23. Jean Quéniart, *Culture et société urbaines dans la France de l'Ouest au 18e siècle*, Paris (Klincksieck), 1978, pp. 160–61.

24. Roger Chartier & Daniel Roche, 'Le Livre: un changement de perspective', in P. Nora & J. Le Goff, eds., *Faire l'histoire*, 3 vols., Paris (Gallimard), 1974, vol. 3, p. 127.

25. Jacques Solé, 'Lectures et classes populaires à Grenoble au 18e siècle: le témoignage des inventaires après décès', in *Images du Peuple au 18e siècle: colloque d'Aix-en-Provence, 1969*, Paris (A. Colin), 1973, p. 97.

26. Roche, *Le Peuple de Paris*, pp. 217–20.

27. Quéniart, *Culture et société urbaines*, pp. 213–24, 253–64, 280–86 & 306–07.

28. Abbé Grégoire, *Rapport sur la nécessité et les moyens d'anéantir les patois et d'universaliser l'usage de la langue française*, presented to National Convention, 16 Prairial Year 2.

29. Augustin Gazier, ed., *Lettres à Grégoire sur les patois de France, 1790–1794*, Geneva (Slatkine reprint of Paris edition of 1880), 1969, Bernadau to Grégoire, 14 Dec. 1790; Martyn Lyons, 'Regionalism and Linguistic Conformity in the French Revolution', in A. Forrest and P. Jones, eds., *Reshaping France: Town, Country and Region During the French Revolution*, Manchester (Manchester UP), 1991, pp. 178–92.

30. Darnton, *Business of Enlightenment*, p. 177 and for all this section.

31. Ibid., p. 526.

32. Ibid., pp. 314–15.

33. Roger Chartier, *The Cultural Origins of the French Revolution*, trans. Lydia G. Cochrane, Durham, NC (Duke UP), 1991, ch. 4.

34. Mornet, *Origines intellectuelles*.

35. Darnton, 'The High Enlightenment' & 'Trade in the Taboo'.

36. Cited by Daniel Roche, 'Printing, Books and Revolution', in Carol Armbruster, ed., *Publishing and Readership in Revolutionary France and America*, Westport, CT (Greenwood), 1993, p. 6.

37. Goulemot, *Forbidden Texts*, p. 92.

38. Chartier, *Cultural Origins*, esp. ch. 4.

39. Robert Darnton, *Forbidden Best-Sellers of Pre-Revolutionary France*, New York (Norton), 1995, and *The Corpus of Clandestine Literature in France, 1769–1789*, New York (Norton), 1995.

40. Darnton, *Forbidden Best-Sellers*, pp. 191 & 245, and 'Paris: The Early Internet', *New York Review of Books*, 29 June 2000, pp. 42–47, and electronic version at www.indiana.edu/~ahr.

41. Daniel Gordon, 'The Great Enlightenment Massacre', in Haydn T. Mason, ed., *The Darnton Debate: Books and Revolution in the Eighteenth Century*, Oxford (Voltaire Foundation), 1998, pp. 129–56; and see the contribution by Jeremy Popkin in this collection.

9   The reading fever, 1750–1830

1. Reinhard Wittmann, 'Was there a Reading Revolution at the End of the Eighteenth Century?' *HORW*, p. 285.
2. Karen Littau, *Theories of Reading: Books, Bodies and Bibliomania*, Cambridge, UK (Polity), 2006, p. 46.
3. Carla Hesse, *Publishing and Cultural Politics in Revolutionary Paris, 1789–1810*, Berkeley, CA (UCP), 1991, pp. 167–77.
4. William St. Clair, *The Reading Nation in the Romantic Period*, Cambridge, UK (CUP), 2004, pp. 118–19.
5. Jeremy D. Popkin, *News and Politics in the Age of Revolution: Jean Luzac's 'Gazette de Leyde'*, Ithaca, NY (Cornell UP), 1989, pp. 123–25.
6. Wittmann, 'Was there a Reading Revolution?', pp. 302–05.
7. James Raven, 'The Book Trades', in Isobel Rivers, ed., *Books and Their Readers in Eighteenth-Century England: New Essays*, London (Leicester UP), 2001, pp. 1–2.
8. François Lopez, 'La edición y la lectura', *HELE*, p. 269.
9. Jean-Marc Buigues, 'Evolución global de la producción', *HELE*, p. 309.
10. Gilles Feyel, 'Les frais d'impression et de diffusion de la presse parisienne entre 1789 et 1792', in Pierre Rétat, ed., *La Révolution du Journal, 1788–1794*, Paris (CNRS), 1989, pp. 77–94.
11. Hugh Gough, 'Continuité ou rupture? Les transformations structurelles de la presse provinciale, 1789–1799', *Annales historiques de la Révolution française*, 273, 1988, pp. 247–53; Antoine de Baecque, 'Pamphlets: Libel and Political Mythology', in Robert Darnton & Daniel Roche, eds., *Revolution in Print: The Press in France*, 1775–1800, Berkeley, CA (UCP), 1989, p. 165.
12. Raven, 'The Book Trades', p. 24.
13. Jack R. Censer, *The French Press in the Age of Enlightenment*, London (Routledge), pp. 185–88.
14. Jean-Claude Bonnet, 'Les Roles du journaliste selon Camille Desmoulins', in Rétat ed., *La Révolution du Journal*, pp. 180, citing *Révolutions de France et de Brabant*, 17 (my translation).
15. Jürgen Habermas, *The Structural Transformation of the Public Sphere: An Inquiry into a Category of Bourgeois Society*, Cambridge, UK (Polity), 1989, chs. 8–9.
16. Daniel Roche, *La France des Lumières*, 1993, p. 392.
17. Daniel Roche, *Le Siècle des Lumières en Province: académies et académiciens provinciaux, 1680–1789*, 2 vols., Paris & The Hague (Mouton), 1978, vol.1, pp. 82–92 and 197.
18. Sarah Maza, *Private Lives and Public Affairs: The Causes Célèbres of Prerevolutionary France*, Berkeley, CA (UCP), 1993, p. 190.
19. Keith M. Baker, 'Politics and Public Opinion Under the Old Regime: Some Reflections', in Jack R. Censer & Jeremy D. Popkin, eds., *Press and Politics in Pre-revolutionary France*, Berkeley, CA (UCP), 1987, p. 239.
20. François Furet, 'La librairie du royaume de France au 18e siècle', in F. Furet & A. Dupront, eds., *Livre et Société dans la France du 18e siècle*, Paris & The Hague (Mouton), vol.1, pp. 3–32; Robert Darnton, 'Reading, Writing

and Publishing in Eighteenth-Century France: A Case-Study in the Sociology of Literature', *Daedalus*, 100, 1971, pp. 214–56.

21. Wittmann, 'Was there a Reading Revolution?' p. 302.
22. David D. Hall, 'The History of the Book: New Questions? New Answers?' *Journal of Library History*, 21:1, 1986, pp. 32–33.
23. William J. Gilmore, *Reading Becomes a Necessity of Life: Material and Cultural Life in Rural New England, 1780–1835*, Knoxville, TN (Tennessee UP), 1989, pp. 248–75.
24. David D. Hall & Elizabeth Carroll Reilly, 'Practices of Reading', in *HOBAmerica1*, pp. 387–88.
25. Renato Pasta, 'Editoria e pubblico nell'Italia del '700', paper delivered to the International Conference on the History of the Book, Prato, 2001.
26. Frédéric Barbier, *Histoire du livre*, Paris (Armand Colin), 2000, p. 185.
27. Roger Chartier, *The Cultural Origins of the French Revolution*, Durham, NC (Duke UP), 1991, ch. 5; Michel Vovelle, 'Le tournant des mentalités en France 1750–1789: la sensibilité pré-révolutionnaire', *Social History*, 5, 1977, pp. 605–29.
28. Cathy N. Davidson, *Revolution and the Word: The Rise of the Novel in America*, New York (OUP), 1986, pp. 10 & 39.
29. Ian Watt, *The Rise of the Novel: Studies in Defoe, Richardson and Fielding*, Berkeley, CA (UCP), 1957.
30. James Raven, 'New Reading Histories, Print Culture and the Identification of Change: The Case of Eighteenth-Century England', *Social History*, 23:3, 1998, pp. 268–87.
31. Harold W. Streeter, *The Eighteenth-Century English Novel in French Translation*, New York (Institute of French Studies), 1936, p. 252.
32. Daniel Mornet, 'Les enseignements des bibliothèques privées, 1750–1780', *Revue d'Histoire Littéraire de la France*, 17, 1910, p. 461.
33. St. Clair, *Reading Nation*, p. 221.
34. Albert Ward, *Book Production, Fiction and the German Reading Public, 1740–1800*, Oxford (Clarendon), 1974, p. 168.
35. Jan Fergus, 'Women Readers: A Case Study', in Vivien Jones, ed., *Women and Literature in Britain, 1700–1800*, Cambridge, UK (CUP), 2000, p. 157.
36. Jacqueline Pearson, *Women's Reading in Britain, 1750–1835: A Dangerous Recreation*, Cambridge, UK (CUP), 1999, cit. p. 22.
37. Ibid., pp. 105 & 197.
38. James Green, 'Subscription Libraries and Commercial Circulating Libraries in Colonial Philadelphia and New York', in Thomas Augst & Kenneth Carpenter, eds., *Institutions of Reading: The Social Life of Libraries in the United States*, Amherst, MA (Massachusetts UP), 2007, pp. 53–71.
39. St. Clair, *Reading Nation*, p. 40 & ch. 7.
40. Rolf Engelsing, *Der Bürger als Leser: Lesergeschichte in Deutschland, 1500–1800*, Stuttgart (Metzlersche Verlag), 1974.
41. Samuel Goodrich, *Recollections of a Lifetime*, 2 vols., New York, 1857, vol. 1, pp. 71–86, cited by David D. Hall, *Cultures of Print: Essays in the History of the Book*, Amherst, MA (Massachusetts UP), 1996, pp. 54–55.
42. Matthew P. Brown, *The Pilgrim and the Bee: Reading Rituals and Book Culture in Early New England*, Philadelphia, PA (Pennsylvania UP), 2007, pp. x–xii.

43. Ibid., cit. p. 81.
44. Hall, *Cultures of Print*, p. 55.
45. Martyn Lyons and Lucy Taksa, *Australian Readers Remember: An Oral History of Reading 1890–1930*, Melbourne (OUP), 1992, ch. 3.
46. Ibid., p. 32.
47. Wittmann, 'Was there a Reading Revolution?' p. 297; Littau, *Theories of Reading*, p. 68.
48. Claude Labrosse, *Lire au XVIIIe siècle: 'La Nouvelle Héloïse' et ses lecteurs*, Lyon (Lyon UP), 1985, p. 87.
49. Robert Darnton, 'Readers Respond to Rousseau: The Fabrication of Romantic Sensitivity', in *The Great Cat Massacre and other Episodes in French Cultural History*, London (Allen Lane), 1984, pp. 215–56.
50. Labrosse, *Lire au XVIIIe siècle*, pp. 27–29.
51. Pearson, *Women's Reading in Britain*, p. 28.
52. John Brewer, *The Pleasures of the Imagination: English Culture in the 18th Century*, New York (Farrar Straus Giroux), 1997, pp. 194–97.

10   The age of the mass reading public

1. David M. Henkin, 'City Streets and the Urban World of Print', *HOBAmerica3*, p. 331.
2. Frédéric Barbier, *L'empire du livre: Le livre imprimé et la construction de l'Allemagne contemporaine*, 1815–1914, Paris (Cerf), 1995, p. 31.
3. Honoré de Balzac, *Illusions perdues*, Paris (Gallimard-livres de poche), 1962, p. 16.
4. James Moran, *Printing Presses: History and Development from the 15th Century to Modern Times*, London (Faber & Faber), ch. 7.
5. Ibid., ch. 9 and p. 185.
6. Balzac, *Illusions Perdues*, p. 13.
7. Moran, *Printing Presses*, p. 110.
8. Ibid., ch. 9 and p. 190.
9. Pilar Vélez i Vicente, 'La industrialización de la técnicas', *HELE*, p. 546.
10. Alexis Weedon, *Victorian Publishing. The Economics of Book Production for a Mass Market, 1836–1916*, Aldershot, UK (Ashgate), 2003, p. 64.
11. Barbier, *L'empire du livre*, p. 327.
12. Simon Eliot, *Some Patterns and Trends in British Publishing, 1800–1919*, London (Bibliographical Society), 1994, section A.
13. Robert Estivals, *La statistique bibliographique de la France*, Paris & The Hague (Mouton), 1965, p. 415.
14. Barbier, *L'empire du livre*, p. 47.
15. Martyn Lyons, 'Britain's Largest Export Market', *HOBA2*, p. 19.
16. Charles Louandre, 'Statistique littéraire de la production intellectuelle en France depuis quinze ans', *Revue des Deux Mondes*, 20, 1847, pp. 681ff.; Martyn Lyons, *Le Triomphe du livre: Une histoire sociologique de la lecture dans la France du XIX siècle*, Paris (Promodis/Cercle de la librairie), 1987, p. 14.
17. Barbara Sicherman, 'Ideologies and Practices of Reading', *HOBAmerica3*, p. 289.

18. Eliot, *Some Patterns*, section C.
19. Ibid., section C.
20. Leslie Howsam, *Cheap Bibles. Nineteenth-Century Publishing and the British and Foreign Bible Society*, Cambridge, UK (CUP), 1991, p. 118.
21. Jean-Yves Mollier, *Michel et Calmann-Lévy ou la naissance de l'édition moderne, 1836–1891*, Paris (Calmann-Lévy), 1984, pp. 322–23.
22. Claire Parfait, *The Publishing History of Uncle Tom's Cabin, 1852–2002*, Aldershot, UK (Ashgate), 2007, pp. 100–08.
23. Adeline Daumard, *Les Bourgeois de Paris au XIXe siècle*, Paris (Flammarion), 1970, p. 75.
24. Richard D. Altick, *Writers, Readers, Occasions: Selected Essays on Victorian Literature and Life*, Columbus, OH (Ohio State UP), 1989, pp. 226–27.
25. Thomas C. Leonard, *News For All: America's Coming-Of-Age with the Press*, New York (OUP), 1995, p. 91.
26. Ibid., pp. 53–56.
27. Elisabeth Parinet, *la Librairie Flammarion, 1875–1914*, Paris (IMEC), 1992, pp. 191–225 & 301.
28. Barbier, *L'empire du livre*, pp. 93–96.
29. Sylve Baulo, 'La producción por entregas y las colecciones semanales', *HELE*, pp. 586–87.
30. John Sutherland, *Victorian Fiction: Writers, Publishers, Readers*, Basingstoke, UK (Macmillan), 1995, pp. 90–91.
31. Lyons, *Triomphe du livre*, p. 61.
32. Nicole Felkay, *Balzac et ses éditeurs, 1822–1837: essai sur la librairie romantique*, Paris (Promodis/Cercle de la librairie), 1987, pp. 138–59 (Mame) and pp. 219–49 (Werdet).
33. Jean-Yves Mollier, *L'Argent et les lettres: histoire du capitalisme d'édition, 1880–1920*, Paris (Fayard), 1988, pp. 227 & 233.
34. Ibid., pp. 236–47 (Garnier) & 356–79 (Calmann-Lévy).
35. Christine Haynes, 'An "Evil Genius": The Construction of the Publisher in the Postrevolutionary Social Imaginary', *French Historical Studies*, 30:4, 2007, pp. 559–95.
36. Jean-Yves Mollier, *Louis Hachette*, Paris (Fayard), 1999, p. 225.
37. Ibid., p. 326.
38. Eliot, *Some Patterns*, section B.
39. Michael B. Palmer, 'Some Aspects of the French Press During the Rise of the Popular Daily, c.1860 to 1890', Oxford University D. Phil thesis, 1972, p. 381.
40. Mollier, *Louis Hachette*, ch. XI; Elisabeth Parinet, 'Les bibliothèques de gare, un nouveau réseau pour le livre', *Romantisme*, 80, 1993, pp. 95–106.
41. Françoise Parent-Lardeur, *Les Cabinets de lecture: La lecture publique sous la Restauration*, Paris (Payot), 1982. This figure includes bookshops that lent books.
42. Barbier, *L'empire du livre*, pp. 502–03.
43. Lyons, *Triomphe du livre*, p. 173.
44. Jean Hassenforder, *Développement comparé des bibliothèques publiques en France, en Grande-Bretagne et aux Etats-Unis dans la seconde moitié du XIXe siècle, 1850–1914*, Paris (Cercle de la librairie), 1967.

45. Abigail A. Van Slyck, *Free to All: Carnegie Libraries and American Culture, 1890–1920*, Chicago (Chicago UP), 1995, pp. 138–39.
46. Ibid., pp. 158–59.
47. Barbier, *L'empire du livre*, p. 161.
48. Lyons, *Triomphe du livre*, pp. 197–200.
49. Barbier, *L'empire du livre*, p. 236; Marie-Claire Bosq, 'L'implantation des libraires à Paris, 1815–1848', in Jean-Yves Mollier, ed., *Le Commerce de la Librairie en France au XIXe siècle, 1789–1914*, Paris (IMEC/MSH), 1997, pp. 27–50.
50. Ana Martínez Rus, 'El libro en la calle. De la venta ambulante a les ferias del libro', in Antonio Castillo Gómez & Verónica Sierra Blas, eds., *Senderos de ilusión: Lecturas populares en Europa y América latina del siglo XVI a nuestros días*, Madrid (TREA), 2007, p. 171.
51. Barbier, *L'empire du livre*, p. 96.
52. Eliot, *Some Patterns*, pp. 106–07.
53. Eugen Weber, *Peasants into Frenchmen: The Modernisation of Rural France, 1870–1914*, London (Chatto & Windus), 1977.

11 New readers and reading cultures

1. Arnould Frémy, 'Comment lisent les français aujourd'hui?' Paris (Calmann-Lévy), 1878, pp. 7 & 67–92.
2. Jonathan Rose, 'Rereading the English Common Reader: A Preface to a History of Audiences', *Journal of the History of Ideas*, 53:1, 1992, pp. 47–70.
3. Wilkie Collins, 'The Unknown Public', in I.B. Nadel, ed., *Victorian Fiction: A Collection of Essays*, New York (Garland), 1986.
4. R. Grew & P.J. Harrigan, *School, State and Society: The Growth of Elementary Schooling in Nineteenth-Century France – A Quantitative Analysis*, Ann Arbor (Michigan UP), 1991, p. 47.
5. Pierre-Jakez Hélias, *The Horse of Pride: Life in a Breton Village*, trans. J. Guicharnaud, New Haven, CT (YUP), 1978, p. 96.
6. Evelyne Sullerot, *La Presse féminine*, Paris (Armand Colin), 1963, pp. 16–30.
7. *Le Journal illustré*, no. 8, 3–10 April 1864.
8. Stendhal, *Correspondance*, ed. A. Paupe & P.-A. Chéramy, 3 vols., Paris (Bosse), 1908, vol. 3, pp. 89–92.
9. Barbara Sicherman, 'Sense and Sensibility: A Case Study of Women's Reading in Late-Victorian America', in Cathy N. Davidson, ed., *Reading in America: Literature and Social History*, Baltimore (Johns Hopkins UP), 1989, pp. 206–07.
10. Georges Duby, ed., *Histoire de la France urbaine, vol.4, La Ville de l'âge industriel: Le cycle haussmannien*, Paris (Seuil), 1983, p. 366.
11. Anne-Marie Thiesse, *Le Roman du quotidien: Lecteurs et lectures populaires à la Belle Epoque*, Paris (Le Chemin Vert), 1984, p. 22 (my translation).
12. Ibid., and Martyn Lyons & Lucy Taksa, ' "If Mother Caught Us Reading!": Impressions of the Australian Woman Reader, 1890–1933', *Australian Cultural History*, 11, 1992, pp. 39–50.

13. John Burnett, ed., *Useful Toil: Autobiographies of Working People from the 1820s to the 1920s*, Harmondsworth, UK (Penguin), 1977, pp. 224 and 231.

14. Emma Goldmann, *Living My Life*, London (Pluto) 1987, vol. 1, p. 12 (first published 1931).

15. Carl F. Kaestle et al, *Literacy in the United States: Readers and Reading Since 1880*, New Haven, CT (YUP), 1991, p. 241.

16. Margaret Penn, *Manchester Fourteen Miles*, Sussex, UK (Caliban reprint), 1979.

17. Martyn Lyons, *Le Triomphe du livre: Une histoire sociologique de la lecture dans la France du XIXe siècle*, Paris (Promodis/Cercle de la librairie), 1987, p. 186.

18. Kelly J. Mays, 'The Disease of Reading and Victorian Periodicals', in John O. Jordan & Robert L. Patten, eds., *Literature in the Marketplace: Nineteenth-Century British Publishing and Reading Practices*, Cambridge, UK (CUP), 1995, ch. 8, pp. 176–78.

19. Kate Flint, *The Woman Reader, 1837–1914*, Oxford (Clarendon), 1993, ch. 4 & p. 219.

20. Ibid., p. 99.

21. Joseph McAleer, *Popular Reading and Publishing in Britain, 1914–1950*, Oxford (Clarendon), 1992, p. 100.

22. Ibid., p. 100.

23. Janice Radway, *Reading the Romance: Women, Patriarchy and Popular Literature*, London (Verso), 1987, p. 221.

24. 'Books That Everybody Should Read', *The Woman's Voice*, 2:24, 29 June 1895, p. 282.

25. Adelheid Popp, *La Jeunesse d'une ouvrière*, Paris (Maspéro), 1979, pp. 30–32, first published with a preface by August Bebel as *Die jugendgeschichte einer Arbeiterin*, Munich, 1909.

26. Ibid., p. 75.

27. Dieter Langewiesche & Klaus Schonhoven, 'Arbeiterbibliotheken und Arbeiterlektüre in Wilhelmischen Deutschland', *Archiv für Sozialgeschichte*, 16, 1976, p. 136.

28. Frédéric Barbier, *L'empire du livre: Le livre imprimé et la construction de l'Allemagne contemporaine, 1815–1914*, Paris (Cerf), 1995, pp. 487–88.

29. Charles Dickens, *Speeches*, ed., K.J. Fielding, Oxford (Clarendon), 1960, pp. 152–54.

30. Lyons, *Triomphe du livre*, pp. 186–87.

31. Martin Hewitt, 'Confronting the Modern City: The Manchester Free Public Library, 1850–80', *Urban History*, 27:1, 2000, p. 73.

32. Ibid., pp. 80–82.

33. Jean-François Botrel, 'Narrativas y lecturas del pueblo en la España del siglo XIX', *Cuadernos Hispanoamericanos*, 516, 1993, p. 83.

34. Lewis C. Roberts, 'Disciplining and Disinfecting Working-Class Readers in the Victorian Public Library', *Victorian Literature and Culture*, 26:1, 1998, pp. 122–23 and 125–27; Michel Foucault, *Discipline and Punish: The Birth of the Prison*, Harmondsworth, UK (Penguin), 1979.

35. Langewiesche & Schonhoven, 'Arbeiterbibliotheken und Arbeiterlektüre', p. 167.

36. Lyons, *Triomphe du livre*, p. 190.

37. Ibid., pp. 182–83.

38. Jean-Baptiste Dumay, *Mémoires d'un militant ouvrier du Creusot, 1841–1905*, ed. Pierre Ponsot, Grenoble (Maspéro), 1976, pp. 116–18.

39. Jonathan Rose, *The Intellectual Life of the British Working Classes*, New Haven, CT (YUP), 2001.

40. Ibid., pp. 100–01.

41. Thomas Augst, *The Clerk's Tale: Young Men and Moral Life in Nineteenth-Century America*, Chicago (Chicago UP), 2003, for example ch. 1 & pp. 161–71.

42. Nöé Richter, *La Conversion du Mauvais Lecteur et la Naissance de la Lecture publique*, Marigné (La Queue du Chat), 1992, pp. 9–22.

43. G.H. Roberts, 'How I Got On', *Pearson's Weekly* (London), 17 May 1906, p. 806c.

44. William Lovett, *Life and Struggles of William Lovett, in His Pursuit of Bread, Knowledge and Freedom*, London (Trubner), 1876, p. 416.

45. Ned Peters, *A Gold Digger's Diaries*, ed. Les Blake, Newtown, Victoria (Neptune), 1981.

46. M. Askew and B. Hubber, 'The Colonial Reader Observed: Reading in Its Cultural Context', in D.H. Borchardt & W. Kirsop, eds., *The Book in Australia: Essays Towards a Cultural and Social History*, Melbourne (Australian Reference Publications), 1988, pp. 129–30.

47. Peters, *A Gold Digger's Diaries*, pp. 80–81, 114, & 124.

48. Kaestle, *Literacy in the United States*, p. 231.

49. Rose, *Intellectual Life of the British Working Classes*, for this section. See pp. 60, 83, 180, 201 & 237.

12   The democratisation of writing, 1800 to the present

1. Françoise Simonet-Tenant, *Le journal intime: genre littéraire et écriture ordinaire*, Paris (Téraèdre), 2004, pp. 36–37.

2. Lynn Z. Bloom, ' "I Write for Myself and Strangers": Private Diaries as Public Documents', in Suzanne L. Bunkers & Cynthia A. Huff, eds., *Inscribing the Daily: Critical Essays on Women's Diaries*, Amherst, MA (Massachusetts UP), 1996, p. 23.

3. Examples include Bunkers & Huff, *Inscribing the Daily*; Harriet Blodgett, *Centuries of Female Days: Englishwomen's Private Diaries*, New Brunswick, NJ (Rutgers UP), 1988; Lorely French, *German Women as Letter Writers: 1750–1850*, Madison (Fairleigh Dickinson UP), 1996.

4. J.-P. Albert, 'Ecritures domestiques', in Daniel Fabre, ed., *Ecritures ordinaires*, Paris (POL/Centre Georges Pompidou), 1993, pp. 78–79.

5. Philippe Lejeune, *'Cher cahier...': témoignages sur le journal personnel*, Paris (Gallimard), 1989, index no.6.

6. Eugénie de Guérin, *Journal*, Albi (Ateliers professionnels de l'Orphelinat St.-Jean), 60th ed., 1977; Martyn Lyons, *Readers and Society in 19th-Century France: Workers, Women, Peasants*, New York & Basingstoke, UK (Palgrave), pp. 103–08.

7. Béatrice Didier, *Le Journal intime*, Paris (PUF), 1976, pp. 56–59.

8. Marie-Claude Penloup, 'Literary Temptations and Leisure-time Copying: Spontaneous Adolescent Writing in Contemporary France', in Martyn Lyons, ed., *Ordinary Writings, Personal Narratives: Writing Practices in 19th and Early 20th-Century Europe*, Bern (Peter Lang), 2007, p. 206.
9. Philippe Lejeune, *Le Moi des demoiselles: enquête sur le journal de jeune fille*, Paris (Seuil), 1993, p. 11.
10. Michelle Perrot & Georges Ribeill, eds., *Le Journal Intime de Caroline B.*, Paris (Montalba), 1985.
11. Ibid., p. 207.
12. Jean-Pierre Baylac, 'Journal Intime', *Les Temps Modernes*, sept. 1951, 71, pp. 495–508.
13. Marie-Claude Penloup, *La tentation du littéraire*, Paris (Didier), 2000.
14. Lejeune, *'Cher cahier…'*, pp. 86–87.
15. Roger Chartier, ed., *La Correspondance: les usages de la lettre au XIXe siècle*, Paris (Fayard), 1991, p. 369.
16. Cécile Dauphin, 'Pour une histoire de la correspondance familiale', *Romantisme*, 90, 1995, pp. 92–93.
17. Chartier, *Correspondance*, p. 87.
18. Ibid., p. 39; David Vincent, *Literacy and Popular Culture in England, 1750–1914*, Cambridge, UK (CUP), 1989, p. 39; New South Wales PMG's Annual Report, 1901.
19. Paolo Macry, 'La Napoli dei dotti: Lettori, Libri, e bibliotheche di una ex-capitale, 1870–1900', *Meridiana*, 4, 1988, pp. 131–61.
20. Annabella Boswell, *Some Recollections of My Early Days, Written at Different Periods*, probably Sydney, no date (?1908), p. 19.
21. Michelle Perrot, 'Le Secret de la Correspondance au XIXe siècle', in Mireille Bossis & Charles A. Porter, eds., *L'Epistolarité à travers les siècles (Actes du colloque de Cérisy)*, Stuttgart (Franz Steiner), 1990, pp. 184–88.
22. Cécile Dauphin *et al*, eds., *Ces Bonnes Lettres: une correspondance familiale au XIXe siècle*, Paris (Albin Michel), 1995, pp. 161–77.
23. Ibid., pp. 70–71.
24. Ibid., pp. 118–19.
25. Ibid., p. 170.
26. Ibid., pp. 106–07.
27. Susan Foley, ' "J'avais tant besoin d'être aimée…par correspondance": les discours de l'amour dans la correspondance de Léonie Léon et Léon Gambetta, 1872–1882', *Clio – histoire, femmes et sociétés*, 24, 2006, pp. 157–58.
28. Marie-Claire Grassi, 'Des Lettres qui parlent d'amour', *Romantisme*, 68, 1990, pp. 23–32.
29. Antonio Castillo Gómez, 'De la suscripción a la necesidad de escribir', in A. Castillo Gómez, ed., *La conquista del alfabeto: Escritura y clases populares*, Gijón (Trea), 2002, pp. 21–51.
30. Anna Kuismin, 'Hymn as the Genre for Self-Educated Women in 19th-Century Finland', unpublished paper.
31. André Loez, 'Mots et Cultures de l'Indiscipline: les graffiti des mutins de 1917', *Genèses*, 59, juin 2005, pp. 25–46.
32. Judy Kalman, *Writing on the Plaza: Mediated Literacy Practice Among Scribes and Clients in Mexico City*, Creskill, NJ (Hampton Press), 1999.

33. Witold Kula & Josephine Wtulich, *Writing Home: Immigrants in Brazil and the United States, 1890–1891*, New York (Columbia UP), 1986, p. 104.
34. Antonio Gibelli, 'Emigrantes y Soldados. La escritura como práctica de masas en los siglos XIX y XX', in Castillo Gómez, ed., *La conquista del alfabeto*, p. 197.
35. Martyn Lyons, 'French Soldiers and Their Correspondence: Towards a History of Writing Practices in the First World War', *French History*, 17:1, 2003, pp. 79–95.
36. www.museostorico.tn.it/asp/approfondimenti.htm.
37. Martène Albert-Llorca, 'Le Courrier du Ciel', in Fabre ed., *Ecritures ordinaires*, pp. 183–221.
38. George T. Blakers, *A Useless Young Man? An Autobiography of Life in Australia, 1849–64*, Melbourne (Australian Large Print), 1989, p. 152.
39. Laura Martínez Martín, 'The Correspondence of Asturian Emigrants at the End of the 19th and Beginning of the 20th Centuries', unpublished conference paper.
40. Barnett Singer. *Village Notables in Nineteenth-Century France: Priests, Mayors, Schoolmasters*, Albany, NY (State University of New York Press), 1983, p. 39.
41. Antoine Sylvère, *Toinou, le cri d'un enfant auvergnat, pays d'Ambert*, Paris (Plon), 1980, pp. 153–54.
42. Cécile Dauphin, *'Prête-moi ta Plume...': les manuels épistolaires au XIXe siècle*, Paris (Kimé), 2000, p. 26.
43. *Beeton's Complete Letter-Writer for Gentlemen*, London (Ward Lock), no date (1890s). p. v.
44. Verónica Sierra Blas, '¡Cuidado con la Pluma! Los Manuales epistolares en el siglo XX', *Litterae*, 3–4, 2003–04, p. 299.
45. *Dymock's Australian Letter-Writer for Ladies and Gentlemen*, Sydney (Dymocks), no date (about 1911?).
46. Marina Roggero, 'La Escritura de los grupos populares en la Italia del Antiguo regimen', in Castillo Gómez, ed., *La conquista del alfabeto*, p. 71.

13   Readers and writers in the digital age

1. D. Giugni & A. Terry, *Challenge: Technological Change*, Roseville, NSW (McGraw-Hill Australia), 1998, p. 11. I am grateful to Claudine Lyons for bringing this to my attention.
2. Jeanette Gilfedder, 'A Contemporary Italian Publishing Phenomenon: The *Millelire* Series', unpublished PhD thesis, Griffith University, Queensland, 1999, pp. 192–99.
3. Isabelle de Conihout, 'La conjoncture de l'édition', *HEF4*, p. 78.
4. Janick Jossin, 'La France se met à lire', *L'Express*, 4–11 nov. 1978, p. 82.
5. Colombe Schneck, *La lecture en Europe: Les pratiques de lecture en France, Allemagne, Grande-Bretagne, Italie et Espagne*, Paris (France Edition), 1993, pp. 8–10.
6. Milan Voykovic, 'The Culture of Thriller Fiction in Britain, 1898–1945: Authors, Publishers and the First World War', unpublished Ph.D. thesis,

University of New South Wales, 1996, for these details from the Hodder & Stoughton Archive.

7. Gideon Reuveni, *Reading Germany: Literature and Consumer Culture in Germany Before 1933*, New York (Berghahn), 2006.

8. Stephen Mogridge, *Talking Shop*, London, 1949, cited in Joseph McAleer, *Popular Reading and Publishing in Britain, 1914–1950*, Oxford (Clarendon), 1992, p. 84.

9. De Conihout, 'La conjoncture de l'édition', *HEF4*, p. 89.

10. Gabriele Turi, 'Cultura e poteri nell'Italia repubblicana, in Gabriele Turi, ed., *Storia dell'Editoria nell'Italia contemporanea*, Florence (Giunti), 1997, p. 439.

11. Gianfranco Pedulla, 'Gli anni di fascismo: imprenditora privata e intervento statale', in Turi, *Storia dell'Editoria*, pp. 346–56.

12. Vadim V. Volkov, 'Limits to Propaganda: Soviet Power and the Peasant Reader in the 1920s', in James Raven, ed., *Free Print and Non-Commercial Publishing since 1700*, Aldershot, UK (Ashgate), 2000, pp. 177–93.

13. D. Milo, 'La Bourse mondiale de la traduction: Un baromètre culturel?' *AESC*, 39, 1984, pp. 92–115.

14. Stephen Lovell, *The Russian Reading Revolution: Print Culture in the Soviet and Post-Soviet Eras*, Basingstoke, UK (Macmillan) & New York (St. Martin's), 2000, chs. 2 & 4.

15. McAleer, *Popular Reading*, p. 59.

16. Richard Hoggart, *Penguin's Progress, 1935–1960*, Harmondsworth, UK (Penguin), 1960.

17. Gilfedder, 'A Contemporary Italian Publishing Phenomenon', for this section.

18. Janice A. Radway, *A Feeling for Books: The Book-of-the-Month Club, Literary Taste and Middle-Class Desire*, Chapel Hill, NC (North Carolina UP), 1997, p. 261.

19. Ibid., pp. 294–300.

20. Ibid., pp. 93–94.

21. Ibid., pp. 114–17.

22. *Le Monde*, 1–2 oct. 2000, p. 16.

23. *The Guardian*, January 2000, cited in Jenny Hartley, *Reading Groups*, Oxford (OUP), 2001, p. 4.

24. http://www2.oprah.com/books

25. Hartley, *Reading Groups*, for all this section.

26. Janice Radway, *Reading the Romance: Women, Patriarchy and Popular Literature*, London (Verso), 1987, p. 221.

27. Elizabeth Long, *Book Clubs: Women and the Uses of Reading in Everyday Life*, Chicago (Chicago UP), 2003, p. 101 & chapter 5.

28. Hartley, *Reading Groups*, p. 48.

29. Jorge Luis Borges, *Fictions*, trans. A. Kerrigan, London (John Calder), 1965, pp. 75–76.

30. Barbara Brannon, 'The Laser Printer as an Agent of Change: Fixity and Fluxion in the Digital Age', in Sabina Alcorn Baron, Eric N. Lindquist & Eleanor F. Shevlin, eds., *Agent of Change: Print Culture Studies after Elizabeth L. Eisenstein*, Amherst, MA (Massachusetts UP), 2007, pp. 353–64.

31. Roy Rozensweig, 'Scarcity or Abundance? Preserving the Past in a Digital Era', in Thomas Augst & Kenneth Carpenter, eds., *Institutions of Reading: The Social Life of Libraries in the United States*, Amherst, MA (Massachusetts UP), 2007, pp. 310–42, cited at page 315.

32. Emmanuel Hoog, 'Internet a-t-il une mémoire?' *Le Monde*, 17 août 2002.

33. Daniel Pennac, *Comme un Roman*, Paris (Gallimard-nrf), 1992, pp. 139–44 and 'les droits imprescriptibles du lecteur'.

34. Antonio Viñao Frago, 'Del Periódico a Internet. Leer y Escribir en los Siglos XIX y XX', in Antonio Castillo Gómez, ed., *Historia de la cultura escrita del Próximo Oriente Antiguo a la sociedad informatizada*, Gijón (Trea), 2002, pp. 329–30.

35. Thomas Augst, *The Clerk's Tale: Young Men and Moral Life in Nineteenth-Century America*, Chicago (Chicago UP), 2003, p. 219.

36. Hermann Hesse, 'Die Schreibmaschine', *März*, 4, 1908, pp. 377–78.

37. Catherine Viollet, 'Ecriture mécanique, espaces de frappe: Quelques préalables à une sémiologie du dactylogramme', *Genesis*, 10, 1996, p. 198.

38. Giulia Giuffre, *A Writing Life: Interviews with Australian Women Writers*, Sydney (Allen & Unwin), 1990, p. 155.

39. Christina Stead, *I'm Dying Laughing: The Humourist*, Melbourne (Penguin), 1989, p. 151.

40. Bernard Lehire, *La Raison des plus faibles*, Lille (Lille UP), 1993, chs. 7 & 8.

41. Yasmine Siblot, ' "Je suis la secrétaire de la famille!" La prise en charge féminine des tâches administratives entre subordination et ressource', *Genèses*, 64, 2006, pp. 46–66.

42. Raymonde Ladefroux, Michèle Petit & Claude-Michèle Gardien, *Lecteurs en Campagnes: Les ruraux lisent-ils autrement?*, Paris (Centre Georges Pompidou/ Bibliothèque publique d'information), 1993, p. 140; for other surveys, see Jossin, 'La France se met à lire', Schneck, *La lecture en Europe*, and Olivier Donnat & Denis Cogneau, *Les pratiques culturelles des français*, 1973–89, Paris (La Découverte/ La Documentation française), 1990.

43. Ladefroux *et al*, *Lecteurs en campagnes*, p. 202.

44. Olivier Péretié & Anne Fohr, 'Mais si, ils aiment lire!', *Le Nouvel Observateur*, 4–10 mars 1999.

45. http://unescostat.unesco.org//Yearbook

Further reading

These suggestions for further reading are confined to major works published in (or translated into) English. More detailed references may be found in the notes to each chapter.

International and national histories, general and collective works

Augst, Thomas and Kenneth Carpenter, eds., *Institutions of Reading: The Social Life of Libraries in the United States*, Amherst, MA (Massachusetts UP), 2007.

Barker, Nicholas, ed., *A Potencie of Life: Books in Society*, London (British Library), 1993.

Bourdieu, Pierre, *Distinction: A Social Critique of the Judgement of Taste*, London (RKP), 1984.

Carpenter, Kenneth, E., ed., *Books and Society in History*, New York (Bowker), 1983.

Cavallo, Guglielmo and Roger Chartier, eds., *A History of Reading in the West*, Cambridge, UK (Polity), 1999.

Certeau, Michel de, *The Practice of Everyday Life*, trans. Steven Rendall, Berkeley, CA (California UP), 1984.

Chartier, Roger, *Cultural History: Between Practices and Representations*, Oxford (Polity), 1988.

Chartier, Roger, *The Order of Books: Readers, Authors and Libraries in Europe Between the Fourteenth and the Eighteenth Centuries*, Cambridge, UK (Polity), 1993.

Colclough, Stephen, *Consuming Texts: Readers and Reading Communities, 1695–1870*, New York (Palgrave Macmillan), 2007.

Davidson, Cathy, N., ed., *Reading in America: Literature and Social History*, Baltimore (Johns Hopkins UP), 1989.

Darnton, Robert, *The Kiss of Lamourette: Reflections in Cultural History*, New York (Norton), 1990.

Finkelstein, David and Alistair McCreery, eds., *The Book History Reader*, London and New York (Routledge), 2002.

Fish, Stanley, *Is There a Text in This Class? The Authority of Interpretive Communities*, Cambridge, MA (HUP), 1980.

Fleming, Patricia, L., Gilles Gallichan and Yvan Lamande, eds., *History of the Book in Canada, vol.1, Beginnings to 1840*, Toronto (Toronto UP), 2004.

Graff, Harvey, ed., *Literacy and Social Development in the West: A Reader*, Cambridge, UK (CUP), 1981.

Hall, David, D., General ed., *A History of the Book in America*, Cambridge, UK (CUP), and Chapel Hill, NC (North Carolina UP and American Antiquarian Society), 5 vols., 2000.

Howsam, Leslie, *Old Books and New Histories: An Orientation to Studies in Book and Print Culture*, Toronto (Toronto UP), 2006.

Lyons, Martyn, 'The History of Reading from Gutenberg to Gates', *European Legacy*, 4:5, 1999, pp. 50–57.

Lyons, Martyn and John Arnold, eds., *A History of the Book in Australia, 1891–1945: A National Culture in a Colonised Market*, St. Lucia (University of Queensland Press), 2001.

Manguel, Alberto, *A History of Reading*, London (Harper-Collins), 1986.

Martin, Henri-Jean, *The History and Power of Writing*, trans. Lydia G. Cochrane, Chicago (Chicago UP), 1994.

McKenzie, D.F., D.J. McKitterick and I.R. Willison, eds., *Cambridge History of the Book in Britain*, 7 vols., Cambridge (CUP), 1999–.

Resnick, Daniel, P., ed., *Literacy in Historical Perspective*, Washington (Library of Congress), 1983.

Zboray, Ronad, J. and Mary Saracino Zboray, *A Handbook for the Study of Book History in the United States*, Washington DC (Library of Congress Center for the Book), 2000.

Anthropology and ethnography

Boyarin, Jonathan, ed., *The Ethnography of Reading*, Berkeley, CA (UCP), 1993.

Goody, Jack, ed., *Literacy in Traditional Societies*, Cambridge, UK (CUP), 1968.

Goody, Jack, *The Logic of Writing and the Organization of Society*, Cambridge, UK (CUP), 1986.

Kintgen, Eugene, R., Barry M. Kroll and Mike Rose, eds., *Perspectives on Literacy*, Carbondale, IL (Southern Illinois UP), 1988.

Olson, David, R., *The World on Paper: The Conceptual and Cognitive Implications of Writing and Reading*, Cambridge, UK (CUP), 1994.

Ong, Walter, J., *Orality and Literacy: The Technologizing of the Word*, London (Methuen), 1982.

Ancient and medieval Europe

The Cambridge History of the Bible, Cambridge, UK (CUP), 1963–1970, vol. 1, ed. P.R. Ackroyd and C.F. Evans.

Clanchy, Michael, T., *From Memory to Written Record: England 1066–1307*, Oxford (Blackwell), 2nd ed., 1993.

Knox, Bernard, M.W., 'Silent Reading in Antiquity', *Greek, Roman and Byzantine Studies*, 9:4, 1968, pp. 421–35.

McKitterick, Rosamond, ed., *The Uses of Literacy in Early Medieval Europe*, Cambridge, UK (CUP), 1900.

Petrucci, Armando, *Writers and Readers in Medieval Italy*, New Haven, CT (Yale UP), 1995.

Saenger, Paul, *Space Between Words: The Origins of Silent Reading*, Stanford, CA (Stanford UP), 1997.

Thomas, Rosalind, *Literacy and Orality in Ancient Greece*, Cambridge, UK (CUP), 1993.

Print, Reformation and Renaissance

Baron, Sabrina Alcorn et al, eds., *Agent of Change: Print Culture Studies After Elizabeth L. Eisenstein*, Amherst, MA (Massachusetts UP), 2007.

Blair, Ann, 'Humanist Methods in Natural Philosophy: The Commonplace Book', *Journal of the History of Ideas*, 53:4, 1992, pp. 541–51.

Chrisman, Miriam Usher, *Lay Culture, Learned Culture: Books and Social Change in Strasbourg, 1480–1599*, New Haven, CT (YUP), 1982.

Eisenstein, Elizabeth, L., *The Printing Press as an Agent of Change: Communications and Global Transformations in Early Modern Europe*, Cambridge, UK (CUP), 1979.

Eisenstein, Elizabeth, L., *The Printing Revolution*, Cambridge, UK (CUP), 1983.

Eisenstein, Elizabeth, L. and Adrian Johns, 'How Revolutionary Was the Print Revolution?', *AmHistRev* forum, 107:1, 2002, pp. 84–128.

Febvre, Lucien and Henri-Jean Martin, *The Coming of the Book: The Impact of Printing, 1450–1800*, London (New Left Book Club), 1976.

Gawthrop, Richard and Gerald Strauss, 'Protestantism and Literacy in Early Modern Germany', *P&P*, 104, 1984, pp. 31–55.

Gilmont, Jean-François, ed., *The Reformation and the Book*, Aldershot, UK (Ashgate), 1998.

Ginzburg, Carlo, 'High and Low: The Theme of Forbidden Knowledge in the 16th and 17th Centuries', *P&P*, 73, 1976, pp. 28–41.

Grafton, Anthony, *Commerce with the Classics: Ancient Books and Renaissance Readers*, Ann Arbor (Michigan UP), 1997.

Jardine, Lisa and Anthony Grafton, 'Studied for Action: How Gabriel Harvey Read his Livy', *P&P*, 129, 1990, pp. 30–78.

Johns, Adrian, *The Nature of the Book: Print and Knowledge in the Making*, Chicago (Chicago UP), 1998.

Kapr, Albert, *Johann Gutenberg, The Man and His Invention*, trans. D. Martin, Aldershot, UK (Scolar Press), 1996.

Lowry, Martin, *The World of Aldus Manutius: Business and Scholarship in Renaissance Venice*, Ithaca, NY (Cornell UP), 1979.

Martin, Henri-Jean, *Print, Power and People in 17th-Century France*, Metuchen, NJ (Scarecrow), 1993.

Martin, Henri-Jean, *The French Book: Religion, Absolutism and Readership, 1585–1715*, trans. P & N. Saenger, Baltimore (Johns Hopkins UP), 1996.

McLuhan, Marshall, *The Gutenberg Galaxy: The Making of Typographical Man*, Toronto (Toronto UP), 1962.

Scribner, R.W., *For the Sake of Simple Folk: Popular Propaganda for the German Reformation*, Cambridge, UK (CUP), 1981.

Scribner, R.W., 'Incombustible Luther: The Image of the Reformer in Early Modern Germany', *P&P*, 110, 1986, pp. 38–68.

Sharpe, Kevin and Steven N. Zwicker, eds., *Reading, Society and Politics in Early Modern England*, Cambridge, UK (CUP), 2003.

Waquet, Françoise, *Latin or the Empire of a Sign from the 16th to the 20th Centuries*, London (Verso), 2001.

Early modern literacy and popular culture

Amelang, James, *The Flight of Icarus: Artisan Autobiography in Early Modern Europe*, Stanford, CA (Stanford UP), 1998.

Barry, Jonathan, 'Literacy and Literature in Popular Culture: Reading and Writing in Historical Perspective', in Tim Harris, ed., *Popular Culture in England, c.1500–1850*, Basingstoke, UK (Palgrave Macmillan), 1995, pp. 69–94.

Brown, Matthew, P., *The Pilgrim and the Bee: Reading Rituals and Book Culture in Early New England*, Philadelphia, PA (Pennsylvania UP), 2007.

Burke, Peter, *Popular Culture in Early Modern Europe*, London (Temple Smith), 1978.

Capp, Bernard, *Astrology and the Popular Press: English Almanacs, 1500–1800*, London (Faber & Faber), 1979.

Chartier, Roger, *The Cultural Uses of Print in Early Modern France*, trans. Lydia G. Cochrane, Princeton, NJ (PUP), 1987.

Ciosáin, Niall Ó., *Print and Popular Culture in Ireland, 1750–1850*, Basingstoke, UK (Palgrave Macmillan) and New York (St. Martin's), 1997.

Cornelius, Janet Duitsman, *'When I Can Read My Title Clear': Literacy, Slavery and Religion in the Antebellum South*, Columbia, SC (South Carolina UP), 1991.

Cressy, David, *Literacy and the Social Order: Reading and Writing in Tudor and Stuart England*, Cambridge, UK (CUP), 1980.

Cressy, David, 'Books as Totems in 17thc England and New England', *Journal of Library History*, 21:1, 1986, pp. 92–106.

Darnton, Robert, 'Peasants Tell Tales: The Meaning of Mother Goose', in his *The Great Cat Massacre and Other Episodes in French Cultural History*, London (Allen Lane), 1984.

Furet, François and Jacques Ozouf, 'Literacy and industrialisation: The Case of the Département du Nord in France', *Journal of European Economic History*, 5:1, 1976, pp. 5–44.

Furet, Francois and Jacques Ozouf, *Reading and Writing: Literacy in France from Calvin to Jules Ferry*, Cambridge, UK (CUP/MSH), 1982.

Ginzburg, Carlo, *The Cheese and the Worms: The Cosmos of a 16th-Century Miller*, trans. J. & A. Tedeschi, London (RKP), 1981.

Guttormson, Loftur, 'The Development of Popular Religious Literacy in the 17th and 18th Centuries', *Scandinavian Journal of History*, 15:1, 1990, pp. 7–35.

Houston, Rab, 'The Literacy Myth? Illiteracy in Scotland, 1630–1760', *P&P*, 96, 1982, pp. 81–102.

Houston, Robert, A., *Literacy in Early Modern Europe: Culture and Education, 1500–1800*, London (Longman), 1992.

Monaghan, E. Jennifer, *Learning to Read and Write in Colonial America*, Amherst, MA (Massachusetts UP), 2005.

Nalle, Sara, T., 'Literacy and Culture in Early Modern Castile', *P&P*, 125, 1989, pp. 65–96.

Perkins, Maureen, *Visions of the Future: Almanacs, Time and Cultural Change*, Oxford (Clarendon), 1996.

Schofield, Roger, S., 'The Measurement of Literacy in Pre-Industrial England', in Goody, J., ed., *Literacy in Traditional Societies*, Cambridge, UK (CUP), 1968, pp. 311–25.

Spufford, Margaret, 'First Steps in Literacy: The Reading and Writing Experiences of the Humblest 17th-Century Spiritual Autobiographers', *Social History*, 4:3, 1979, pp. 407–35.

Spufford, Margaret, *Small Books and Pleasant Histories: Popular Fiction and Its Readership in 17th-Century England*, Cambridge, UK (CUP), 1981.

Stone, Lawrence, 'Literacy and Education in England, 1640–1900', *P&P*, 42, 1969, pp. 69–139.

Thomas, Keith, 'The Meaning of Literacy in Early Modern England', in Gerd Baumann, ed., *The Written Word: Literacy in Transition*, Oxford (Clarendon), 1986, pp. 97–131.

Tóth, István György, *Literacy and Written Culture in Early Modern Central Europe*, Budapest (Central European UP), 2000.

Williams, Heather Andrea, *Self-Taught: African American Education in Slavery and Freedom*, Chapel Hill, NC (North Carolina UP), 2005.

The Ancien Regime, the reading revolution and the public sphere

Censer, Jack, R. and Jeremy D. Popkin, eds., *Press and Politics in Pre-Revolutionary France*, Berkeley, CA (UCP), 1987.

Chartier, Roger, *The Cultural Origins of the French Revolution*, trans. Lydia G. Cochrane, Durham, NC (Duke UP), 1991.

Darnton, Robert, *The Business of Enlightenment: A Publishing History of the Encyclopédie, 1775–1800*, Cambridge, MA (Belknap), 1979.

Darnton, Robert, *The Literary Underground of the Old Régime*, Cambridge, MA (HUP), 1982.

Darnton, Robert, 'Readers Respond to Rousseau: The Fabrication of Romantic Sensitivity', in his *The Great Cat Massacre and Other Episodes in French Cultural History*, London (Allen Lane), 1984, pp. 215–56.

Darnton, Robert, *The Forbidden Best-Sellers of Pre-Revolutionary France*, New York (Norton), 1995.

Darnton, Robert, 'Paris: The Early Internet', *New York Review of Books*, 29 June 2000, pp. 42–47 and at www.indiana.edu/~ahr.

Darnton, Robert and Daniel Roche, eds., *Revolution in Print: The Press in France, 1775–1800*, Berkeley, CA (UCP), 1989.

Davidson, Cathy, N., *Revolution and the Word: The Rise of the Novel in America*, New York (OUP), 1986.

Habermas, Jürgen, *The Structural Transformation of the Public Sphere. An Inquiry into a Category of Bourgeois Society*, Cambridge, UK (Polity), 1989.

Hall, David, D., *Cultures of Print: Essays in the History of the Book*, Amherst, MA (Massachusetts UP), 1996.

Hesse, Carla, *Publishing and Cultural Politics in Revolutionary Paris, 1789–1810*, Berkeley, CA (UCP), 1991.

Lough, John, *Writer and Public in France from the Middle Ages to the Present Day*, Oxford (Clarendon), 1978.

Mason, Haydn, T., *The Darnton Debate: Books and Revolution in the 18th Century*, Oxford (Voltaire Foundation), 1998.

Melton, James Van Horn, *The Rise of the Public in Enlightenment Europe*, Cambridge, UK (CUP), 2001.

Nathans, Benjamin, 'Habermas's Public Sphere in the Era of the French Revolution', *French Historical Studies*, 16:3, 1990, pp. 620–43.

Pearson, Jacqueline, *Women's Reading in Britain, 1750–1835: A Dangerous Recreation*, Cambridge, UK (CUP), 1999.

Popkin, Jeremy, *Revolutionary News: The Press in France, 1789–1799*, Durham, NC (Duke UP), 1990.

Raven, James, Helen Small and Naomi Tadmor, eds., *The Practice and Representation of Reading in England*, Cambridge, UK (CUP), 1996.

Rivers, Isobel, ed., *Books and Their Readers in Eighteenth-Century England: New Essays*, London (Leicester UP), 2001.

St. Clair, William, *The Reading Nation in the Romantic Period*, Cambridge, UK (CUP), 2004.

Vovelle, Michel, 'Le tournant des mentalités en France 1750–1789: la 'sensibilité' pré-révolutionnaire', *Social History*, 5, 1977, pp. 605–29 (English text).

Ward, Albert, *Book Production, Fiction and the German Reading Public, 1740–1800*, Oxford (Clarendon), 1974.

Nineteenth century

Allen, James Smith, *In the Public Eye: A History of Reading in Modern France, 1800–1940*, Princeton, NJ (PUP), 1991.

Allen, James Smith, *Popular French Romanticism: Authors, Readers and Books in the Nineteenth Century*, Syracuse, NY (Syracuse UP), 1981.

Altick, Richard, *The English Common Reader: A Social History of the Mass Reading Public, 1800–1900*, Chicago (Chicago UP), 1957.

Brooks, Jeffrey, *When Russia Learned to Read: Literacy and Popular Literature, 1861–1917*, Princeton, NJ (PUP), 1985.

Collins, Wilkie, 'The Unknown Public' (1858), *Victorian Fiction: A Collection of Essays*, ed. I.B. Nadel, New York (Garland), 1986.

DeMarco, Eileen, S., *Reading and Riding: Hachette's Railroad Bookstore Network in 19th-Century France*, Bethlehem, PA (Lehigh UP), 2006.

Eliot, Simon, *Some Patterns and Trends in British Publishing, 1800–1919*, London (Bibliographical Society), 1994.

Flint, Kate, *The Woman Reader, 1837–1914*, Oxford (Clarendon), 1993.

Hewitt, Martin, 'Confronting the Modern City: The Manchester Free Public Library, 1850–80', *Urban History*, 27:1, 2000, pp. 62–88.

Hoock-Demarle, Marie-Claire, 'Reading & Writing in Germany', in G. Fraisse and M. Perrot eds., *A History of Women, v.4: Emerging Feminism from Revolution to World War*, Cambridge, MA (Belknap), 1993, pp. 145–165.

Howsam, Leslie, *Cheap Bibles: Nineteenth-century Publishing and the British and Foreign Bible Society*, Cambridge, UK (CUP), 1991.

Lyons, Martyn, *Readers and Society in Nineteenth-Century France: Workers, Women, Peasants*, Basingstoke, UK, and New York (Palgrave), 2001.

Lyons, Martyn, *Reading Culture and Writing Practices in Nineteenth-Century France*, Toronto (Toronto UP), 2008.

Parfait, Claire, *The Publishing History of* Uncle Tom's Cabin, *1852–2002*, Aldershot, UK (Ashgate), 2007.

Patten, Robert, L., *Charles Dickens and His Publishers*, Oxford (Clarendon), 1978.

Roberts, Lewis, C., 'Disciplining and Disinfecting Working-Class Readers in the Victorian Public Library', *Victorian Literature and Culture*, 26:1, 1998, pp. 105–32.

Rose, Jonathan, 'Rereading the *English Common Reader*: A Preface to a History of Audiences', *Journal of the History of Ideas*, 53:1, 1992, pp. 47–70.

Rose, Jonathan, 'How Historians Study Reader Response: or, What Did Jo Think of *Bleak House*?' in John O. Jordan and Robert L. Patten, eds., *Literature in the Marketplace: Nineteenth-century British Publishing and Reading Practices*, Cambridge, UK (CUP), 1995, chapter 9.

Rose, Jonathan, *The Intellectual Life of the British Working Classes*, New Haven, CT (YUP), 2001.

Vincent, David, 'Reading in the Working-Class Home', in J.K. Walton and J. Walvin, eds., *Leisure in Britain 1780–1939*, Manchester (Manchester UP), 1983.

Webb, R.K., *The British Working-class Reader, 1790–1848: Literacy and Social Tension*, London (Allen & Unwin), 1955.

Weedon, Alexis, *Victorian Publishing: The Economics of Book Production for a Mass Market, 1836–1916*, Aldershot, UK (Ashgate), 2003.

Writing

Augst, Thomas, *The Clerk's Tale: Young Men and Moral Life in Nineteenth-Century America*, Chicago (Chicago UP), 2003.

Chartier, Roger, ed., *Correspondence: Models of Letter-Writing from the Middle Ages to the 19th Century*, Cambridge, UK (Polity), 1997.

Dekker, Rudolf, ed., *Autobiographical Writing in Its Social Context Since the Middle Ages*, Hilversum (Verloren), 2002.

Kalman, Judy, *Writing on the Plaza: Mediated Literacy Practice Among Scribes and Clients in Mexico City*, Creskill, NJ (Hampton), 1999.

Lyons, Martyn, ed., *Ordinary Writings, Personal Narratives: Writing Practices in the 19th and Early 20th Centuries*, Bern (Peter Lang), 2007.

Lyons, Martyn, *Reading Culture and Writing Practices in Nineteenth-Century France*, Toronto (Toronto UP), 2008.

Petrucci, Armando, *Public Lettering: Script, Power and Culture*, Chicago (Chicago UP), 1993.

Sinor, Jennifer, *The Extraordinary Work of Ordinary Writings: Annie Ray's Diary*, Iowa City (Iowa UP), 2002.

Traugott, Mark, ed., and trans. *The French Worker: Autobiographies from the Early Industrial Era*, Berkeley, CA (UCP), 1984.

Vincent, David, *Bread, Knowledge and Freedom: A Study of 19th-Century Working-class Autobiography*, London (Europa), 1981.

Twentieth century

Fishburn, Matthew, *Burning Books*, Basingstoke, UK (Palgrave Macmillan), 2008.

Hartley, Jenny, *Reading Groups*, Oxford (OUP), 2001.

Hoggart, Richard, *The Uses of Literacy: Aspects of Working-class Life*, Harmondsworth, UK (Penguin), 1958.

Kaestle, Carl, F., et al, *Literacy in the United States: Readers and Reading Since 1880*, New Haven, CT (YUP), 1991.

Long, Elizabeth, *Book Clubs: Women and the Uses of Reading in Everyday Life*, Chicago (Chicago UP), 2003.

Lovell, Stephen, *The Russian Reading Revolution: Print Culture in the Soviet and Post-Soviet Eras*, Basingstoke, UK (Palgrave Macmillan) and New York (St. Martin's), 2000.

Lyons, Martyn and Lucy Taksa, *Australian Readers Remember: An Oral History of Reading in New South Wales*, Melbourne (OUP), 1992.

McAleer, Joseph, *Popular Reading and Publishing in Britain, 1914–50*, Oxford (Clarendon), 1992.

Radway, Janice, *Reading the Romance: Women, Patriarchy and Popular Literature*, London (Verso), 1987.

Radway, Janice, A., *A Feeling for Books: The Book-of-the Month Club, Literary Taste, and Middle-Class Desire*, Chapel Hill, NC (North Carolina UP), 1997.

Reuveni, Gideon, *Reading Germany: Literature and Consumer Culture in Germany Before 1933*, New York (Berghahn), 2006.

Van Slyck, Abigail, *Free to All: Carnegie Libraries and American Culture, 1890–1920*, Chicago (Chicago UP), 1995.

Index

Note: Page numbers in bold type (e.g. **79–81**) refer to the most detailed discussion of the topic. Page numbers in italics (e.g. *114*) refer to illustrations.

CPSIA information can be obtained
at www.ICGtesting.com
Printed in the USA
LVOW05s0053300817

546888LV00027B/562/P